First Crossing

First Crossing

Alexander Mackenzie,
His Expedition Across North America, and the Opening of the Continent

Derek Hayes

SASQUATCH BOOKS
SEATTLE

Originated in Canada by Douglas & McIntyre Ltd. and published simultaneously in the United States of America by Sasquatch Books, Seattle.
Printed in Hong Kong by C&C Offset

05 04 03 02 01   5 4 3 2 1

Cover design: Karen Schober
Interior design and layout: Derek Hayes
Interior photographs: Derek Hayes unless otherwise credited
Copy editor: Naomi Pauls

Library of Congress Cataloging-in-Publication Data

Hayes, Derek, 1947-
      First crossing : Alexander Mackenzie, his expedition across North America, and the opening of the continent / Derek Hayes.
         p. cm.
      Includes bibliographical references and index.
      ISBN 1-57061-308-7
      1. Mackenzie, Alexander, Sir, 1763-1820. 2. Northwest, Canadian—Description and travel. 3. Northwest, Canadian—Discovery and exploration. 4. Explorers—Northwest, Canadian—Biography. 5. Overland journeys to the Pacific. 6. Canada—Description and travel. 7. Canada—Discovery and exploration. 8. Indians of North America—Northwest, Canadian—History—18th century. 9. Fur trade—Northwest, Canadian—History—18th century. I. Title.
F1060.7.M1783 H39 2001

917.1204'1—dc21 2001031374

Sasquatch Books
615 Second Avenue
Seattle, Washington 98104
(206) 467-4300
www.SasquatchBooks.com
books@SasquatchBooks.com

Derek Hayes
derek@derekhayes.ca
www.derekhayes.ca

Previous page: View southwestward from Mackenzie Rock, near Bella Coola, B.C. This was the farthest west Mackenzie attained, and this was his reward – a view of the Pacific Ocean or, at least, Pacific tidewater in Dean Channel, one of many long arms of that ocean.

Contents

Acknowledgments

I would like to acknowledge all those who assisted me in the writing of this book: Tammy Hannibal, Map Archivist with the Hudson's Bay Company Archives in Winnipeg, who was so very helpful when I visited to examine and photograph many of their maps and journals, including Peter Fidler's notebooks; Debra Moore, Still Images Archivist with the Hudson's Bay Company Archives; Brad Otelie and Carol Urness of the James Ford Bell Library at the University of Minnesota, where Samuel Hearne's map of the Coppermine River is located; Edward Redmond of the Library of Congress Geography and Maps Division, who was most helpful and allowed me to examine the original map drawn by Alexander Henry; Nick Doe, who helped me understand the way longitude was observed and calculated astronomically in Mackenzie's time; Bruce Ward of the B.C. Map Society, who helped identify some features on old maps; Bruce, a pilot with Pacific Coastal, who flew me from Bella Coola to Mackenzie Rock, and David, of BeauDel Air, who flew me from Inuvik to Garry Island in the Arctic Ocean; Martha King of the National Gallery of Canada for allowing me to use a photograph I took of Mackenzie's portrait hanging in the gallery; B.C. Hydro for allowing me to access their archival material and to reproduce photographs they took before the building of the W.A.C. Bennett Dam; Dan Savard of the Royal British Columbia Museum; Louis Campeau of the Canadian Museum of Civilization; Kathryn Bridge of the British Columbia Archives; Karen Haughian of Nuage Editions for allowing me to use the photograph of Jean Steinbeck's birchbark journal; Larry Mensching of the Joslyn Art Museum in Omaha; the staff of the Special Collections Department at the Vancouver Public Library, helpful as always; the staff at the Peace River Museum, Peace River, Alberta; and last but not least my wife, Carole, for her unerring support, not to mention accompanying me to the Arctic and the Peace River country, flying in seemingly rickety planes and driving endless miles. Naomi Pauls did a superb job of cleaning up my text, and the book is much better for it; nevertheless, any remaining errors are my responsibility alone. In addition I would like to thank Scott McIntyre of Douglas and McIntyre for his support of my vision of Canadian history and for agreeing to publish this book; and also Joan Gregory of Sasquatch Books, Seattle, for her continued support.

Illustration Credits

Numbers refer to pages. Photographs not otherwise credited were taken by the author. Maps and other images not credited are in the author's or other private collections.

National Gallery of Canada, 9; National Archives of Canada, 5, 21, 38, 46, 74, 83, 84, 87, 164–65, 181, 183, 195, 231, 273; James Ford Bell Library, 26–27; Hudson's Bay Company Archives, 30, 33, 34 (top), 53, 54, 85, 86, 88, 93, 94 (top), 94 (bottom), 98, 133, 148, 149 (top), 149 (bottom), 150 (bottom left), 171, 192, 194, 243 (bottom), 264–65, 276, 279, 280–81, 294, 298; Library of Congress, 34 (bottom); Public Record Office, 48–49, 56–57, 64, 89, 95 (top), 109 (top), 114, 118 (top), 131, 151 (top), 159, 175, 198, 250–51, 288; British Library, 60, 247; Yale University Library, 69; Joslyn Art Museum, 77; Provincial Archives of Alberta, 78–79; Nuage Editions, 82; Natural Resources Canada, Aeronautical and Technical Services, 91, 199; Natural Resources Canada, Centre for Topographic Information, 104, 107, 150 (top), 180 (top); Vancouver Public Library, 115, 122, 127, 151 (bottom), 157, 162, 180 (bottom), 234 (left), 255, 282, 285; Smithsonian Institution, 140; Peace River Museum, 160 (top left), 161; B.C. Hydro, 170, 174 (top); British Columbia Archives, 172, 230, 299, 303; Royal British Columbia Museum (Neg. PN 7195–B), 208–9; Canadian Museum of Civilization, 204 (top), 205 (bottom), 206–7 (bottom left), 206–7 (bottom middle), 208, 304; American Museum of Civilization, 206–7 (top); National Archives and Records Administration (U.S. National Archives), 234 (right); McCord Museum, Montreal, 241; Seattle Public Library, 260, 261; Her Majesty the Queen in Right of Canada, reproduced from the collection of the National Air Photo Library with permission of Natural Resources Canada, 173 (© 1949), 301 (© 1929).

Author's Note

This book relies heavily on Mackenzie's own words, both in journals and letters. When using quotes, I have followed the capitalization and spelling in the journal or other contemporary source being quoted. Many of the fur traders did not have much formal education, and in any case English spelling and grammar were much looser then than they are now. Words were often capitalized for no apparent reason. "Canoe," for example, is almost always capitalized, perhaps underlining its importance to the fur traders. I have kept the original form and spelling because I think it adds to reality and immediacy and brings history to life. I think it is well worth the slightly greater degree of difficulty in reading. The journal of the semi-literate Peter Pond cannot fail to bring a smile to the face of any who read it.

I have spelled Mackenzie's own name as he spelled it in his book, but in fact Mackenzie himself used "McKenzie" much of the time. Some letters are signed one way, some the other.

With Mackenzie's words there is another difficulty. Only one of his journals survives, and that, unfortunately, is not an original but a copy made by hand, as they often were in the days before the ubiquitous photocopier we today take for granted. The surviving journal is of his first "voyage" (for that is what it was, an expedition by canoe), Mackenzie's travels to the Arctic Ocean in 1789. There is no reason to believe it is not an exact copy of his words, and I have followed this journal.

For his second "voyage," to the Pacific in 1793, we have to follow the "cleaned up" version of Mackenzie's words as published in his book of 1801. This is known to have been edited by one William Coombe (see page 253) in order to make the book more suitable for publication. Although it contains many examples of language that is clearly more flowery than Mackenzie would likely himself have written, the sense is not changed or embellished to the point where it is not a valid record of his exploits. We can make this judgement, of course, because we can compare the "before" and "after" text of his first expedition.

I have included endnotes but they are not numbered. Instead the notes on pages 312–13 refer to page numbers. This I think makes notes much easier to refer to, but leaves any numbering system well alone. I have used this method after years of being annoyed by systems that require you to know what chapter you are reading before you can find the correct notes.

To Cross the Continent

Mackenzie's Portrait

This famous portrait of Alexander Mackenzie was painted in 1800 or 1801 by Sir Thomas Lawrence, a well-known British artist of the time. It seems to be the only extant portrait of Mackenzie painted from life; all others are copies that use this painting as their source. Our intrepid explorer, jauntily dressed and clearly back in "civilization," would have been somewhere between thirty-six and thirty-nine years old when he sat for Lawrence.

Soon after this book was written, I happened to be in Ottawa, and so resolved to visit Mackenzie. After a little searching in the glass and concrete halls of the National Gallery of Canada, I found him. There he was, between a French plaster bust and a medieval-looking *Salutation of Beatrice,* by Dante Rossetti.

The painting was life-size, and carefully hung at Mackenzie's likely height. It was an interesting moment for me, finally meeting the man I had been learning and writing about for several years. I wished I could have spoken to him!

It is fitting that this unique portrait now belongs to the Canadian people and hangs in the capital of the country he first explored to the Pacific Ocean.

Both Mackenzie's expeditions made such immense and basic contributions to geographical knowedge that their interest is perpetual and their importance self-evident.

– W. Kaye Lamb, 1970

[Mackenzie] may be standing waist deep in a rushing river, holding on to a wrecked canoe, but this battered craft is still the needle drawing behind it a thread which, knotted with those drawn across the world's greatest oceans by Cook and Vancouver, will form the basis of a network on which Canada still depends for its economic survival.

– Roy Daniells, 1969

Alexander Mackenzie was the first person to cross the continent of North America north of Mexico. He completed this momentous trek in 1793, a full twelve years before Meriwether Lewis and William Clark reached the Pacific Ocean with the Corps of Discovery. A partner in the North West Company, based in Montreal, Mackenzie was driven by the need to find a commercial route to the Pacific Ocean to enable his company to compete with its rival, the Hudson's Bay Company, which shipped its furs out through Hudson Bay, a much shorter route than that through Montreal. But he was also driven to explore the unknown.

Mackenzie paddled and trekked 6 400 km or 4,000 miles to find tidewater on the Pacific, the culmination of years of planning and puzzling over inaccurate maps. He had even made a previous attempt, in 1789, a 2 500 km or 1,600 mile canoe trip that proved a monumental dead end, reaching the Arctic Ocean instead of the Pacific. But in 1793 he succeeded in his quest, and in so doing for the first time established the relationship of the inland river and lake system to the coast, revealing much of the geography of western North America for those, including Lewis and Clark, who would follow.

Mackenzie was, first and foremost, an explorer in the true sense of the word. Although his bread and butter was the fur trade, he also had a large dose of that idea of wanting to know the unknown, of wanting to see for himself what was over the next mountain. His urge to explore went far beyond the point of any direct interest from his fur trade point of view. He proved this when he continued north after the Mackenzie River curved northward when he wanted to go westward to the Pacific; he was an intelligent man, and must very soon have realized that the route he was following was not likely to be a commercially viable one.

Those scions of American exploration literature and legend, Meriwether Lewis and William Clark, have received much more attention than Alexander Mackenzie. A book published as late as 1922 still proclaimed Lewis and Clark as "first across the continent." But Mackenzie was first. The comparative neglect of Mackenzie is perhaps partly due to the fact that his original journals have disappeared, whereas those of Lewis and Clark survive to give a superb immediacy to their tale; their journals have become, as Stephen Ambrose put it, the American national epic poem. Yet Mackenzie wrote Canada's own epic saga, one equally important to the future national geography of that country and the entire continent.

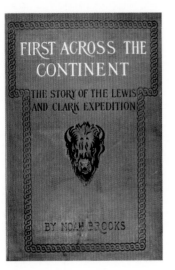

This is at root a book about geography: the way in which an unknown but anticipated geography of the Northwest was revealed to Alexander Mackenzie, whose concepts of what to expect led him to discover what was really there. Without the geographical motivation – in his case the search for a navigable river flowing to the Pacific Ocean – and the economic motivation – the idea that this river could be used for commerce, the easier making of money in his business, the fur trade – Mackenzie would not have been fired to push westward and would not have found out how the river and lake system already known to his company, the North West Company, could be linked to the Pacific. The fact that the route Mackenzie found was not itself commercially practicable does not matter, for he was the pioneer, proving it was possible; others could fill in the details and find a better route.

Mackenzie was essentially gathering information to try to put together a coherent and comprehensive picture of the geography of the Northwest. He was doing this primarily for commercial reasons: to find additional regions for the fur trade to exploit and to find an easier route for the transportation of those furs to their market, that is, via the Pacific by sea instead of the long and laborious canoe routes to Montreal. In doing so he was, in the modern vernacular, thinking globally but acting locally. His knowledge was pan-continental or approaching that; he knew of the world and its markets outside the area he was exploring, and he was trying to link the regions as yet unknown to him and his peers into their knowledge of the rest of the world. In a word, he was trying to fill in the gap in the map.

Because some of the gap had been filled by Mackenzie, Lewis and Clark knew with much greater certainty than he did how far they would have to travel. They even knew what their intended destination was, for the mouth of the Columbia had been found and mapped thirteen years earlier by the American Robert Gray – in his ship the *Columbia Rediva,* after which the river is named. By the time of Lewis and Clark's trek the coast had been irrevocably surveyed with what, for the time, was stunning exactness, by George Vancouver. Unlike Mackenzie, Lewis and Clark were able to carry with them Vancouver's maps; Vancouver had been surveying the coast the same year Mackenzie reached the ocean. Lewis and Clark also had Aaron Arrowsmith's rapidly improving map of "all the interior discoveries" of North America, and several more, even including the maps from Mackenzie's own book.

The best Mackenzie may have had was Arrowsmith's first great map, his world map of

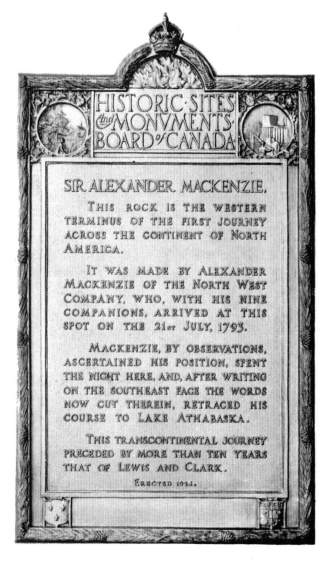

SIR ALEXANDER MACKENZIE.

THIS ROCK IS THE WESTERN TERMINUS OF THE FIRST JOURNEY ACROSS THE CONTINENT OF NORTH AMERICA.

IT WAS MADE BY ALEXANDER MACKENZIE OF THE NORTH WEST COMPANY, WHO, WITH HIS NINE COMPANIONS, ARRIVED AT THIS SPOT ON THE 21st JULY, 1793.

MACKENZIE, BY OBSERVATIONS, ASCERTAINED HIS POSITION, SPENT THE NIGHT HERE, AND, AFTER WRITING ON THE SOUTHEAST FACE THE WORDS NOW CUT THEREIN, RETRACED HIS COURSE TO LAKE ATHABASKA.

THIS TRANSCONTINENTAL JOURNEY PRECEDED BY MORE THAN TEN YEARS THAT OF LEWIS AND CLARK.

ERECTED 1926.

The original plaque placed in 1927 (despite the 1926 date) on the Mackenzie monument at Mackenzie Rock on Dean Channel, near Bella Coola. Note the specific reference to beating Lewis and Clark! The plaque was replaced by a bilingual one, shown on page 222.

1790, still with many tentative parts, and we know he also had with him John Meares' semi-fictitious effort of 1790, which was of little real help. And of course he had James Cook's map, drawn in 1778 and published in 1784, which although fixing for the first time the longitude of some points still left a huge expanse of the coastline of present-day British Columbia as a very tentative dotted line. All these maps together left considerable doubt as to exactly what Mackenzie would encounter west of the mountains, or even where he might expect to meet the coast. And he, like Lewis and Clark, was expecting a single ridge of mountains and a short portage to Pacific waters. As it turned out, Mackenzie did find a short portage to Pacific waters, but they were waters of such turbulence and length that he was forced to seek a more direct, overland route, unlike Lewis and Clark, whose portage – if it can be called that – became a long and arduous quest for water flowing westward. Once found, however, the going rapidly became much easier for them.

The question of whether Mackenzie "discovered" anything considering that the places he visited had all been "discovered" by indigenous peoples long before is one that presents itself in any discussion of Euro-American exploration in North America. The geographical knowledge of the indigenous peoples was essentially local. For example, the lives of the coastal natives in the late eighteenth century revolved around the sea and the salmon; some penetrated inland to trade and in so doing passed on and collected geographic information, creating a chain of knowledge coherent for some larger area, perhaps in the possession of, but not in the experience of, a single individual. The areas over which there was comprehension could be quite large, as is shown by many of the native maps drawn for Peter Fidler, the Hudson's Bay Company surveyor. But it was never global or even continent-wide. For their lives, for their survival, indigenous peoples only needed what they had – the more local view. Not knowing or needing what was beyond their regional trading horizon, the natives felt no need to go looking for it. Mackenzie and his peers possessed the one thing that the natives did not have, a *motivation* for their travels across continents.

The characterization of Alexander Mackenzie as the first *white man* to cross North America north of Mexico denigrates his achievement by suggesting that a non-white person had done it before. Could this reasonably be the case? Travel by natives before the coming of European traders only occurred for the purposes of trade, to make war, or to obtain food in a different location, not to "explore" regions beyond their current knowledge. Mackenzie's vision was what drove him, to show that it was *possible* to get to the Pacific. Native people, at this time, if they knew of oceans either side of the continent, cared less. They had no *motivation* to cross the continent the way Mackenzie did, and it is thus highly unlikely that anyone did so before him. Fear of enslavement by a distant tribe would itself have ensured this. Let us therefore give Mackenzie his due – he was almost certainly the first person to cross the North American continent, period.

Having said that, whether he was first or twenty-first is not really the issue. He is certainly the first documented person to cross the continent, and certainly the first to return to disseminate news of his crossing to the rest of the world. But the significant thing is that he successfully undertook his epic journey *at that point in history,* and by so doing drove the North West Company and eventually others to the Pacific, starting a process which would ultimately ensure that the Pacific coast would become part of Canada rather than of Russia or the United States.

I now mixed up fome vermilion in melted greafe, and infcribed, in large charaƈters, on the South-Eaƒt face of the rock on which we had ƒlept laƒt night, this brief memorial—" Alexander Mackenzie, from Canada, by land, the twenty-ƒecond of July, one thouƒand ƒeven hundred and ninety-three."

Passage from Mackenzie's book, *Voyages from Montreal.*

Lure of the Western Sea

A great river which flows westward
and discharges into the sea

Previous page: This superbly bizarre map shows a classic Northwest Passage from Hudson Bay to the Pacific and a huge Sea of the West stretching eastward to Nebraska at about 98° W. It is part of *Mappe Monde ou Globe Terrestre en deux Plans Hemispheres. Dressee sur les observations de Mrss de L'Academie Royal Des Sciences,* by Jean Covens and Corneille Mortier, about 1780. The Sea of the West as depicted here was copied from a map first produced by Mortier's father, Pierre, about 1700.

When the European explorers Columbus and Cabot found the North American continent in the late sixteenth century, they were actually searching for Asia. And they thought they had found it. The search for Cathay or Cipango, China and Japan, or the Spice Islands, via a route to the west, was to continue for centuries. By about 1525 it had become clear to the knowledgeable that America was not Asia but a distinct new continent blocking the way to Asia, and from that time forth the search was on for a way through it – the fabled Northwest Passage, a strait, or if not, perhaps a great river.

In 1520, Ferdinand Magellan had discovered a strait at the tip of South America. At that time the Strait of Magellan was considered a passage through an otherwise continuous continent stretching to a great southern continent, and since a widely held theory supposed that geographical features ought to balance themselves in their distribution around the earth, it was quickly hyphothesized that there must be a corresponding strait through the northern part of the American continent.

For a long period beginning in earnest in 1576, English maritime exploration focused on a search for this strait. Thus we have the voyages of Martin Frobisher in 1576–78, finding Frobisher "Strait" – today Frobisher Bay, at the head of which sits Iqualuit, the capital of Nunavut; those of John Davis in 1585–87, finding and mapping what is today Davis Strait; and those of Humfray Gylbert, whose searches for a passage didn't get very far, but who in the process claimed English ownership of Newfoundland and set in motion a chain of

Left: This engraving of a river providing an easy route to exotic climes is a typical representation of the idea of a River of the West. Always over the next horizon was the way to Cathay. From *A New Discovery of a Vast Country in America*, by Father Louis Hennipin, published in 1698.

events that is probably responsible for that island today being a province of Canada.

Then in 1610 came the voyages of Henry Hudson, again looking for a passage through the continent but instead finding the eastern part of the great bay that now bears his name. A host of others followed, expanding the original English knowledge of the bay and exploring possible ways out of it toward the west or north – Thomas Button in 1612–13; William Baffin and Robert Bylot to the north in 1612–16; Luke Foxe in 1631; Thomas James the same year; not to mention the efforts of the Dane Jens Munk in 1624, who reached the west side of Hudson Bay. James had noted in his journal that the shores of the bay "were the home of many of the choicest fur-bearing animals in the world" – for the cold climate made for thick furs. The knowledge of the bay and the realization that it had a wealth all its own culminated in the decision by the English to establish the Hudson's Bay Company, chartered by Charles II in 1670.

It was from bases on the shores of Hudson Bay that the British were to eventually explore the region away from the bay and push ever westward, first in competition with the French, and later in competition with British and Canadian fur traders based in Montreal.

The French had early established a presence farther south than these northern probes. In 1534, the French navigator Jacques Cartier sailed to the eastern part of the St. Lawrence, and in 1535 he sailed up that broad river thinking he had found the passage to Cathay. Later, after the French found it was not their passage, and after a number of earlier abortive attempts to establish settlements, Samuel de Champlain finally established the French presence in what is now Quebec in 1608 and then set out to exploit the resources of the new colony. Thus began a series of attempts to penetrate the interior of the continent to search for new fur areas and to perhaps find a way to Cathay through the lakes and rivers that seemed to be so well linked.

It is a peculiar fact of Canadian exploration that it all progressed over hundreds of years from east to west; nobody penetrated from the Pacific eastward. This is not surprising, however, when one realizes that the east coast was that nearest to Europe, and that the Pacific coast was essentially unknown by Europeans until the last quarter of the eighteenth century. The first map of the Pacific coast of Canada

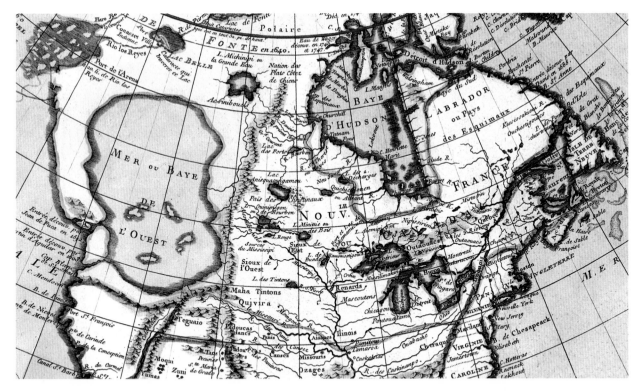

based on exploration was not drawn until 1774, and it would be many years after that before there would be any exploration of the interior eastward from the west coast.

Until the French loss of virtually all of their North American colonies after the Treaty of Paris in 1763, it was the French fur traders who provided the impetus for westward exploration, as the British seemed content to sit passively on the shores of Hudson Bay.

Two enduring myths surfaced early: that of a Western Sea and that of a River of the West flowing to that sea, *somewhere* to the westward, usually round the next bend in the river or over the next mountain. They were really partial myths, since there were in the Pacific Ocean and the Columbia River some truth to them. The one about a Western Sea probably originated in a reference to the Great Lakes, but as European knowledge pressed west, so the sea migrated just out of reach. There are, of course, enough large bodies of water and large and long rivers in the northern part of North America for confusion to have kept alive such myths for a long time. Even after the idea of a viable marine Northwest Passage had died, there was still the idea that the lake and river system would somehow provide an equivalent. Add to this the fact that the width of the North American continent was

A vastly fantastic conception of the geography of western North America by French map-maker Joseph-Nicolas de L'Isle, 1752. A Sea of the West, complete with islands and rivers flowing into it, occupies a huge area of western Canada immediately west of a mountain chain. A river, the Rio los Reyes, flows to the Pacific north of the sea. Part of: *Carte Des Nouvelles Découvertes au Nord de la Mer Tant a l'Est de la Siberie et du Kamtchatka Qu'a l'Ouest de la Nouvelle France: Dressée sur las Mémoires de Mr Del'isle, Professeur Royale et de l'Académie des Sciences Par Philippe Buache de la même Académie et Presentée a l'Académie, dans son Assemblée Publique de 8 Avril 1750 Par Mr De l'Isle 1752.*

unknown until James Cook in 1778 finally established the position of the west coast using the newly invented chronometer to find his longitude. Thus it seemed there was always the possibility that the Western Sea might be reached over the next horizon. The motivational origins of Alexander Mackenzie's treks to the Arctic and Pacific were, as we shall see, based on a penultimate concept of this search for a Western Sea.

In 1615, Samuel de Champlain had ventured as far west as Lake Huron. The Great Lakes provided a practical pathway for deep inland penetration, and French fur traders and Jesuit missionaries pushed west. By 1659 Pierre Esprit Radisson and Medard Chouant, Sieur de Groseilliers, had reached Lake Superior, though they claimed to have reached Hudson Bay. In 1670 Father Claude Jean Allouez reached the western end of Lake Superior, and in 1686, Jacques de Noyon went up the Kaministiquia River probably as far as the Lake of the Woods, in the process receiving reports from the natives of a river which flowed into a Western Sea. The reference was probably to the Winnipeg River and Lake Winnipeg, but the intelligence added to the endurance of the myth.

Radisson and Groseilliers became convinced that the best way to bring out furs was through Hudson Bay, but they were unable to garner support for their idea from the government in New France. Thus they sailed to England, where they did interest investors, one of whom was Prince Rupert. After an initial foray in the famous *Nonsuch* in 1668, when Groseilliers reached the mouth of the Rupert River at the southern end of James Bay and returned to England with a cargo of furs, the Hudson's Bay Company was chartered in 1670, with rights granted by the English king to all of the drainage basin of Hudson Bay, which they named Rupert's Land.

The English were to prove more desirous of waiting on the shore of the bay for furs to come to them than of going out to seek them, but since it was essential to announce their presence if they expected the natives to come to them, in 1690 Henry Kelsey was sent up the Nelson River from York Fort, which had been established in 1684. Kelsey was a good choice, for "The Boy Henry Kelsey," said a Company report, was "a very active Lad Delighting much in Indians Compa.[ny] being never better pleassed then when hee is Travelling amongst them." Accompanying a group of natives returning from York Factory to their wintering ground, he continued up the Saskatchewan River and became the first European to reach the prairies. Kelsey was perhaps the first to show that the best progress and results were obtained from traveling light and adapting to the native methods of survival, a lesson, however, that would take a long time in the learning.

After the Treaty of Utrecht in 1713, Hudson Bay was confirmed as English, and the French were denied access to the bay and so were forced to concentrate on a route to the interior farther south. As early as 1717 a French government report stated what the French had deduced, based on assumptions about symmetrical geography, popular at the time. Every geographical feature had to be balanced by another. The French had heard of "a large river which is understood to issue from the same mountain that holds the source of the Missouri. It is believed, even, that a branch of it falls into the Sea of the West." Men were to be sent west to discover it, and, it was hoped, they would soon open a commerce with China and Japan.

In 1728 Pierre Gaultier de Varennes, Sieur de La Vérendrye, was placed in charge of the French trading posts west of Lake Superior. Here he heard reports from the Cree about "a great river which flows towards the setting sun." As the French traders extended their posts to Lake Winnipeg and Lake Manitoba, it became evident that the reports referred only to the Winnipeg River. But they heard a report

Carte que les Gnacsitares . . . and *Carte de la Riviere Longue . . .* by French adventurer Louis-Armand de Lom d'Arce, Baron de La Hontan, drawn in 1703. This map was the product of Hontan's imagination combined with native information; two maps combined into one. Despite this fact, the map was very influential. Hontan managed to convince many people that the map was the result of his personal explorations, and as a result the information about a long river flowing to or from the west was incorporated into many later maps, even those by more reputable mapmakers.

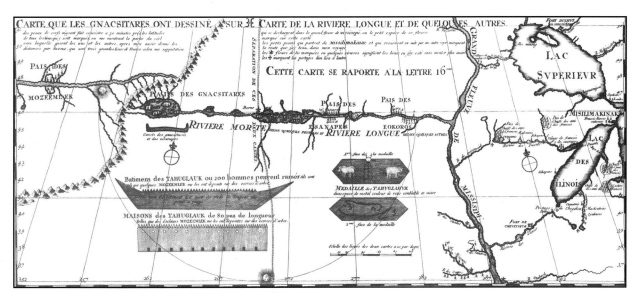

from the Jesuit Father Charlevoix that "after sailing up the Missouri as far as it is navigable you come to a great river which flows westward and discharges into the sea." In 1738 Vérendrye went southward to the Missouri in search of this river, and in 1742 he sent two of his sons, Louis-Joseph, known as the Chevalier, and François, to go yet farther in their search for a Western Sea. They reached, it is thought, the Black Hills of Dakota, the most easterly outpost of the Rocky Mountains. No doubt they expected to see the ocean from the crest of the hills, but were still 1 600 km or 1,000 miles from the Pacific. They were, however, probably the first non-natives to see the Rocky Mountains.

In 1754, Anthony Henday of the Hudson's Bay Company left York Fort on a massive reconnaisance of the western interior, designed to encourage distant native groups to bring their furs to the shores of Hudson Bay rather than trade with the French. By October Henday had reached the foothills of the Rocky Mountains near present-day Calgary. Later he found the North Saskatchewan River, passing what is now Edmonton in March 1755. Henday is generally credited with being the first English explorer to see the Rocky Mountains. He was unable to persuade the natives to bring furs to York Factory, however, as they considered it, quite reasonably, to be too distant. He also found the French had pre-empted much of the fur trade of the prairies. Henday was sent out again in 1759 and presumably made a similar trip to the foothills of the Rockies, but no record of his later expedition survives.

In 1766 Jonathan Carver was sent to explore "uncharted western territories" by Robert Rogers, an army captain who thought he could discover the Northwest Passage. Although Carver only got as far as the Minnesota River, his ideas were enormously influential, for the book he wrote became a best-seller in its day, eventually going through some thirty editions in several languages. The map in Carver's book showed a large and long River of the West flowing to the Pacific, as well as an undefined Western Sea. Another of Carver's maps named the river the "Origan," from whence came the name of the state, Oregon, and one of the early names for the Columbia River. So here, in 1778, was the Columbia, as yet unmapped by actual exploration, depicted on a widely disseminated map.

After the end of the Seven Years War between Britain and France, the Treaty of Paris was signed in 1763, ceding all of Canada to Britain.

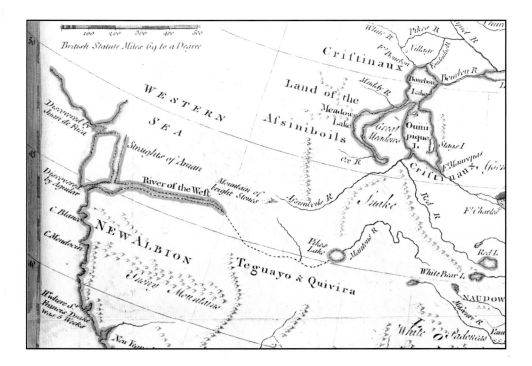

It seemed as though the Hudson's Bay Company, despite a reluctance to expand westward, would control the entire fur trade. But this was not to be. The French fur-trading infrastructure was taken over by another group, which would compete against the Hudson's Bay Company. It was financed by British and American business interests; the French *coureurs du bois* and *voyageurs* were now employed by different masters, and competition for the Hudson's Bay Company in fact became more intense. Before long various groups of traders realized that it was more advantageous to cooperate with each other than to compete, and after several temporary arrangements the North West Company was created. Competition between the North West Company and the Hudson's Bay Company was to spur much westward exploration and expansion in the search for advantage and for new fur regions to supply bigger and bigger volumes of furs, as the "pedlars" based in Montreal became increasingly aggressive. One of these fur-trading businesses in Montreal would later recruit a young Alexander Mackenzie as a promising trainee trader.

Another enormously influential map, published in a book which went through thirty editions. A River of the West is shown flowing past the "Mountain of bright Stones" into the strait "Discovered by Aguilar" (from Spaniard Sebastian Vizcaíno's voyage in 1602). The "Straights of Anian" connect it with the Strait of Juan de Fuca, and an inland "Western Sea" covers an undefined area of the Pacific Northwest.

A New Map of North America From the Latest Discoveries 1778 Engrav'd for Carvers Travels. From J. Carver, *Travels through the Interior Parts of North America in the Years 1766, 1767 and 1768,* London, 1778.

ue levell ground the banks of the
 st steep to. in general about 30. & 40 Feet high.

Fine Marshey Ground

The Coppermine River. by Sam. Hearne. July 1771.

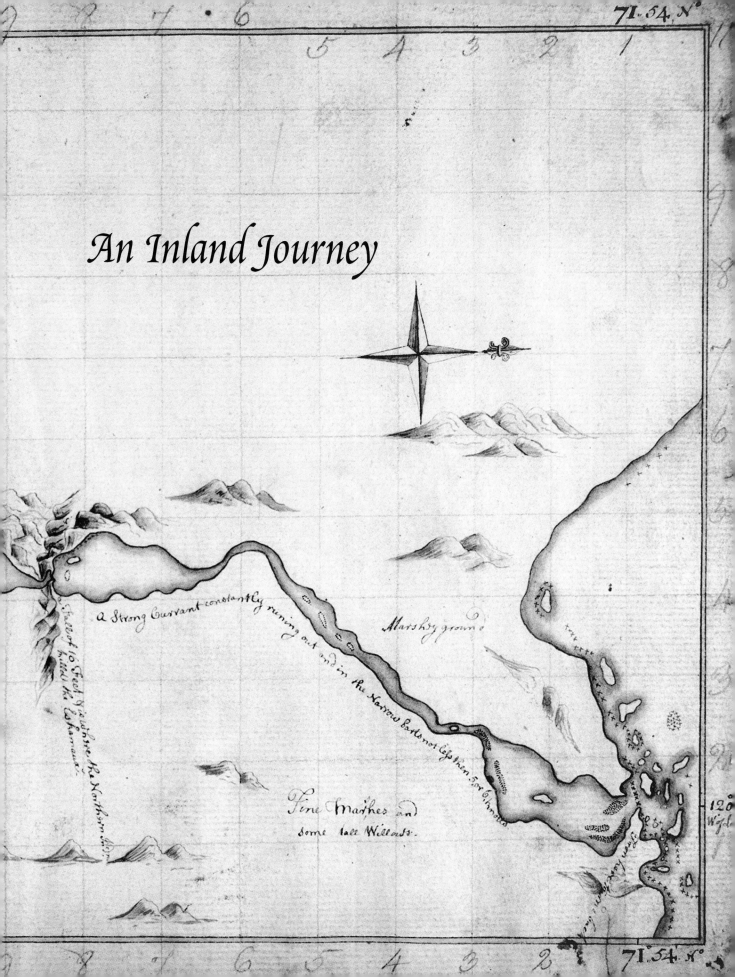

An inland journey, far to the north of Churchill, to promote an extension of our trade, as well as for the discovery of a North West Passage, Copper Mines, &c.

Above: Engraved portrait of Samuel Hearne, from the frontispiece of his book, published posthumously in 1795.

Previous page: Northern part of *A Plan of the Coppermine River by Sam Hearne July 1771*, original manuscript copy. The map is orientated south-north, with north, and the Arctic Ocean, on the right. Note the "Fall of 16 Feet is where the Northern Ind[ia]ns killd the Eskamaux" – Bloody Falls.

Although Alexander Mackenzie was to be the first documented person to descend the Mackenzie River to the Arctic Ocean, he was not the first European explorer to make it overland to that sea; that distinction goes to Samuel Hearne, an employee of the Hudson's Bay Company.

Hearne was a young naval veteran who joined the Company in 1766 and, three years later, at the age of twenty-four, was chosen by Moses Norton, the governor at Prince of Wales Fort on the shores of Hudson Bay, to undertake an expedition to find a river reported by the natives to have sustantial copper deposits. This river apparently flowed northward into a polar sea. The expedition was coincidentally to find a Northwest Passage, should there be one, for the Hudson's Bay Company had been criticized for not attempting to locate this elusive geographical feature, to the extent that Arthur Dobbs, the Surveyor-General of Ireland and a big booster of the concept, had actually petitioned the British Parliament to cancel the Company's monopoly of trade into Hudson Bay.

The Hudson's Bay Company, in a letter to Hearne, stated:

Mr. Norton has proposed an inland journey, far to the north of Churchill, to promote an extension of our trade, as well as for the discovery of a North West Passage, Copper Mines, &c.; and as an undertaking of this nature requires the attention of a person capable of taking an observation for determining the longitude and latitude, and also distances, and the course of rivers and their depths we have fixed upon you . . . to conduct this Journey.

After two false starts, in 1769 and 1770, Hearne set off a third time in December 1770, taking with him a Chipewyan leader named Matonabbee and a large entourage as guides, including seven or eight of the chief's wives – Hearne wasn't sure of the number. More natives joined them as they moved northward, with the result that his party finally numbered more than two hundred.

What Hearne didn't know was that the Chipewyan considered the Eskimo – the Inuit – to be enemies, and were intending to attack them. At the beginning of June 1771 Matonabbee left behind his women, children, and dogs and continued north with only sixty warriors. Hearne by this time had figured out what was going on, but his protestations fell on deaf ears, and since he was quite dependent on the natives for his survival, he had to go along with the plan, and went north with the war party. On 13 July 1771, Hearne and the small army arrived at the Coppermine River, a short distance from its mouth. The Coppermine is 845 km or 525 miles long and flows north to Coronation Gulf, on the Arctic Ocean. Far from being easily navigable, as he had been led to believe by the natives, the river was "at that part scarcely navigable for an Indian canoe." There, a little farther downstream, the natives found a party of Inuit camping by a waterfall. They rushed them during the night and massacred the entire group, much to Hearne's horror, for he was unable to stop them. On the large-scale map that Hearne drew (at the beginning of this chapter), the waterfall is shown "where the Northern Ind[ns] killd the Eskamaux."

On 17 July Hearne finally made it to the shores of the Arctic Ocean. In contrast to what would be Alexander Mackenzie's experience, he immediately realized he was at an ocean, remarking on the presence of a tide; although it was low tide when he arrived at the river's mouth, he noted from marks on the edge of the ice the position of high tide. Again in contrast to Mackenzie,

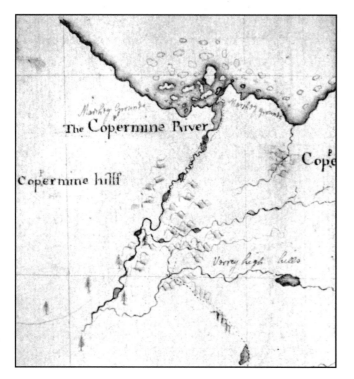

The Coppermine River and the Arctic Ocean, from Hearne's original pen-and-ink map, *A Map of part of the Inland Country to the N[h] W[t] of Prince of Wales Fort H[s], B[y], Humbly Inscribed to the Gov[nr] Dep[y], Gov[nr] and Committee of the Hon[ble] Hud[ns] B[y] Comp[y] By their Hon[rs], moste obediant humble servant. Sam[l] Hearne; 1772.*

Hearne tasted the water, and on finding it fresh he noted:

I am certain of it being the sea, or some branch of it, by the quantity of whalebone and seal-skins which the Esquimaux had at their tents, and also by the number of seals which I saw on the ice.

Hampered now by fog and rain, Hearne did not set up his instrument – a quadrant – to determine his latitude but estimated his position from courses and distances (dead reckoning) from a place he had recently fixed his position, at the Burnside River, which he called by his interpretation of the native name, the mouthful Congecathawhachaga River. The only problem was, he had calculated his position there as 240 km or 150 miles too far north. Not only that, but this was the only fix of his position recorded in his journal that he did during the entire trip – not a good idea. As a consequence his calculated position at the mouth of the Coppermine River was also out. This, he calculated, was 71° 54´ N, and it is shown as such on his map. However, this latitude, which he considered "may be depended upon within twenty miles at the most," was in fact 67° 49´ N, so he was just over 4°, 450 km or 280 miles, too far north. Similarly, Hearne's longitude for the mouth of the Coppermine River was out. He placed it at 120° 34´ W; the correct longitude is 115° 05´ W.

This incorrect latitude was to have far-reaching consequences, for when Hearne finally reached England he found he had been harshly criticized, in particular by Alexander Dalrymple, then Hydrographer to the East India Company. Dalrymple, an advocate of a Northwest Passage, disputed Hearne's claim to have reached nearly 72° N, based on the fact that no grass grew on the coast of Greenland north of 65° N. Since Hearne reported grass (scurvy grass) and trees (stunted pines) near the mouth of the Coppermine, Dalrymple concluded that Hearne must have been no farther north than 65° N. He was wrong, of course; the climate changes sufficiently as you progress westward that the treeline trends farther and farther north.

On his second attempt, Hearne's expedition had returned because he had broken his Hadley's quadrant, used for measuring latitude. Due to tensions between Hearne and Moses Norton, when he departed for his third expedition he had only been allowed an older and inferior

Elton's quadrant; even this was later broken in a storm. This may or may not have been the reason Hearne incorrectly calculated his latitude, but it certainly gave his detractors more ammunition.

On his way back to Prince of Wales Fort, Hearne crossed Great Slave Lake using a route that would later be used by Mackenzie, although Hearne crossed in winter, when the lake was frozen.

Hearne's depiction of the lake showed an outlet to the west, actually the Mackenzie River, but he had obtained the information from natives living around the lake, not from visiting the west end of the lake itself. This outlet had first been shown on a map drawn in 1769 by Moses Norton, Hearne's superior at Prince of Wales Fort, and had been derived from native sources including Matonabbee, Hearne's guide (see page 34). It was native report of this western outlet that was to excite pioneering Nor'Wester Peter Pond to conclude that here must be the link to the Pacific Ocean (see chapter 4).

Hearne returned to Prince of Wales Fort in June 1772 with a single lump of copper ore. The Hudson's Bay Company was pleased with his work but did not consider it important enough to publish. This despite Hearne's conclusion that he has "the pleasure to think that . . . it has put a final end to all disputes concerning a North West Passage through Hudson's Bay."

In 1776 Hearne was put in charge of the fort, and in 1782 he surrendered it to the French naval force under Jean François Galaup, Comte de la Pérouse; the latter is best known for his scientific voyage around the world intended to rival that of James Cook. La Pérouse found Hearne's journal and, recognizing its significance, gave it back to Hearne on the condition that he publish it. When Hearne retired in 1787 he set about doing just that, but he died in November 1792, and the book, *A Journey from Prince of Wales's Fort, in Hudson's Bay, to the Northern Ocean. Undertaken By Order of the Hudson's Bay Company.*

Arathapescow Lake (Great Slave Lake), from the engraving in Hearne's 1795 book, based on his own drawing.

For the Discovery of Copper Mines, A North West Passage, &c. In the Years 1769, 1770, 1771, & 1772, was published posthumously in 1795.

One wonders whether Hearne heard before he died about Alexander Mackenzie's expedition to the Arctic Ocean; he died the same year Mackenzie was in London, and after that visit. It is fascinating to consider the possibility of Samuel Hearne discussing the geography of the Northwest with Mackenzie, but as their affiliations were to competing companies, and they were in London, not the wilderness, it is unlikely such a discussion ever happened.

Hearne's map of Great Slave Lake (Arathapescow Lake), showing the undefined outlet to the west he had heard about from the natives in the region. From the pen-and-ink map drawn by Hearne, *A Map of part of the Inland Country to the N^h W^t of Prince of Wales Fort H^s, B^y, Humbly Inscribed to the Gov^{nr} Dep^y, Gov^{nr} and Committee of the Honble Hud^{ns} B^y Comp^y By their Hon^{rs}, moste obediant humble servant. Saml Hearne; 1772.*

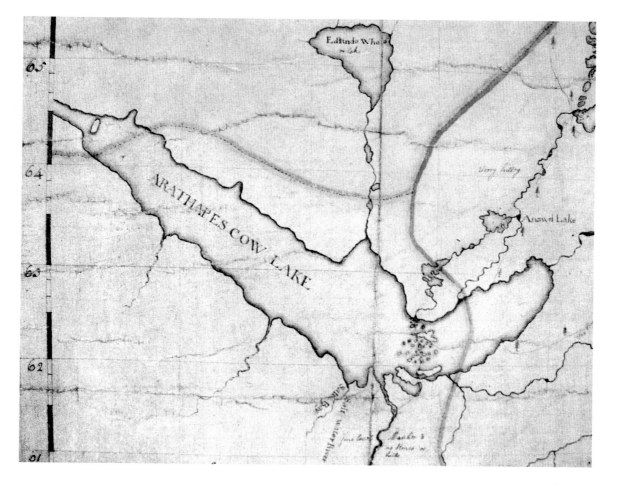

An Explanation of a Draught brought by two Northern Indians Leaders Calld Meatonabee & Idotlyazee Of Ye Country To Ye Northward of Churchill River. Drawn by Moses Norton, c1767.

This hard-to-see pencil-drawn map is the first to show Great Slave Lake and the Mackenzie River flowing from the lake's west end, labeled with the Cree name of "Kis-Ca-Che-Wan."

"Meatonabee," or Matonabbee, was a native chief who had been born at Prince of Wales Fort, the Hudson's Bay Company post on the shores of Hudson Bay. He served as Samuel Hearne's guide during his trek to the Arctic Ocean at the mouth of the Coppermine River in 1771. One of Matonabbee's followers, known as the "English Chief" from his assistance to Hudson's Bay Company traders, became Mackenzie's guide on his first voyage. Moses Norton was the governor at Prince of Wales Fort.

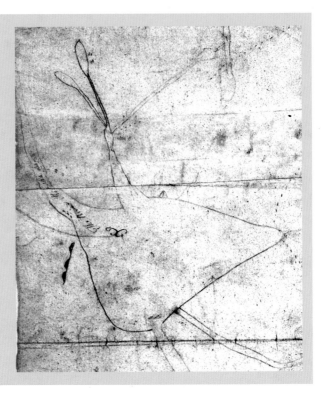

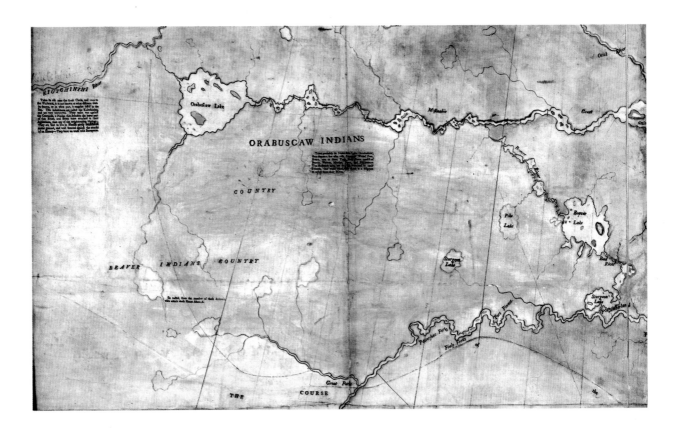

Alexander Henry

One of the first fur traders based in Montreal to travel to the Northwest was the New Jersey–born trader Alexander Henry, called "the elder" to distinguish him from his nephew, Alexander Henry "the younger," who entered the fur trade in 1791. Henry the elder's memoir, *Travels and Adventures in Canada and the Indian Territories Between the Years 1760 and 1776* (1809), is considered a classic of Canadian travel literature.

On 18 August 1775, Henry was on Lake Winnipeg, where his journal records, "I was joined by Mr. Pond, a trader of some celebrity in the northwest."

On 1 July 1776, probably on Lac Île-à-la-Crosse, at the point farthest west and north that he reached, Henry made an entry in his journal of significance to our story of Alexander Mackenzie. Henry was here close to the Arctic drainage system of the Athabasca, though he did not know it.

Our customers [natives selling furs] *were from Lake Arabuthcow* [in this case, Henry is talking about Lake Athabasca, not Great Slave Lake, to which the Arabuthcow name, or its variants, are usually applied], *of which, and the surrounding country, they were the proprietors, and at which they wintered. They informed us, that there was, at the further end of that lake, a river, called Peace River, which descended from the Stony or Rocky Mountains, and from which mountains the distance to the salt lake, meaning the Pacific Ocean, was not great; that the lake emptied itself by a river, which ran to the northward, which they called Kiratchinini Sibi* [or, Henry footnoted, *Yatch-inini Sipi*], *or Slave River, and which flows into another lake, called by the same name; but whether this lake was or was not the sea, or whether it emptied itself or not into the sea, they were unable to say. They also made war with the Indians who live at the bottom of the river, where the water is salt. They also made war on the people beyond the mountains, toward the Pacific Ocean, to which their warriors had frequently been near enough to see it.*

Henry traded a huge number of furs, reportedly some 12,000 beaver as well as otter and marten. It would be the quantity and quality of the furs from the Athabasca country that would encourage the traders to pool their trade goods and send one of their number, Peter Pond, into the region, into the Arctic watershed, and thus push the fur-trading frontiers farther west. The end result would be the formation of a partnership arrangement to deal with the increasing logistics of distance – the North West Company.

In 1781, Henry proposed an expedition to the Pacific, by traveling northwest in high latitudes. The proposal was contained in a letter to the influential president of the British Royal Society, Joseph Banks. Here Henry was influenced by the concepts of Northwest geography that were being developed by his associate Peter Pond. It was the first suggestion for an expedition, one that would ultimately be carried through by Alexander Mackenzie.

Left: Part of a large map of the Northwest drawn by Alexander Henry in 1776, and presented to Guy Carleton, Governor of Quebec. Cumberland House ("Fort Cumberland"), founded by Hearne in 1774, is shown at bottom right. Beaver Lake is Lac Île-à-la-Crosse, Beaver River is La Loche River, and Missinabie River is the Clearwater River; Orabuscow Lake is Lake Athabasca. Methye Portage is at the angle formed by La Loche River and the Clearwater. The Kiutchinini River could be the Peace, Slave, or even Mackenzie River; it is impossible to say for sure. All information west of Lac Île-à-la-Crosse was derived from native reports.

To Undertake the
Perilous Enterprise

I was led, at an early period of life, by commercial views, to the country North-West of Lake Superior, in North America.

Above: The "country North-West of Lake Superior" as shown on a British map of 1785 entitled *The British Colonies in North America.* The boundary between American and British territory, just agreed to by the Treaty of Paris in 1783, is drawn from Lake of the Woods westward to meet with the "headwaters of the Mississippi," the Missouri River. In fact a line drawn west from Lake of the Woods never meets the Missouri, but this was not known at the time.

*A*lexander Mackenzie was a Scot from the Outer Hebrides, rugged and isolated islands off Scotland's west coast. It is not certain when he was born; his emigrant record of 1774 says he was then twelve, so this would make his year of birth 1762; his grandson wrote to an author in 1906 that it was 1763, and notes derived from his sister's descendants said it was 1764. The exact date is not important, but it is interesting to note that this means that Mackenzie was at most only twenty-seven when he went on his first voyage in 1789, and at most thirty-one when he reached the Pacific Ocean in 1793.

He was born in Stornoway, the chief settlement of the Outer Hebrides even to this day, but nevertheless just a village. It has often been pointed out that the latitude of Stornoway is the same as that of Fort Chipewyan, the post on Lake Athabasca from which Mackenzie began both of the epic voyages that were to make him famous. Although the climates of the two places are substantially different, it is likely Mackenzie would not have thought himself particularly far north at Fort Chipewyan.

Mackenzie's mother died when he was still a child, no doubt instilling self-reliance that would stand him in good stead later in life. His family lived at Melbost, a farm very close to the sea, and Mackenzie grew up in an environment where he would have been comfortable with boats. This skill would assist him in the Canadian West, where virtually all travel was by water. A fact often overlooked is that Mackenzie's first language was presumably Gaelic, but even if it was not, he would have grown up familiar with the tongue. Negotiating

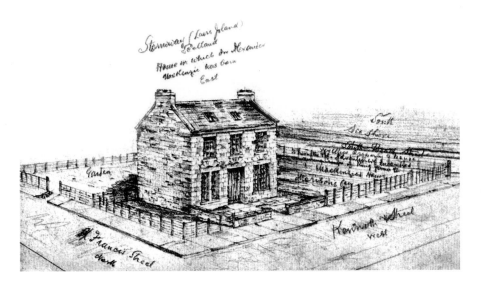

Mackenzie's birthplace, Luskentyre House, Stornoway, Outer Hebrides, Scotland.

with peoples who spoke other languages, trying to decide whether what an interpreter was saying was a true translation, would be a skill perhaps enhanced by this early exposure to two languages. In true Canadian style, Mackenzie probably grew up bilingual.

Overpopulation, rising rents, poor crops, and relatively hard times were the order of the day in much of Scotland at this time, and many Scottish families left their homeland for good and emigrated to America. Young Alexander's family, it seems, were not terribly poor, but not wealthy either, and in 1774 Kenneth Mackenzie, Alexander's father, decided to emigrate as well.

Alexander and two of his four sisters sailed for New York. His father may have preceded him, but by the end of the year the family was in America.

It was not good timing. Only a few months after the Mackenzies arrived in the American colonies, the American Revolution broke out. Kenneth and his brother John signed up with the British army. Alexander's father died while stationed near Kingston in 1780. Alexander was left with two aunts who, in 1778, sent him for safety to Canada, where he briefly attended school in Montreal.

In 1779, when sixteen or seventeen, he entered the fur trade, easily the most exciting occupation likely to appeal to a lad of his age. Montreal had been established as the center of the fur trade by the French, and had been essentially taken over by the British after the fall of Quebec in 1760 and the Treaty of Paris in 1763, the latter dispossessing the French from everywhere in North America except

St. Pierre and Miquelon. Mackenzie joined the firm of Finlay, Gregory and Company and, as an early biographer put it a hundred years ago, "His keenness and daring at once attracted the attention of his employers, and his selection, after a very short experience, to lead a trading expedition to Detroit, on the lower lakes, was a remarkable example of confidence."

In fact it was five years later, in 1784, that Mackenzie was tried out in this way, and sent to Detroit to trade. While there, at the age of twenty-one or twenty-two, he was offered a partnership in the firm, reconstituted the year before as Gregory, McLeod and Company following the retirement of one of the original partners. The partners must have seen qualities of leadership and commercial acumen, for Gregory, wrote Mackenzie, "without any solicitation on my part, had procured an insertion in the agreement, that I should be admitted a partner in this business, on condition that I would proceed to the Indian country in the following spring, 1785." The "Indian country" was the Canadian Northwest. Mackenzie jumped at the opportunity.

This renewed push to the northwest was the result of a new Treaty

This mid-nineteenth-century Ordnance Survey map shows Stornoway much as Mackenzie would have known it as a child. The family farm, Melbost, is clearly marked, close to the sea on two sides.

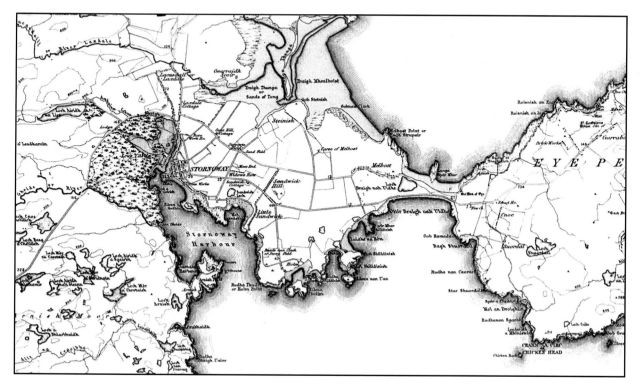

of Paris, signed in 1783, which ended the American Revolutionary War and ceded to the newly recognized independent United States the entire region south of the Great Lakes. Up till that time this area had been a major fur catchment area for the Montreal-based trade, which had inherited the French trading areas south to the Mississippi. Key fur trade posts – Detroit, Michilmackinac, and even Grand Portage, at the western end of Lake Superior – were now in American territory, and no one knew how long British traders would be able to continue to use them. It would be more than ten years before the British would finally have to give up these posts, but in the meantime, they were to be utilized as much as possible, and the thrust of new business, as they say, was to be in the Northwest, the area safe at least for now from American incursions.

The renewed emphasis on the Northwest was to lead to more competition and eventually to the formation of a new trading partnership, much bigger than any of the individual trading firms to that time, the North West Company. Groups of traders had before informally and for a single season sometimes pooled their resources so as to cover more area and not compete against each other for furs traded from the natives. In the winter of 1783–84 a more broadly encompassing five-year partnership emerged and the name North West Company, sometimes applied to the previous looser partnerships, became its official designation. The company was to endure until 1821, when it would merge with the Hudson's Bay Company under the latter's name. But it was the North West Company that would be responsible for much of the thrust to the west, and it would be the North West Company that would first set up a post on the Pacific coast.

For the time being, Mackenzie's company did not join the North West Company, but decided to compete against it. Mackenzie was sent to the English (Churchill) River Department, based at Île-à-la-Crosse. In September 1784 Alexander's cousin Roderic McKenzie had arrived in Canada and, no doubt because of his relative's presence, had become employed by Gregory, McLeod and Company as an apprentice clerk. He was to become the one person Alexander could rely on to hold the fort, literally, while he was away on his voyages in search of the western ocean.

John Ross, one of Mackenzie's partners, had been assigned to the then farthest regions that fur trading had reached, the Athabasca country, the route to which, across the Methye Portage, had been found by Peter Pond in 1778. Now one of the partners in the North West Company, Pond had a reputation for violence, and in 1787 Pond, or at least one of his men, killed Ross when a firearm discharged into Ross' leg and he expired from lack of blood. This event became the catalyst for the merging of Gregory, McLeod and Company with the larger group, to eliminate the competition that was proving so deadly. Thus Alexander Mackenzie, at the age of twenty-four or twenty-five, became a partner in the reconstituted and enlarged North West Company, now pretty much the only show in town other than the Hudson's Bay Company, which at this time was not competing effectively in the interior, away from Hudson Bay.

Pond, too much of a liability, was to be retired as soon as possible, but he knew too much to be kicked out on the spot. Thus it was that the following year, 1788, he was sent back to the Athabasca country with the person selected as being the one most likely to be able to handle him – Alexander Mackenzie. Pond, because of the concepts of the geography of the Northwest that he had developed, was to provide the motivation for Mackenzie's two voyages. And Mackenzie, having received what was essentially another quick promotion, was bursting to prove himself. His discussions with Pond were to give him the ideas that would enable him to do just that.

Mackenzie wrote his own capsule version of his rise within the fur trade and to the point where he would be ready for his voyages in the preface of his book:

I was led, at an early period of life, by commercial views, to the country North-West of Lake Superior, in North America, and being endowed by Nature with an inquisitive mind and an enterprising spirit; possessing also a constitution and frame of body equal to the most arduous undertakings, and being familiar with toilsome exertions in the prosecution of mercantile pursuits, I not only contemplated the practicability of penetrating across the continent of America, but was confident in the qualifications, as I was animated by the desire, to undertake the perilous enterprise.

Beavers on a riverbank,
engraved from a painting by
Karl Bodmer, about 1830.

The North West Company

It has been said that a fashion in men's hats was responsible for the creation of the North West Company, the organization to which Alexander Mackenzie belonged at the time of his two expeditions. Indeed it was responsible for the entire Canadian fur trade. The hats were made of beaver.

The fur of beaver pelts was ideal for making very high-grade felt, which was warm and waterproof in a climate where it rained a lot and little was truly waterproof. This demand for beaver led to the formation of the Hudson's Bay Company, chartered in 1670 and given a monopoly by the King of England covering all the lands draining into Hudson Bay, which was considered, by right of first exploration, to be English. In any case the St. Lawrence was already claimed and occupied by the French. All that changed in 1763, when, by the Treaty of Paris, Britain came into possession of all the French territories in North America, save St. Pierre and Miquelon.

The British simply took over the management of the French fur trade. Individual entrepreneurs saw a way into the North American fur trade that would get around the Hudson's Bay Company monopoly: they didn't need to use Hudson Bay; they would use Montreal and the St. Lawrence. After the end of the American War of Independence, another Treaty of Paris in 1783 meant that the trade routes to the south would be cut off, thus necessitating a concentration north of the 49th parallel, east of the Rockies.

The problem for the fur traders was they needed to be in the interior trading furs with the natives and in Montreal selling and shipping the furs to Europe, and sometimes in England arranging financial matters. It took years for a fur traded in the Northwest to find its way to Europe and for the payment for it to find its way back again.

A selection of contemporary hats, all made from beaver pelts.
From top: naval cocked hat; military helmet; "the Regent"; "the Paris beau"; army tricorn.

It was the need to act cooperatively in order to deal with these long times and the vast distances now presenting themselves that forced the fur traders of Montreal to begin loose associations, and then initiate formal partnership arrangements, the major one being the formation of the North West Company. This way some partners could be in Montreal and some, the wintering partners, in the interior. Both needed each other. Long-term financing was also needed due to the length of time between cost outlays for the interior trading organization and the return of profits from the fur sales, as well as for financing of exploration to extend the area over which furs could be gathered as the closer areas became depleted of beaver. This favored larger companies. Mackenzie needed to be part of a larger organization in order to be able to finance his explorations, which of course did not yield any immediate return.

The North West Company was a partnership of partnerships, since the businesses that grew up in Montreal were all groups of individuals. It was the Montreal partnership of Finlay, Gregory and Company that Mackenzie joined in 1779, the year after he first arrived in Canada and the same year the first temporary partnership that became known as the North West Company was formed. It was reorganized the following year, and in the winter of 1783–84 became a permanent organization, albeit renewed every few years. The partnership that Mackenzie was part of, which had been renamed Gregory, McLeod and Company in 1783, became part of the North West Company group in 1787, after the killing of John Ross, who was also one of the Gregory, McLeod partners, by (we assume) Peter Pond.

The North West Company lasted until 1821, when it merged with the Hudson's Bay Company, taking the latter's name. It is an interesting and ironic footnote to history that the company that purchased the chain of northern stores from the Hudson's Bay Company in the 1980s renamed itself the North West Company.

Coat of arms of the North West Company. A beaver and a canoe figure prominently.

Mackenzie's Illustration of the Need for Capital and Cooperation in the Fur Trade

In *The General History of the Fur Trade*, which precedes the accounts of his two expeditions in his book *Voyages from Montreal,* Mackenzie gave this account of the long times required for furs to yield a return to the business, thus emphasizing the need for considerable capital resources and cooperation:

The agents are obliged to order the necessary goods from England in the month of October, eighteen months before they can leave Montreal; that is, they are not shipped from London until the spring following, when they arrive in Canada in the summer. In the course of the following winter they are made up into such articles as are required by the savages; they are then packed into parcels of ninety pounds weight each, but cannot be sent from Montreal until the May following; so that they do not get to market until the ensuing winter, when they are exchanged for furs, which come to Montreal the next fall, and from thence are shipped, chiefly to London, where they are not sold or paid for before the succeeding spring, or even as late as June; which is forty-two months after the goods were ordered in Canada; thirty-six after they had been shipped from England, and twenty-four after they had been forwarded from Montreal; so that the merchant, allowing that he has twelve months credit, does not receive a return to pay for those goods, and the necessary expences attending them, which is about equal to the value of the goods themselves, till two years after they are considered as cash, which makes this a very heavy business. There is even a small proportion of it that requires twelve months longer to bring round the payment, owing to the immense distance it is carried, and from the shortness of the seasons, which prevents the furs, even after they are collected, from coming out of the country for that period.

This will be better illustrated by the following statement:

We will suppose the goods for 1798;

The orders for the goods are sent to this country	25th Oct. 1796
They are shipped from London	March 1797
They arrive in Montreal	June 1797
They are made in the course of that summer and winter	
They are sent from Montreal	May 1798
They arrive in the Indian country, and are exchanged for furs the following winter	1798–9
Which furs come to Montreal	Sept. 1799
And are shipped to London, where they are sold in March and April, and paid for in	May or June 1800

Even the time required for information to travel was long. An "express" was a canoe and two or three men traveling light, with little more than letters and their own supplies. In winter they traveled by foot and only in later years by sled and dogs. Interesting information on the times required was given by Alexander's cousin Roderic McKenzie in his later reminiscences. According to him, the first winter express left Fort Chipewyan on 1 October 1798 and reached Sault Ste. Marie on 17 May 1799, taking 229 days. Distance and time were major considerations in fur trade travel.

Continent

RICA

by Capt. Cook

Here according to the account of the Natives the water ebbs and flows and they know of no Land further to the Northward

Here the Ochipawayons from No. 21 kill'd a number of Eskimaux in the Summer of 1787.

Dog Rib Indians

no wood to be seen in these parts

in Cook found the water on this Coast to be much fresher
alt or Sea water: likewise, a quantity of drift wood, no doubt
d there by the Rivers Aurabascha, Peace and Mountain, especially as
y annually overflow their banks in the months of May and August: the former
g to the Ice breaking up; the latter to the great quantity of Snow upon the
ountains where they take their source, melting at that time, and at each of
ese periods there, drives down a large quantity of Wood such as is not to be
et with to the Northward of the aforementiond Rivers.

Bear L.

Red Knife People

Birch L.

much Ice
15 July 87

Great Slave Lake

A broken Country

Ochipawayon's In'.

many Lakes & Rivers

A Great Waterfall

Mt. of the Mountain

Salt R'.

Lake of the Hills discov'd by P. Pond.

a number of small Lakes call'd little Aurabascha

Sandwich Sound

Mt. St. Elias

Hare Indians

Variation 16°.30 East

Hinchinbrooke I.

Cape St. Elias

Cape Suckling

River of Peace

Pelican R'

Cook's R.

Aurabaska

Fire Steel R'

Beef L.

L. Clair

Cross Cape

Pike Indians

Strong Bow Indians

These parts are the least frequented by the Natives it being a War Road

Aurabaska

Esclave L.

Water hen L.

Cape Edgecombe

Port Briccarelli discover'd by the Spaniards

Gt. River

Beaver R'. Ind'

Beaver R'

I.t St. Charles

Cottonohis In'

Pike L.

This chain of Mountains extends from New Mexico

Raven In'.

ORTH

CIFIC

King George's Sound where Capt. Cook repair'd

going Northw. 1778

River of the West discover'd 1603

CEAN

You Will Readily Conjecture

There can be no doubt, but the Source of Cook's River
is now fully discovered and known.

– Isaac Ogden on Peter Pond, 1790

Mr. Pond's Assertion was nothing but conjecture.

– Alexander Mackenzie, 1794

Previous page: Part of a copy of the map Peter Pond prepared for presentation to Catherine, Empress of Russia. The river flowing from the west end of Great Slave Lake is now shown close to Cook Inlet, strongly hinting at a connection. See page 64 for complete map.

O f central importance to our story of Alexander Mackenzie is the Connecticut fur trader Peter Pond. He was the first trader to breach the Arctic watershed and thus bring a whole new realm of fur potential into the trade; not only was the Athabasca region large and untapped, but the quality of the fur was significantly better, due to lower temperatures.

It was Pond who first interested Mackenzie in the idea that at Lake Athabasca you were near enough to the Pacific Ocean to attempt to traverse the intervening land. Mackenzie undoubtedly knew of earlier attempts to reach the fabled Western Sea, but it was Pond who convinced him that it was now possible, and that he should be the one to do it if Pond himself could not.

Peter Pond has always been a bit of an enigma, but he was also far-sighted, one of Canada's pioneer geographers, and probably quite brilliant, a fact often obscured by his lack of formal education, which meant he was only semi-literate. The only contemporary description of Pond is by Roderic McKenzie, Alexander's cousin, who said Pond "thought himself a philosopher, and was very odd in his manners." An apt enough description, as we shall see.

Pond was born in Milford, Connecticut, in 1740, when, of course, it was still part of a British colony. He joined the British army when he was sixteen to fight the French in New France. Then he became involved in the fur trade along the Mississippi, and by 1765 he was a trader at Detroit. In 1775 he expanded his horizons and made his first foray into the Canadian Northwest; by 1776 he was trading along the Saskatchewan River. Clearly he had a flair for the fur trade. By 1778 he had acquired such a reputation for his ability to collect furs very quickly that a group of traders chose him to represent them in an attempt to pool stock and avoid unnecessary competition.

It was then that Pond first found his way into the Arctic watershed (with rivers flowing to the Arctic Ocean, as distinct from those flowing to Hudson Bay), the Athabasca country.

There is no direct record of Pond's first exploration, but a letter from Alexander Henry the elder to Sir Joseph Banks, dated at Montreal, 18 October 1781, enclosed a memo on an overland route to the Pacific that instructed: "Proceed to Orrabuscow [Athabasca] carrying place, two hundred and fifty leagues, from where you fall on the Great River, course, near west, supposed to be in sixty degrees lattitude." Since Henry had not himself gone beyond Île-à-la-Crosse the account seems to be based on that of Peter Pond.

Mackenzie's own book notes that

some of the traders on the Saskatchiwine River, finding they had a quantity of [trade] goods to spare, agreed to put them into joint stock, and gave the charge and management of them to Mr. Peter Pond, who, in four canoes, was directed to enter the English [Churchill] River . . . and proceed still further; if possible to Athabasca, a country hitherto unknown but from Indian report. In this enterprise he at length succeeded, and pitched his tent on the banks of the Elk [Athabasca] River . . . about forty miles from the Lake of the Hills [Lake Athabasca].

Pond had traveled to Lac Île-à-la-Crosse, the farthest point at that time reached by fur traders. Then, following a well-established native route, he had canoed to Lac La Loche, then dragged his canoes about thirteen miles across a portage to the Clearwater River. This was the famous Portage La Loche, or Methye Portage, which became the principal route to the Northwest from that point on until the coming of the railway. The Clearwater River has also been called the Swan River, or the Pelican River on Pond's 1785 map (page 56).

This was a momentous occasion, for here at last was a river flowing westward, apparently toward the Western Sea. Although Pond did not believe this river flowed directly there, he did believe that it would be connected to rivers that did. Following the Clearwater to the Athabasca,

The Grand Rapids on the
Athabasca River, photo-
graphed about 1910 by a
Hudson's Bay Company
photographer. Pond was the
first fur trader to descend
the Athabasca, which he
called the Elk River.

Hudson's Bay Company Archives,
H. A. Tremayne (1987/245/3).

which it meets at today's Fort McMurray and which he named the
Elk River, Pond established a post about 30 miles upstream from
Lake Athabasca, which would be his headquarters for the next six
years. In this region there was a good supply of birch trees of sufficient size to be able to supply bark for making canoes, a valued
commodity everywhere but even more so in these more northern
latitudes. The post would remain the only one in the region until
Mackenzie established Fort Chipewyan on the south shore of Lake
Athabasca in 1788.

All the evidence points to the fact that Pond was not a very like-
able character, to say the least. We know that while he was based in
Detroit, he killed a man in a duel. A surviving part of Pond's semi-
literate journal says: "We met the Next Morning Eairley & Discharged
Pistels in which the Pore fellowe was unfortenant. I then Came Down
the Countrey & Declard the fact But thare was none to Prosacute
me." It was a pattern that would be repeated.

Proof that Pond had developed some of his theories of the geography of the Northwest quite early came from Alexander Henry, who
wrote of them in 1781:

Proceed down this great river [presumably the river Pond had flowing from the western end of Great Slave Lake] *untill you come to the sea, which cannot be at any great distance. Suppose it should be thirty, or forty degrees of longitude unless some accidents should intervene, it can be done in thirty days which will be in July; here* [on the coast] *an establishment may be made in some convenient bay or harbour, where, shipping may come to. In the meantime a small vessel may be built, for coasting and exploaring the coast which can be no great distance from the streight* [Bering Strait] *which separates the two continents.*

The year after establishing his Athabasca post, Pond was at Lac la Ronge, back in the Churchill watershed, where he was joined by another partner in the enterprise, Etienne Wadin. "Two men of more opposite characters could not have been found" was Mackenzie's assessment. In March 1782 Wadin was killed, probably by Pond or one of his men, but although Pond was tried at Montreal for the murder, there was not enough evidence to convict him. This was to happen again in 1787 when another trader, John Ross, was also killed under dubious circumstances that everyone thought had to be Pond's doing, or at least one of his men's. According to Hudson's Bay Company surveyor Philip Turnor's journal, the culprit was a voyageur named Péché,

As on many northern rivers, the only way to ascend sections of the Athabasca River was by pulling your canoe on a line from the bank. This photograph of Hudson's Bay Company men lining, or tracking, fur-laden scows up the Athabasca was taken in the 1890s.

one of Pond's men; but again there was not enough evidence. In the wilderness it was difficult to find witnesses. But circumstantial evidence or not, it would be the latter incident that would finally end Pond's career; however, it would also advance that of Alexander Mackenzie, who would be sent to replace Pond.

Aware that their explorations in the Athabasca were both valuable and potentially stategically significant, the group of fur traders with whom Pond was associated at the time, one of the precursor groups to the North West Company already calling themselves by that collective name, composed a petition that they sent to Frederick Haldimand, "Captⁿ General and Commander in Chief in and over the Province of Quebec and the Territories thereon depending." Signed by Benjamin and Joseph Frobisher and dated at Montreal, 4 October 1784, the memorial asked for a ten-year monopoly over trade to the northwest from Lake Superior, in

consideration . . . of exploring at their own expence between the Latitudes of 55, and 65, all that Tract of Country West of the Hudsons Bay to the North Pacific Ocean, and communicating to Government such Surveys and other information respecting that Country, as it may be in their power to Obtain.

This was followed up with another memorial sent to Henry Hamilton, the Lieutenant-Governor (Halimand having retired), by "Peter Pond, on behalf of the North West Company," dated at Quebec, 18 April 1785. In it, Pond wrote:

Your Memorialist begs leave to Assure Your Honor, that the persons connected in the North West Company are able and willing to Accomplish the important discoveries proposed in their Memorial to His Excellency General Haldimand, provided they meet with due encouragement from Government; having men among them who have already given proof of their genius and unwearied industry, in exploring those unknown regions as far as the Longitude of 128 degrees West of London; as will appear by a Map with remarks upon the Country therein laid down.

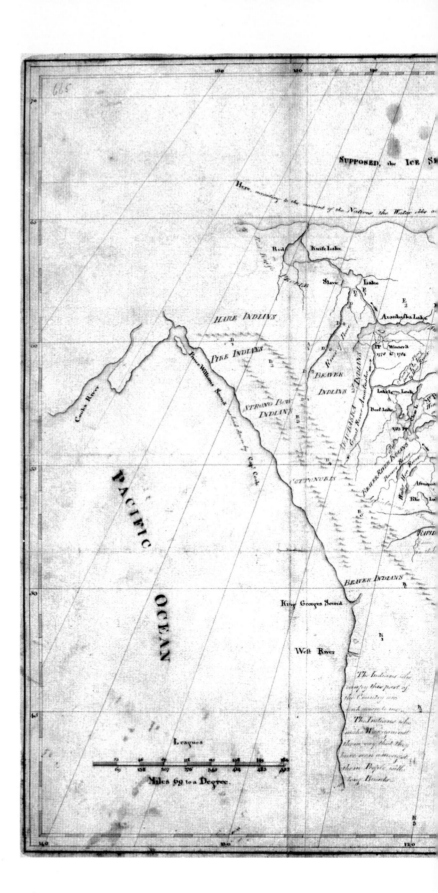

Map of western Canada presented to the
Lieutenant-Governor of Quebec, Lord
Hamilton, in 1785 by Peter Pond.

Pond's map correctly places King George
Sound (Nootka Sound) at about 126° W,
but the interior features between Hudson
Bay and the coast are considerably
compressed. The Rockies are shown not far
from the Pacific coast. Great Slave Lake and
Lake Athabasca are shown about 20° W of
their true location, but correctly emptying
into the Arctic. They would be shown
draining to the Pacific in Pond's later maps.

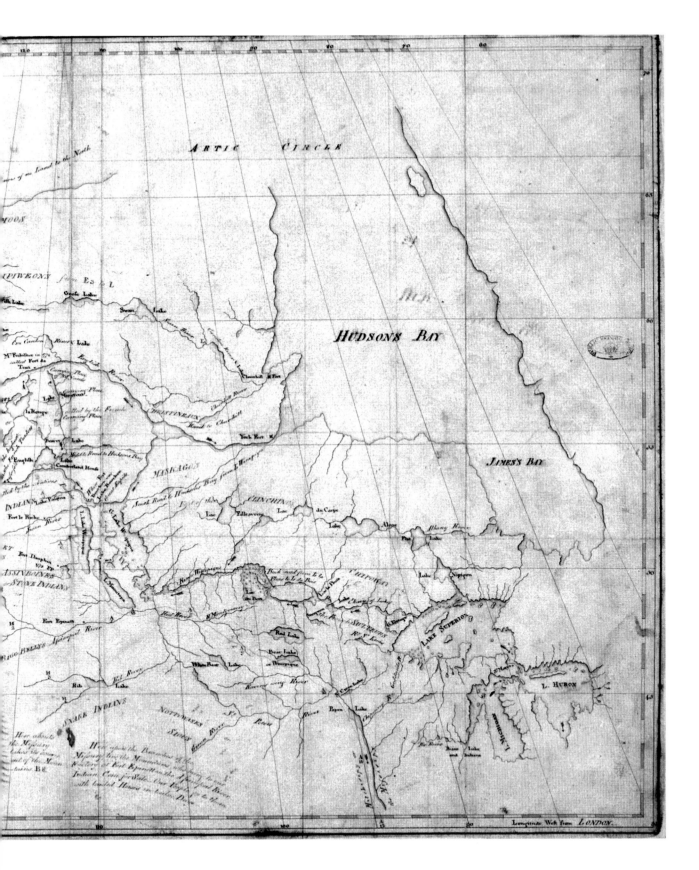

ARTIC CIRCLE

HUDSON'S BAY

JAMES'S BAY

LAKE SUPERIOR

L. HURON

MANICAGO

CHIPIWEONS

ASSINEBOINS
or STONE INDIANS

SNAKE INDIANS

NOTTOWAYS
STONE

Longitude West from LONDON

57

Pond went on to say:

Your memorialist humbly begs leave to inform your honor, that he has had positive information from the Natives, who have been to the Coast of the North Pacific Ocean that there is a trading post already established by the Russians: And your memorialist is credibly informed that Ships are now setting out from the United States of America, under the Command of Experienced Sea-Men who accompanied Captain Cook in his last Voyage in order to establish a furs trade upon the North West Coast of North America, at or near to Prince William's Sound.

Here Pond was referring to the fact that the Russians had indeed established at least one post for fur-trading operations on the island of Unalaska, which had been visited by James Cook on his third voyage, in 1778. Pond could have known about this from the account of Cook's voyage of 1778, which had been published in 1784; other accounts had been published by some of Cook's men before that, in particular one account attributed to John Rickman in 1781 and another by John Ledyard in 1782, both in the United States, so they seem the most likely source for Pond's assertion. A permanent Russian post was established on Kodiak Island in 1784, but it is unlikely Pond would have known about that only one year later.

Pond's reference to American ships is a bit more questionable; although preparations were likely under way, the first voyage to the Northwest Coast did not leave Boston until 1787. This was the voyage of Robert Gray and John Kendrick in the *Lady Washington* and *Columbia Rediva*. The latter ship would later (1792) lend its name to the mighty river flowing into the Pacific.

Hamilton was anxious to support Pond and the North West Company, not least of all because he was concerned that the Americans might try to assert influence leading to claims of sovereignty in the Northwest. He therefore urged the British government to support them, and eventually it would try – by ordering the mounting of an expedition of its own that aimed to do very much what Mackenzie actually did in 1789; the expedition of Captain John Frederick Holland was canceled only after word arrived of Mackenzie reaching the Arctic Ocean in 1789 (see page 140).

The map presented to Hamilton by Pond was not the first he had drawn; Pond drew a number of maps, copies of a few of which survive. They admirably demonstrate the evolution of his concept of the geography of the Northwest, which at its apex must have been the one he would pass to Mackenzie in the winter of 1787–88.

Pond was by all accounts very good at dealing with native peoples, and this manifested itself in his considerable success in acquiring a large number of furs. At the same time he was able to acquire information as to the geography of areas beyond those he had personally visited. There was, however, a significant difference between native mapping concepts and those of western cultures, and Pond, in his attempts to interpret native information, often got his distances, scales, sizes, and directions confused. Of particular significance was the fact that Pond did not have the instruments or skills to determine longitude accurately, and hence he tended to overestimate how far west he was, which had the effect of making him think he was nearer to the Pacific Ocean than he was in reality.

The earliest of Pond's maps that survive is a copy of one he presented to the United States Congress in New York in March of 1785, which was probably a map he had drawn at least a year earlier. It is not clear why he presented it to the Congress, but Pond had been born in Connecticut, by then in the United States of America, and may have hoped to encourage American interest in his ideas. This is possibly why this map dispenses with any notions of rivers flowing to the Pacific Ocean and concentrates on illustrating the ease with which the United States could move northward into the Northwest country. This map is the first to show the Mackenzie drainage system, and an embryonic Mackenzie River is shown, correctly flowing to the Arctic Ocean. The Rocky Mountains are shown as a single line of mountains, following the belief at the time, but no sea coast (apart from a small section in the southwest). The accuracy of the river and lake systems shown declines from east to west, as might be expected.

Attached to the copies of this map in the British Library are some notes, in French, which throw some considerable light on Pond's thinking; one can almost hear Pond elucidating his reasoning to Mackenzie as they pored over his maps in his cabin on the Athabasca River in the winter of 1787–88.

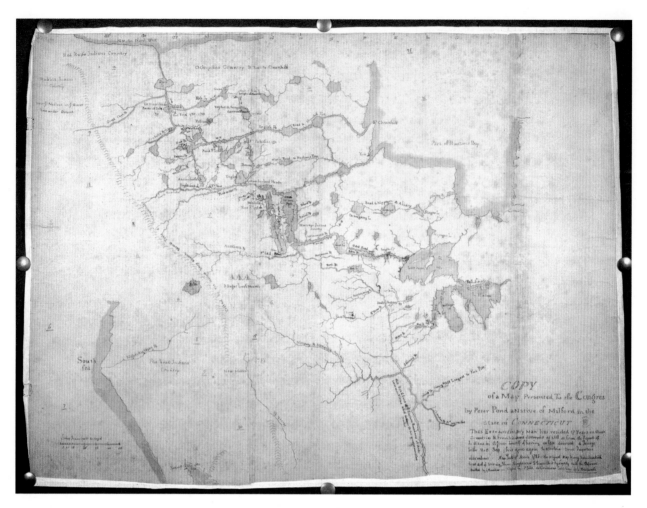

Copy of a Map presented to the Congress by Peter Pond, a native of Milford in the State of Connecticut. 1785 copy of a 1784 map originally drawn by Peter Pond. The legend under the title states: *This extraordinary man has resided 17 years in these countries & from his own Discoveries as well as the reports of Indians, he assures himself of having at last Discovered a passage to the N.O.* [Nord Ouest] *Sea, he is gone again to ascertain some important observations. New York 1st March 1785. The original Map being incumbered with great deal of writing I have thought it best to transcribe it separately with the references marked, by ye numbers. Copied by St. John de Crevecoeur for his Grace of La Rochefoucauld.*

This is the first of Peter Pond's surviving map copies, presented to the United States Congress, then sitting in New York, in 1785. Copied by J. Hector St. John de Crèvecoeur. There are several versions of this map still extant; this is the one from the British Library. The transcript referred to giving the meaning of numbers on the map has been lost, but it seems likely many of them were "forts," in the sense of camping or stopping places. Flowing from the west into the Slave River, between Pond's Arabasca Lake (Lake Athabasca) and Great Slave Lake, is "Great Cave R." This is the Peace River, the river Mackenzie eventually would take to the Pacific.

Pond calculated:

I suppose that there is 140° East of distance between St Petersburg and the Bearing Strait, from St Petersburg to Churchill 126° West, from there to Arabasca 23° West; in all 289° already discovered; in consequence, there is no more to be discovered but 74° between Arabosca and Bearing Strait.

There are several other points Pond uses to promote his theories. He says he had

a conversation with forty of the natives who live a small distance from the sea of the North West. Other tribes call them the people of the red knives. This name comes from their articles being made of red copper, which they have lots of in their country. They confirm the ebb and flow of the waters of that sea.

That Pond knew that the sea he was talking about here was the Arctic Ocean is borne out by the following: "They told me about the length of the days and the nights; there is no total darkness during the summer but always dusk. I imagine that the new sea is on the Arctic Circle."

Pond's initial idea seems to have been to go north to the Arctic Ocean, and then find the Pacific Ocean by going westward along the coast. To this he added, after gaining information from Cook's third voyage, the idea of following the river flowing westward from Great Slave Lake, which would, he presumed, end up at the Pacific more directly. "All the rivers on the west side of the [Rocky Mountains] run to the Pacific or Eastern Ocean," he concluded, this time, for once, correctly.

The reader will be delighted to know, looking at Pond's map, that he did not "claim scrupulous exactitude for the map which accompanies this memoir because being lost in the wood with little paper, I was making my observations as best as I could."

The United States Congress was not interested in Pond's map or the Northwest, because they had just received a large tract of land to the westward of the original thirteen colonies and were trying to figure out what to do with that. What a marked difference there would be in the American attitude to the Northwest only fifty or sixty years in the future, when they would threaten the British with war to get the Oregon country.

Finding no interest in his ideas in the United States, Pond returned to Canada. The map Pond presented to Lieutenant-Governor Hamilton, ostensibly only a month later than the one he presented to the U.S. Congress, shows a progression of ideas and a marked change, the insertion of the outline of the sea coast. Cook's River is shown at 152° W; James Cook had placed it at 208° E, which, surprise, is 152° W. This is too much of a coincidence to have us believe anything other than that Pond copied it from Cook. Nootka Sound, Cook's King George Sound, is also correctly placed at about 126° W. It is worth mentioning, incidentally, that Cook was the first to carry then experimental chronometers for determining longitude accurately, and so the fixing of the position of the west coast of North America by Cook was the first time it had been done correctly, and also the first time, therefore, that the true width of the continent of North America had been determined.

The most immediately noticeable thing about the map presented to Lieutenant-Governor Hamilton is the depiction of the rivers and lakes of the Northwest, and the line of the Rocky Mountains, as too far west by about 20° of longitude, which is about 1 000 km or 600 miles.

Pond was clearly beginning by this time to get a notion of his main theme – that there might be a direct connection from the rivers and lakes to the North Pacific. James Cook had not surveyed Cook Inlet, in Alaska, south of today's Anchorage, to its termination in Turnagain Arm. The published maps show the extreme east-

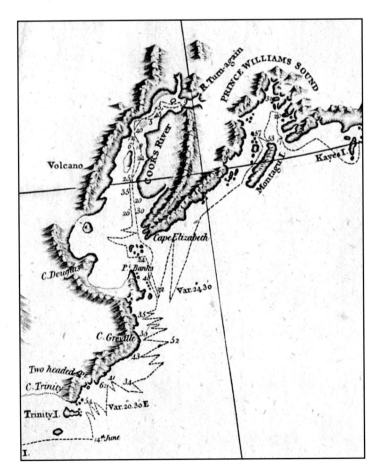

Part of Cook's published map of the entire Northwest Coast. The northeast extremity of Cook's River (now Cook Inlet) is Turnagain Arm. It was not explored by Cook right to its termination, leaving open the way for Pond and others to suggest that it might be the mouth of a large interior river. Part of: *Chart of the NW Coast of America and the NE Coast of Asia explored in the years 1778 and 1779 The unshaded parts of the coast of Asia are taken from a MS chart received from the Russians.* From James Cook, *Voyage to the Pacific Ocean,* 1784.

ern end of the inlet left open. As a result, the whole inlet had been named Cook's River; it would not be explored completely until George Vancouver did so in 1794, at which time he would change its name from Cook's River to Cook's Inlet. In the interim, even the name suggested to many people, not least of all Peter Pond, that there must be some large westward-flowing river that terminated in the inlet. Cook had not found a Northwest Passage, but perhaps it could still be found through the river and lake systems of the Northwest.

By 1785 Pond had not made this leap, but two years later it seems he had, or very closely at any rate. Shown below, and at the beginning of this chapter, is a copy (the original is lost) of a rather beautiful map Pond first made in 1787. It is likely the same or very similar to one he showed to his new wintering partner in 1787–88 at his post on the Athabasca River, Alexander Mackenzie. In fact, it was this map that he gave to Mackenzie in expectation of his being able to present it to Catherine, the Empress of Russia, after Mackenzie had traversed to the Pacific, found a Russian post, and been transported on a Russian ship to the east coast of Russia. The map for this reason shows a good deal of Russia and the North Pacific Ocean in order to convey to the Empress the correct relationship of her realm to North America. The whole map is shown on page 64, and the detail of western North America is the double page map (pages 48–49) at the beginning of this chapter. Needless to say, the map never made it to Russia, but it does summarize the significant concepts of the geography of the Northwest that Pond and then Mackenzie must have had by the time Mackenzie was to set out on his first expedition in 1789. It also explains, as we shall see later, why Mackenzie must have been disappointed when he reached the Camsell Bend on the Mackenzie River, where it turns sharply northward, away from its directional trend to the Pacific, which is maintained up to that point.

The overriding characteristic of this map is the way the river and lake system of the Northwest has inched slowly westward so that it now seems no distance at all from their western extremities to the ocean. It particular, the river flowing westward out of Great Slave Lake, which was undoubtedly the Mackenzie River as related to Pond by native people, flows to within shouting distance of Cook's River and a river flowing into Sandwich Sound (Prince William Sound). It was this

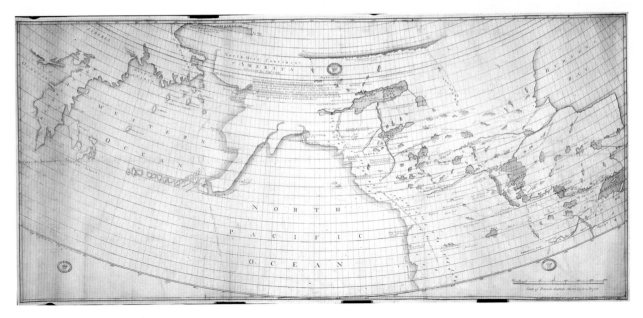

Copy of the map Peter Pond prepared for presentation to Catherine, Empress of Russia. The river flowing from the west end of Great Slave Lake is now shown close to Cook Inlet, strongly hinting at a connection, although a river flowing from the north shore of the lake is shown flowing, as the Mackenzie River does, to the Arctic Ocean. Mackenzie may well have taken this map with him on his first voyage, in case he did indeed end up in Russia. An enlarged part of this wonderful map is shown at the beginning of this chapter (pages 48–49).

river, of course, that Mackenzie would be persuaded to explore in expectation of a speedy arrival at the Pacific Ocean. Pond had decided, contrary to the native reports, that the Rocky Mountains ended at about 62° 30´ N, in order to allow this geographic sleight of hand.

It is perhaps a little ironic that this map actually shows somewhat correctly the Peace River (River of Peace) flowing westward from Slave River, just north of its beginnings at the western end of Lake Athabasca, here shown by the name Pond gave to it, Lake of the Hills. For this is the river that Mackenzie would eventually take on his *second* attempt to find the Pacific Ocean, which would succeed. Even here, the river is shown flowing virtually to the ocean.

Pond even more explicitly developed his ideas to the point of actually showing a connection between Great Slave Lake and Cook's River, as is depicted on his last map (shown at right). Here Pond hedges his bets a bit by showing a connection both to Cook Inlet and Prince William Sound. Again this is not the original map but one taken from *Gentleman's Magazine,* March 1790, published with a letter sent by a Quebec court clerk later to be a judge, Isaac Ogden, to his father, dated the preceding November. His father, David Ogden, had in turn sent a copy of the letter to the British government, in the form of Evan Neapean, the Under-Secretary of State.

Isaac Ogden had had several conversations with Peter Pond and had

Gent.Mag.March 1790. Pl.I.p.197.

A MAP *shewing the communication of the* Lakes *and the* Rivers *between* Lake Superior *and* Slave Lake *in* NORTH AMERICA.

A Map shewing the communication of the Lakes and the Rivers between Lake Superior and Slave Lake in North America. From *Gentleman's Magazine,* March 1790. This representation of the final geographical ideas of Peter Pond now shows a river, labeled "Cook's or Slave R," flowing from Great Slave Lake to Cook Inlet, then known as Cook's River. His dream of an inland Northwest Passage was complete! This was undoubtedly the concept Pond passed on to Alexander Mackenzie in the winter of 1787–88.

been shown his latest map. Ogden must have been impressed by Pond, as he referred to him as a "Gentleman of Observation and Science." Ogden refers to the Athabasca watershed onwards:

when with a small Portage [Methye] *they* [fur traders] *enter into Rivers and Lakes that run a North West Course and empty into other Lakes and Rivers, which all finally communicate with and empty into a great Lake called the Slave Lake, which lays between the Lat. of 63 and 65. being 3 degrees in Width and Long. from 125 to 135. and this Lake is the last water before you come to the great Northern Ocean, which lays in Lat. 68½ and in the Long. 132. where the water ebbs and flows, of which the Gentleman gave me indubitable Proofs.*

One wonders what these "proofs" could have been, but undoubtedly they would have been the same "proofs" that convinced Alexander Mackenzie the year before.

"From out of the Great Slave Lake," Ogden continues,

runs a very large River which runs almost South West, and has the largest Falls on it in the known world, it is at least two miles wide where the Falls are, and an amazing Body of Water. This River leaves the Lake in Lat. 64 and Long. 135 and the Falls are in Long. 141.

Pond had, it seems, misinterpreted native reports. He also couldn't measure longitude; where the Mackenzie leaves Great Slave Lake is in fact 117° W, not 135° W, as Pond maintained, 18° and 900 km or 565 miles too far west. Ironically, Mackenzie would only get to 135° W in 1789 on reaching the Arctic Ocean.

Ogden continues:

You will readily conjecture what River the above Slave lake River is known by, when it empties into the Ocean. To save you much trouble I will tell you it is Cook's River . . . There can be no doubt, but the Source of Cook's River is now fully discovered and known.

Ogden gives some of Pond's "proofs." He thought the great quantities of driftwood Cook found on the beaches of the Northwest Coast must have come from the river. Also, in 1787 Pond received a blanket that had come from "Vessels which were at the Mouth of the River." That a blanket had come from a ship is of course quite possible, but what Pond failed to realize was that the blanket had reached his donors by a trade chain, not directly. The native groups in this region, as in most of North America, had extensive trade networks so that an item could pass from one tribe to another and then to another, many times, traveling a considerable distance in the process.

As to the accuracy of the information, Ogden had no doubt.

The Person from whom I had my Information is Peter Pond, who was supplied with the proper Instruments here to take his Latitude and instructed fully in the Knowledge of Astronomy, etc etc – His Latitude is undoubtedly Right, and his Longitude is near Right, [and, he concluded,] *no great Mistake can be made.*

The final paragraph of Ogden's letter is of particular interest.

Another Man by the name of McKenzie was left by Pond at Slave Lake with orders to go down the River, and from thence to Unalaska, and so to Kamskatska [the Kamchatka peninsula], *and thence to England through Russia, etc. If he meets with no accident you may have him with you* [in England] *the next year.*

Pond was clearly exaggerating his role now; he had essentially been drummed out of the fur trade after he was suspected of killing John Ross, and Mackenzie certainly did not receive any instructions from Pond. But he had clearly received a lot of inspiration!

In the spring of 1788, the year before he espoused his geographical theories to Ogden, Pond had left Athabasca for good and returned to the United States, where he died in 1807. Although Pond was the first fur trader to enter the Athabasca watershed, and perhaps the first to reach Great Slave Lake or even farther north, he has received little credit for this. He has also to date received but little mention in regard to his influence on the young Alexander Mackenzie, but there seems little doubt that without Pond's initial inspiration at least, Mackenzie might well not have embarked on the explorations that made him famous. It would be Mackenzie's first expedition, in 1789, that would prove "that Mr. Pond's Assertion was nothing but conjecture."

Peter Pond drew the first maps, based on exploration, of a huge area of Canada. Even though they had considerable errors, they did correctly show many of the linkages in the river and lake system of the Northwest that Mackenzie was able to build on and correct. Pond's maps were major achievements, the more so because of his lack of instruments, and deserve to be recognized as such. He had what historian Bernard DeVoto called "the continental consciousness . . . of thought and the feel for the land's reality that underlies thought." This man, though of dubious character, was a vital link in the exploration and mapping of the Canada we know today, a link from the previous non-existent or, worse, imaginary concepts of the geography of the West, to the maps of Alexander Mackenzie, which would finally begin the process of filling in the massive blanks in the map based on actual exploration.

To quote Canadian historian Arthur Morton, "Mackenzie took the torch from Peter Pond's hand and pressed on with a masterfulness, self-control, and judgement all his own."

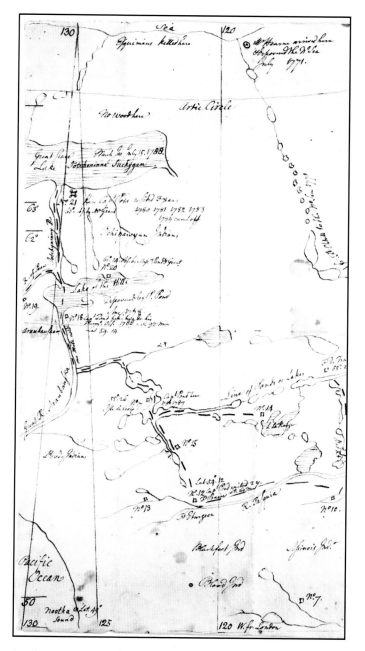

Another variant in Pond's ideas is shown in this map, which is a copy made by Ezra Stiles, then president of Yale University, near Pond's hometown in Connecticut. Pond visited Stiles in 1790, and Yale still has the map he copied. The interesting and unique thing about this map is that now not only does it show the Coppermine River and Samuel Hearne's route to the Arctic Ocean, but it specifically names Hearne and the date – July 1771. Pond's previous maps had shown the route but always attributed it to "Indian report." This map shows that somehow Pond found out the specifics of Hearne's explorations, even though Hearne's employer, the Hudson's Bay Company, was a rival company, and his book was not published until 1795. The year and month were unlikely to have been obtained from native sources.

Determined on Undertaking

a Voyage of Discovery

Determined on undertaking a voyage of discovery the ensuing Spring by the water communications reported to lead from Slave Lake to the Northern Ocean.

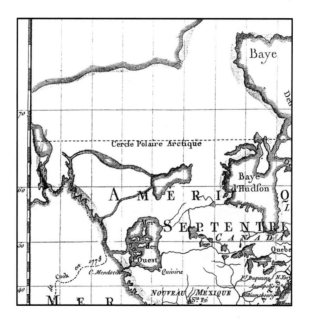

Above: Part of a map of the world published in France, probably c1788–90. A massive river – a strait, really – flows from Great Slave Lake to the Pacific Ocean at Prince William Sound, in Alaska, while another stream flows more directly to the Pacific coast. A Sea of the West covers much of British Columbia and Washington State. If Mackenzie saw such maps before his voyage to the Arctic Ocean they must have encouraged a belief that the passage to the Pacific would be short and not that difficult.

*H*astily reorganized in 1787 to limit the costly competition between it and other groups, the North West Company sent Alexander Mackenzie into the Athabasca country late that year as second-in-command to Peter Pond, for whom the coming winter would be the last he spent in the Northwest. It was so late in the season that when Mackenzie attempted to travel down the Clearwater River to the Athabasca River in October 1787, ice prevented him from getting there with his trade goods for the winter; he had to temporarily cache some of the goods and proceed to the Athabasca post without them.

Mackenzie spent the winter with Peter Pond, as we have seen, going over the latter's ideas of the geography of the Northwest. In January 1788, in the middle of winter, Mackenzie went to Île-à-la-Crosse to visit his cousin Roderic McKenzie. He was evidently formulating his idea of a expedition to the Pacific by then, for on his way back to Athabasca, he wrote a note to Roderic in which he said:

I have already mentioned to you some of my distant intentions. I beg you will not reveal them to any person, as it might be prejudicial to me, though I may never have it in my power to put them in execution.

This is the first documented mention of Mackenzie's plans.

Peter Pond left Athabasca for good in May 1788, leaving Mackenzie in sole command of the district for the North West Company. Now Mackenzie could plan his more immediate future, but he wanted Roderic to be his assistant in Athabasca; Roderic had planned to leave

Mackenzie's cousin and friend, Roderic McKenzie.

the fur trade. But sometime in 1788, according to Roderic's later reminiscences, which have been preserved, Alexander told Roderic

that he had determined on undertaking a voyage of discovery the ensuing Spring by the water communications reported to lead from Slave Lake to the Northern Ocean, adding, that if I [Roderic] could not return and take charge of his department in his absence, he must abandon his intentions. Considering his regret at my refusal, and the great importance of the object he had in view, I, without hesitation, yielded to his wishes, immediately set to work and accompanied him into Athabasca.

Roderic arrived in the Athabasca country later in 1788, and in October he was building a new post that Mackenzie had decided to establish on the south side of Lake Athabasca, or Lake of the Hills, as it was called then, to which Mackenzie would move as the starting point for his expedition only just before his departure. The winter of 1788–89 was spent at Pond's old Athabasca post on the Athabasca River.

Although the intended expedition may have been Mackenzie's idea, it was certainly not without at least the tacit approval of the other partners of the North West Company. If such approval was given, it would have been at Grand Portage in June 1788, at the annual rendezvous of agents and wintering partners. In a letter Mackenzie sent to the "Agents of the North West Company" at Grand Portage dated Athabasca, 22 May 1789, he refers to being back in time, and to passing clerk Laurent Leroux's trading post on Great Slave Lake "on my voyage for a supply of provisions." Leroux would in fact accompany Mackenzie as far as his post when Mackenzie set out on his voyage the following month.

The Explorer's Staple Food: Pemmican

Much has been written about pemmican, for it was very important to the fur trade. Pemmican was dried meat, usually buffalo meat, which was pounded to a powder and then mixed with melted fat. Sometimes berries would be mixed in too. Paul Kane, an artist who was in the Northwest between 1845 and 1848, recorded in his diary the method of making pemmican and the origin of its name.

The thin slices of dried meat are pounded between two stones until the fibres separate; about 50 lbs. of this are put into a bag of buffalo skin, with about 40 lbs. of melted fat, and mixed together while hot, and sewed up, forming a hard and compact mass; hence its name in the Cree language, pimmi signifying meat, and kon, fat.

Credited as having been introduced to the fur trade by Peter Pond in 1779 after he saw natives in the Athabasca country make and use it, pemmican quickly became a staple of the trade, and a huge subindustry was created to manufacture it. It was the fuel of the fur trade, so to speak. With luck it would keep for a whole winter, and it allowed many a trading post and many a traveling fur trader to survive. It was often cached to allow traders on the move to have food without the necessity of hunting, which took time and slowed them down; they were often racing against freeze-up in any case.

Mackenzie used pemmican on both of his expeditions. On 13 August 1789, on his return up the Mackenzie River, he recorded:

At 7 o'Clk we came opposite the Island where we had hid our Pemmican . . . [We] found it as we had left it, and it is very acceptable to us, as it will enable us to get out of the River without losing much time to hunt.

Marriage 'In the Fashion of the Country'

In 1804, the journal kept at Fort Chipewyan recorded the death of the Catt, Sir Alexander Mackenzie's wife. It seems that Mackenzie married her *au façon du nord* or *au façon du pays*, as most fur traders did, probably in the period 1785 to 1787. As had become common, a native girl would be selected for marriage, probably as much by her father as by the trader, and in return trade goods would be given to the family. Mackenzie's book records that, for natives,

the ceremony of marriage is of a very simple nature. The girls are betrothed at a very early period to those whom the parents think the best able to support them: nor is the inclination of the woman considered.

A fur trader would no doubt be considered very much a good choice in terms of support. Once married, the woman would assist the trader in every way, particularly as an interpreter, cooking, making moccasins, and doing all the domestic chores, leaving the trader more free to concentrate on trade. The passing of the long solitary winters would undoubtedly have been made more comfortable. The trader would also receive the benefit of all the furs his wife's family could acquire.

The only problem with this arrangement was that when the trader left the Northwest, he usually left his wife and children behind too, often giving her back to her family. There is an interesting reference in a letter Mackenzie wrote to his cousin Roderic from the ship taking him to England in October 1799.

"I requested of you at parting to send fifty pounds to Mrs. Mackenzie of Three Rivers on my account . . . This sum I mean to continue to her annually while Kitty remains Single." It seems unlikely that the Catt would have been in Three Rivers, but the reference to "Kitty" seems unmistakably to point to her.

Many fur traders, Mackenzie's partner William McGillivray included, often were married to two women at the same time, often with the knowledge and acquiescence of their European wives. But whatever the judgment today of the custom, it was widespread and accepted at the time.

It seems likely that Mackenzie left behind some children when he left Canada. A later North West Company trader, Daniel Harmon, recorded in his journal on 20 March 1809 "the melancholy news of the death of Mr. Andrew McKenzie (natural Son of Sir Alexander McKenzie) who departed this life at Fort Vermilion on the 1st Inst."

Interesting evidence of Mackenzie's possible Canadian descendants is contained in a letter written by John Hosie, Provincial Librarian and Archivist of British Columbia, in September 1930. He wrote:

While at Bella Coola three years ago [1927] *on the occasion of the unveiling of the Mackenzie Monument I met a young man, with evidence of Indian blood, who told me that he was a descendant of Sir Alexander Mackenzie. He would be about 26 years of age. He might possibly be a . . . great-great-grandson of Sir Alexander.*

The Trapper's Bride. Oil on canvas by Alfred Jacob Miller, 1837.

All of Opinion That It Was the Tide

JOURNAL
OF A
VOYAGE, &c.

I went this expedition in hopes of getting into Cook's River; tho' I was disappointed in this it proved without a doubt that there is not a North West passage below this latitude and I believe it will generally be allowed that no passage is practicable in a higher latitude the Sea being eternally covered with Ice.

Previous page: This wonderful photograph of a supply scow shooting rapids on the Slave River about 1900 was found in the Provincial Archives of Alberta. If you don't look too closely at the details of the scow itself, this could be Mackenzie and his men on their way to the Arctic in 1789.

With the approach of the summer of 1789, Mackenzie was ready, and on 3 June his party left Fort Chipewyan for, as they thought, the Pacific Ocean. It is interesting that the only surviving copy of Mackenzie's journal is entitled

Journal of a Voyage performed by Order of the N.W. Company, in a Bark Canoe in search of a Passage by Water through the N.W. Continent of America from Athabasca to the Pacific Ocean in Summer 1789

The *Pacific* Ocean.

The journal begins, simply and unpretentiously: "Wednesday, June 3 at 9 oClock embarked at Fort Chepwean, Mr. Leroux with Canoe for Slave Lake in Company." Laurent Leroux, one of Mackenzie's trading assistants, was to trade for furs that summer on Great Slave Lake. Mackenzie's party consisted of himself; four voyageurs that would do much of the actual paddling work, Joseph Landry, Charles Ducette, François Barrieau, and Pierre de Lorme; two of the voyageurs' native wives; a German, Johann Steinbruck, who was probably an ex-Hessian mercenary soldier who had obtained work in the predominantly French-Canadian voyageur part of the fur trade. In another canoe with his two wives was the man who was to be Mackenzie's guide, called the "English Chief," a Chipewyan native, Nestabeck, known as a follower of Matonabbee, the native chief who had helped Samuel Hearne reach the Arctic coast in 1771 and with whom Mackenzie had become

Johann Steinbruck's Unusual Journal

Alexander Mackenzie's lone German voyageur, Johann (or John or Jean) Steinbruck came to Canada as part of a group of mercenary soldiers called Hessians, because they were from Hesse in Germany. The soldiers were brought in to fight on the side of the British in the American War of Independence. Steinbruck stayed in Canada when the war ended in 1783, deserting to do so, and found employment in the fur trade.

After accompanying Mackenzie in 1789, Steinbruck advanced himself somewhat in the North West Company, and by 1802 he seems to have become a clerk. As such, in the winter of 1802–3 he was in charge of a small temporary trading post called Fort des Couteaux Jaunes (Fort of the Yellow Knives) at the west end of Great Slave Lake.

Supplies to the depot on the lake, Fort Resolution, had not arrived before the freeze-up that fall, and so Steinbruck was short of everything, including paper. Thus he kept his journal, a record of the trading activities at the post, on pages made of birchbark. Pieces of birchbark were always kept available to mend canoes made of this material. Thus when searching for a paper substitute, the birchbark would have come readily to hand. This was probably not unusual; what is unusual is that this birchbark journal has survived.

Now in private hands, the journal is in French, the language of the voyageurs. Steinbruck would have likely learned French before English. The journal was the subject of a recent book, *The Yellowknife Journal*.

First page of Steinbruck's Yellowknife journal. It is now in the Prince of Wales Northern Heritage Centre in Whitehorse, Yukon.

Photograph of Henry Hind's expedition of 1858. It could easily be a picture of Mackenzie's camp. Mackenzie's equipment was essentially identical.

acquainted during his time in charge of the English (Churchill) River region; in addition there was another small canoe with the chief's followers, "two young Indians." Mackenzie's book tells us "these men were engaged to serve us in the twofold capacity of interpreters and hunters."

In contrast to what was to come, they quickly found their way out of Lake Athabasca (which is referred to as Lake of the Hills, the name Peter Pond had given to it) and into the main channel of the Slave River, before camping for the night. The hunters killed a goose and two ducks, and the canoe was gummed. This would prove to be a common routine, as their birchbark canoes were sealed with resins that did not seem to last very long without giving way to a leak.

The following morning they passed Peace River on their left and thus unknowingly set themselves on a route that would not take them to the Pacific Ocean, but to the Arctic.

On the third day they encountered the series of rapids near today's Fort Smith, the Cassette, Pelican, and Mountain Rapids, and the awfully but aptly named Rapids of the Drowned. This of course involved

Pelican Rapids on the Slave River, as painted by George Back, with John Franklin's expedition, in 1821.

considerable portaging around the unnavigable parts of the river. Mackenzie notes that they "had some Difficulty in loading there being a quantity of Ice not yet thawed." The weather had turned cold. On 6 June it was "so cold the Indians made use of their Mittens," and on 9 June, when they arrived at the point where Slave River joins Great Slave Lake, they "found a great change in the Weather, it being excessive Cold. The Lake is covered all over with Ice and does not seem to have yet moved, excepting along the shore." Great Slave Lake is normally frozen over for nearly half the year, and these were simply the normal conditions for the season. The cold and ice was not the only inconvenience. Mackenzie notes another that they were to find a problem often again: "We were much troubled with Muskettows and Gnatts," he wrote.

It was to take Mackenzie almost three weeks to travel the roughly 150 km, or a little less than 100 miles, the distance as the crow flies from the mouth of the Slave River to the entrance to the Mackenzie River. But the ice and wind conditions did not allow a straight line of travel and presumably meant that a route along the south shore was not possible. To all intents and purposes it was like coming to an open sea, with partially broken up pack ice conditions; Great Slave Lake is the tenth largest lake in the world, with 28 600 square km or 11,170 square miles of water. The western half of the lake, where Mackenzie wished to go, is open water.

Knowing that the eastern half of the lake was full of islands, Mackenzie decided that his best chance of getting across this large lake was by traversing across the islands one at a time. He may have known, from his guide, that Samuel Hearne had found his way across the lake in January 1772 coming in the opposite direction across these same islands when, of course, the lake was frozen and thus much easier to cross. The water between the northernmost island, Blanchet, and the mainland is today called Hearne Channel.

Mackenzie's journal during the twenty days they were on Great Slave Lake is littered with comments about the ice, the wind, and the mosquitoes. "It blew very hard from the Northerd this morning which prevented our embarking. A vast quantity of floating Ice," he wrote on 16 June. "Pestered by Muskettoes, tho' we are in a manner surrounded by ice," he wrote on 20 June. "Making our way thro' much broken Ice," he wrote the next day. The same day the hunters were able to kill seven caribou because they had been trapped on a small island by ice breaking up. The islands are likely the same as those today called the Caribou Islands.

Rapid des Noyers – Rapids of the Drowned – on the Slave River, photographed by James McDougall in July 1892.

Hudson's Bay Company Archives (1987/13/176).

But they progressed slowly around the perimeter of the open lake water. By 23 June they were crossing a deep bay, now the bay on which the modern city of Yellowknife stands. Just north of that point, on 25 June, Mackenzie made a dash across about 13 km or 8 miles of open water as he cut across the northern arm of Great Slave Lake at a place now called Whitebeach Point.

Now he followed the northern shore of the lake, continuing a slow progress to the west. He still didn't sound like he was having much fun. "We made our way thro' some Broken Ice tho' at the Risk of damaging our Canoe," he wrote on 25 June, and "A very restless Night being tormented by Musquittoes" on 27 June.

On 25 June he parted from Laurent Leroux, his assistant trader, who was to stay at Great Slave Lake gathering furs. "Mr. Leroux got his Men and Indians to salute us with several Vollies, to which we returned a few shot," to preserve ammunition, for from this point on he was to be in territory previously unknown to Europeans.

His native guides didn't seem to know the local geography either. Mackenzie's main problem now was to find the exit from the lake to the river, the Mackenzie, that he sought. The previous day, he had found that the local "Redknife Indians" (so-called from their copper knives) did not know anything about the river except the entry from

Native camp on the shores of Great Slave Lake at Fort Resolution, July 1892.

Hudson's Bay Company Archives, James McDougall (1987/13/182).

the lake. Thus he had engaged a native to "conduct us thither to prevent loss of time in Circumnavigating Bays." But two days later he found "Our guides quite at a loss they do not know what course to take, he says its 8 Winters since he has been here."

The English Chief was unhappy with the Redknife guide. On 28 June Mackenzie wrote:

George Back's painting of canoes under sail in a storm, painted in his sketchbook in 1821, during John Franklin's first expedition. This was in Melville Sound, in the Arctic, but the conditions can be every bit as treacherous on Great Slave Lake. Traveling in a canoe could be difficult at times!

The Mackenzie River (in foreground) at its confluence with the Liard (in background) is shown in this 1892 photograph from the Hudson's Bay Company Archives.

The English Chief was in a great passion with the Red Knif wanted to shoot him for having undertaken to guide us in a Road he did not know, indeed none of us are well pleased with hime, but we don't think with the English Chief that he merits such severe punishment.

The weather was not cooperating either; they had to resort to using their large kettle to keep the canoe from swamping, even though they had very little sail up.

Finally, on 29 June, twenty days after they had entered Great Slave Lake, they found the passage they were searching for, actually the North Channel of the entrance to the Mackenzie River. (There are two entrances, north and south of Big Island.) They entered the wide channel known as Beaver Lake, which is really part of the river, passed the site of today's Fort Providence, and found another widening of the river, called Mills Lake. The river continues from an unexpected almost southern exit from this lake, and Mackenzie was temporarily at a loss to know which direction to take. His local guide was no help. "Our Red Knife Indian has never been further than this," Mackenzie wrote. Just beyond this point the Mackenzie River begins to flow in a generally northwesterly direction, which must have pleased our explorer, as this was what he was expecting if the river was to flow to the sea at

Cook's River, Cook Inlet. Only three days later he would be disappointed as the river's flow changed to a northerly one.

On 1 July, the party passed a large river flowing in from their left, the Liard, the site of modern Fort Simpson. "The River of the mountain falls in from the southerd," noted Mackenzie. Later that day they hid bags of pemmican, the dried buffalo meat that was a staple of the fur trade, on an island, for their return trip. This shows that Mackenzie had expectations of returning that season, for the pemmican would not last until the following year.

The next day, the bad news. Mackenzie wrote: "At 9 oClock A.M. perceive very high Mountains ahead," the tops of which "hid in the Clouds . . . as far as our view could carry to the southerd." He had sighted the Camsell Range of the Rocky Mountains, where, at Camsell Bend, the river makes a sharp turn away from that northwesterly direction so pleasing to Mackenzie and begins its flow to the north. The river seemingly is deflected by the mountain range from the

Great Slave Lake and the Mackenzie to Camsell Bend is shown in this part of Mackenzie's map.

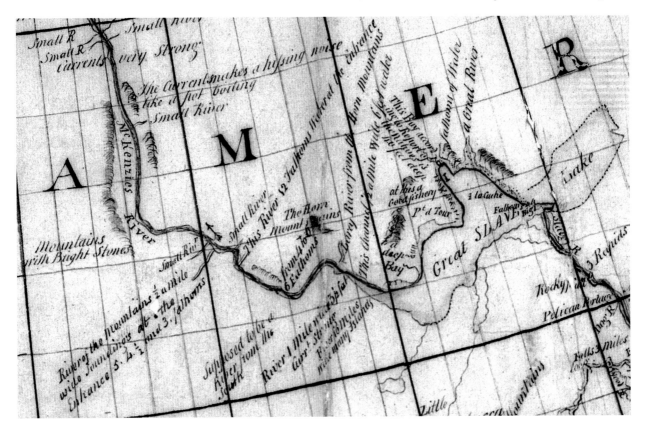

northwesterly direction it wants to flow. Although this was perhaps the most significant part of his journey, Mackenzie did not realize or record it as such, noting simply: "Our course changes to W.b.N. [West by North] along the Mountains 12 Miles N.b.W. [North by West] 21 Miles." His map only records "Mountains with Bright Stones," a name for the Rockies.

The map published in Mackenzie's book in 1801 emphasizes this

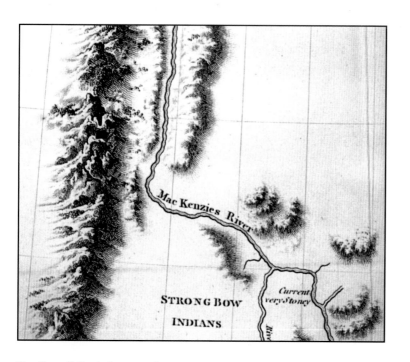

The Camsell Bend shown on the map published with Mackenzie's book.

directional change more, as the wall of mountains, this time unnamed, is depicted three-dimensionally. Only later would Mackenzie come to realize the significance of this direction change. Perhaps at the time he thought that the directional change was temporary, and indeed the river does resume a more northwesterly direction below today's settlement of Wrigley, after following a northerly section for 100 km or 60 miles north of Camsell Bend, but it is to prove too late to reach the southern coast of Alaska, for here we are above 63° N, whereas the tip of Cook Inlet is at 61° N, a latitude Mackenzie would have known full well. Now the river would have had to have trended due west to have had any chance of meeting his coveted objective. It was truly the turning point in his expedition!

The next day, 3 July, the going got tougher. There was heavy rain, a strong head wind, and colder weather again. That evening they camped below a mountain that rose 350 metres or 1,200 feet from the river; it was part of a small range that crosses the Mackenzie River at this point, just south of modern Wrigley. Mackenzie took the opportunity to climb the mountain for a better view of what lay ahead and found the remains of a native encampment on the top, but no sign of natives. "We were obliged to shorten our Stay here," wrote Mackenzie, "on account of the Swarms of Muskettoes that attacked us and were the only Inhabitants of the Place."

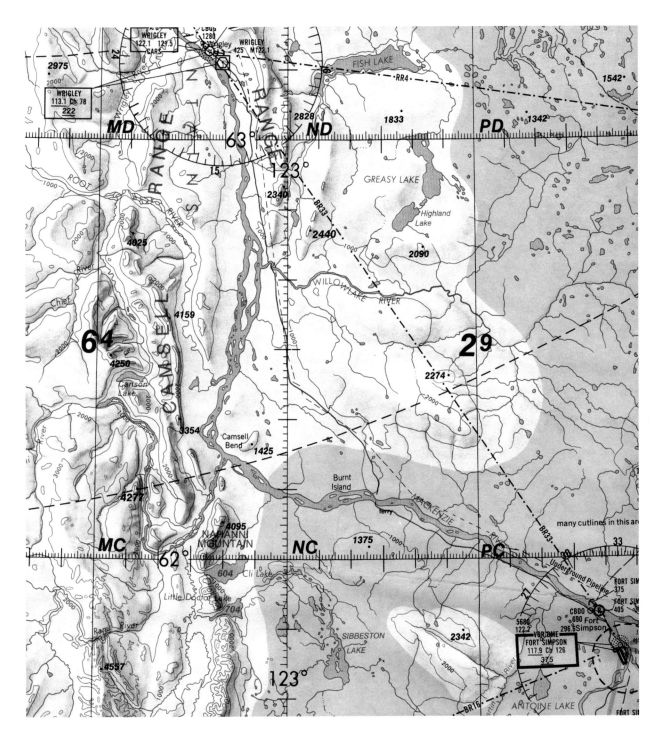

This section of a modern 1:1 000 000 scale aeronautical map shows dramatically how the Mackenzie River changes its course from northwest to north at Camsell Bend.

The increasingly northern situation was becoming evident. On 5 July Mackenzie recorded, "Last Night the sun set at 55 minutes past 9 by my watch and rose before 2 this morning."

They at last made contact with some of the inhabitants of the area, Slave and Tlicho (Dogrib). Seeing rising smoke, Mackenzie made for the encampment as fast as possible, but most of the natives ran away. His hunters managed to land before all had made their getaway, however, and persuaded the frightened natives that they were not to be hurt, and so, slowly, the rest of what turned out to be five families came out of hiding. It was intelligence that Mackenzie was after, but he did not get any useful information. After the "Distribution of Knives, beads, awls, Rings, garlering [gartering], Fire Steels, Flints and a couple of Axes," Mackenzie recorded:

The Information they gave us respecting the River, seems to me so very fabulous that I will not be particular in inserting, Suffice it to say that they would wish to make us believe that we would be several Winters getting to the Sea, and that we all should be old men by the time we would return. that we would have to encounter many Monsters (which can only exist in their own while [wild?] Imaginations) Besides that there are 2 impracticable Falls or Rapids in the River, the first 30 Days March from us.

Although this nonsense had no effect on Mackenzie's resolve, it did on that of the English Chief and his followers, who immediately tried to persuade him to give up and return upstream, adding their own opinions that there would be no animals below where they were, and that as a consequence the party would surely starve. Mackenzie brooked no hint of giving up, instead ordering re-embarkation, despite the fact that it was three in the afternoon. He also bribed one of the local natives to accompany them with an offer of kettles, an axe, a trencher (used for serving food), and a knife.

Mackenzie here entered in his journal a detailed ethnographic-type description of the local natives.

They are of Middle Stature & as far as could be discerned thro' Dust & Grease that cover their whole Body fairer than the generality of Indians, who inhabit warmer climes . . . The Men have no covering on their Private Parts except a small Tassel of Paring of Leather, which hang loose by a small Cord, before them in order to keep off the Flies which otherwise wou'd be very troublesome . . . Their ornaments consists of Bracelets, Gorgets [necklaces], Arm & Wrist Bands made of Wood, Horn, or Bone[;] Belts, Garters & a kind of Cap which they wear on the Head made of a Piece of Leather 1½ Ins. wide embroidered with Porcupine Quills & stuck round with the Claws of Bears or wild Fowls inverted to each of which hangs a few parings of fine white Ferrit Skins in fashion with a Tassel.

Leaving these natives, Mackenzie continued downriver, and soon passed the Great Bear River, which flows out of Great Bear Lake. There they camped for the night. His new "Conductor," as Mackenzie calls the local native he bribed to go with them, was unhappy. "He was very uneasy with us, pretending sickness that we might let him return to his relations to prevent which we be obliged to watch him all Night." They were at Bear Rock, just north of Fort Norman.

The next day, 6 July, Mackenzie recorded that a "Ridge of Snowy Mountains" was always in sight. This was the northern part of the Rocky

Bear Rock, a distinctive landmark at the point near Fort Norman that the Great Bear River, flowing from the lake of the same name, joins the Mackenzie, 1892.

Hudson's Bay Company Archives, James McDougall (1987/13/198).

Mountains range now called the Mackenzie Mountains. That night he again tried to climb a mountain to get a better view of the way ahead, but, he says, "We were obliged to relinquish our design half way up it being nearly suffocated by Swarms of Musquittoes."

The same day Mackenzie would have passed the site of the modern settlement of Norman Wells, and would no doubt have been astonished had he been making the journey 200 years later to find the river strewn with small rectangular artificial islands created as oil well platforms *in* the river.

These photographs by James McDougall were taken in July 1892. They show a native encampment on the river near Fort Norman and native women in front of the Hudson's Bay Company post.

Hudson's Bay Company Archives, James McDougall (*right:* 1987/13/195; *below:* 1987/13/196).

a Manitoe in the River

to the Eastward by...

middling tare River comes from a Lake

Peninsula

2. The River is here 300 yds wide & 50 fathoms deep behind 2 precipices

Small River

Hare Indians many Inhabitants near the Rapids

Snowy Mountains

River of the Great Lake 250 yards wide

1 Rapid

River   *Many Islands*

River Widens Current Slackens

Small River

Small River

Small R

Small R

Currents very strong

The Current makes a hissing noise like a pot boiling

Small River

Mackenzies

A   M

River 12 Fathoms Water at the...

Above: The middle part of the Mackenzie River, from Mackenzie's map.

Right: Plaque at Norman Wells airport; the date is wrong!

The Mackenzie River   Deho

Always known as Deh Cho — Big River to the Dene people, the Mackenzie was named after Alexander Mackenzie, who navigated it in 1796.

It is the fourth largest river in North America, draining almost one-fifth of Canada.

The Mackenzie remains frozen from November to mid-May. Breakup of the ice in spring is a spectacular sight, with huge ice-floes uprooting trees from the river banks in their rush to reach the sea.

Denewá ke gólǫ gots'é Deho, Deh Cho gókǝdı yı́le, 1796 gú Mǫ́la Alexander Mackenzıe yegá dáʔa gots'ę nıyá Mǫ́la k'ę́ Mackenzıe Rıver gohįzı kǝhsı̨.

Derı neh North Amerıca bek'e ráhıdǝ gota de xáhwere hı̨sha yáwǝlı ta Deho dı k'e weda, gú Canada tu ʔareyǫné lak'e gú lak'ets'eyıhtl'ı nidé derı ta lát'ǝ ʔaréht'e ya Deho ts'ę káyı̨lı̨.

Derı Deho xat'ą́ November tadǝtı̨ gots'ę May gots'é gǫ́htę. ʔuyálele ludǝdáwı nidé goshó ʔagot'ı̨. Ludéwé begháré tl'ánı bǝhdlá ts'u ráweʔa daı teyátl'e gú hı̨dá tushoho ts'éyá dedéwe.

At the Ramparts, just south of Fort Good Hope, the Mackenzie narrows dramatically as it passes between limestone cliffs. The Ramparts Rapids are at the entrance to the gorge. This view is toward the south; the river is flowing north, toward the camera. The river flowing in from the west (right) is the Ramparts River.

The next day, traveling fast, they came to a series of rapids, called today the Sans Sault Rapids, which they traversed without a problem. These were presumably the first rapids referred to by the natives a few days earlier and they "convinced me," Mackenzie wrote, "in my Opinion respecting the falsity of the Natives Information." Then they met more natives, who, again after initial fears, with all except an elderly man running off, were persuaded that Mackenzie meant no harm. They told him of another great rapid close by, the Ramparts Rapid, but this time they showed Mackenzie which channel to take to go down these rapids. His new guide had to be forced to continue, as he "wanted absolutely to return."

Now they passed through the Ramparts, just above today's Fort Good Hope, where high limestone cliffs confine the river for about 11 km or 7 miles to a narrower channel, 400 to 800 m (1,300 to 2,600 feet) wide as compared to about 4 km or 2½ miles wide above it. The river narrows quite spectacularly. Nevertheless, because of increased depth, the speed of the current does not increase appreciably. "We came between the steep Rock . . . but did not find the Current stronger than elsewhere," recorded Mackenzie.

His guide now told Mackenzie that they should not continue on account of "the Eskmeaux [Eskimo; Inuit] who he says are very wicked and will kill us all." He had reason to be apprehensive, he said. "It is but two summers since a great Party of them came up this River and killed a Number of his Relations." This information must have given Mackenzie pause, as he probably knew from the English Chief of the battle between Chipewyan and Inuit that Samuel Hearne was later to document in his book.

The next day, 8 July, they began their paddling at two-thirty in the morning. It had been the expedition's normal habit to start very early in the morning. Of course, this was long before the advent of daylight saving time, so it is equivalent to three-thirty in the morning now, but

The Ramparts.
Engraving from John Franklin's 1828 book.

since at these northern latitudes it was essentially daybreak at this time, it no doubt seemed natural to get going early.

Mackenzie was getting fed up with the reluctance of his guide to continue. "He was become very troublesome obliged to watch him Night and day except when upon the Water," Mackenzie recorded. So when he met some more natives, now K'áshot'ine (Hare), he changed "his Conductor." But he didn't do much better with his replacement. "This Fellow had likewise no sooner consented [to act as guide] but he repented, alledging that he had not seen much of the River." Telling Mackenzie that others of his tribe could do much better than he, the native was forced to take the job when others failed to turn up. Naturally he took the first opportunity to desert, which was the next day.

At this Mackenzie again forced another, from a small group he had encountered that day, to take his place. He seems to have had no qualms about forcing individuals to act as his guide, although he was doing very well by himself. It seems clear that a number of Mackenzie's guides initially agreed to accompany him because of the rewards they were being offered, but they did not want to fulfill their part of the bargain, quite likely because they feared for their lives venturing into enemy teritory with only a few others for protection. It also seems clear that neither this guide nor the previous two actually knew much about the route downriver, at least that they were prepared to communicate to Mackenzie. The general game plan for guides seems to have been accept the gifts, go a little way, then escape!

Native encampment,
lower Mackenzie.

Near today's Thunder River, Mackenzie met with another small
native group that, from the page of ethnological information he gives
us, seems to have had much more interaction with Inuit groups than
those before. Mackenzie wrote:

*They have no Iron ecept for small Pieces that serve them for Knives,
which they get from the Eskmeaux. Their arrows are made of light
wood and have only two Feathers at the end. They had a Bow which is
diff[eren]t in Shape from theirs, and say they had it from the Eskmeaux
who are their Neighbours.*

Mackenzie persuaded one of the group, whom the English Chief
was able to understand, to accompany them. He would stay with them
the rest of their downriver journey, though not without apprehensions, as we shall see. The previous guide was delighted to be let off
the hook.

The party's new guide told them "that we will sleep 10 Nights more
before we come to the Sea." Perhaps it is a measure of the speed at
which Mackenzie was traveling that they were actually going to reach
the sea in only three more days. Mackenzie thought his new guide
better than the previous ones. He recorded:

[The guide] spoke much in derision of the last Indians who we had seen, that they were all like old Women & great Liars etc. which coincides with the Opinion I had already entertained of them.

An interesting example of how the original journal was "cleaned up" for publication to an English audience occurs in a passage from Mackenzie's observations about his new guide. The journal for 9 July says the new guide

pull'd his Penis out of his Breeches laying it on his hand & telling us the Eskmeaux name of it. In short he took much Pains to shew us that he knew the Eskmeaux and their Customs.

The published book says

when he began to display various indecencies, according to the customs of the Esquimaux, of which he boasted an intimate acquaintance.

This change was probably the work of Mackenzie's editor, William Coombe (see page 253).

Later that day Mackenzie "saw a Smoak upon the West Shore traversed & landed." After causing considerable confusion and uproar, probably because they thought they were being attacked, the native group was "introduced" by their guide, and after being given presents, they followed Mackenzie downstream to another encampment on the east side of the river, where Mackenzie was able to obtain some more information. These people, which he called "Diguthe Dinees or the Quarrelleas," were probably Gwich'in: Dinjii Zhuh or Loucheaux. Mackenzie wrote:

Those Indians told me that from where I met the first of their People this Morning it was not far to go to the Sea over Land on the East Side & from where I found them it was but a short way to go to it to the Westwd that the land on both Sides of the River was like a Point.

Although perhaps a fair description of the morphology of the Mackenzie Delta itself, it was not an accurate description of their current situation.

The Mackenzie River between Thunder River and Arctic Red River. At this point the river is flowing nearly due west.

Mackenzie's map (page 109) shows at this point (near Thunder River) "This point is near the Sea to the Eastward by Indian Report" and at the river bend to the west, probably placed there just for convenience when drawing the map, is the notation "By the Indian Account the Sea is but a short way to the Westward."

Now Mackenzie's new guide made overtures to leave them.

He was afraid that we should not come back this way, & besides that the Eskmeaux would perhaps kill us & take their Women from my Men & Indians, & that he was afraid of them too.

Reassured by the English Chief and his followers, the guide was persuaded to continue.

The next day they passed through the Lower Ramparts, a short stretch of the river just upstream of Arctic Red River (the river) and the modern community of Tsiigehtchic (whose name was recently changed from Arctic Red River, the village). Here the channel narrows, though it is still wide by any normal standards. The banks here

View downstream from
Tsiigehtchic (Arctic Red
River). Point Separation,
where the river begins its
split into multiple channels,
is not far away.

are up to 90 m or 300 feet high. Then they came to Point Separation, where the Mackenzie River begins its split into a multitude of channels, which can be thought of as the start of the delta. Mackenzie was now in view of "Snowy Mountains ahead," the Richardson Mountains on the west side of the delta and the most northerly extension of the Rocky Mountains. He recorded:

Lower Ramparts
at Tsiigehtchic.

The River widens & runs in many Channels amongst Islands some of which are nothing but a Bank of Land & Mud without a Tree, other are covered very thick with a kind of White Spruce & largir Trees than any we have seen this 10 days.

His map shows "Many Channels & Islands are in the Riv." A decision had to be made:

We were much at a loss what Channel out of some hundreds to take. Our Conductor was for taking the Eastmost, on account as he said that the Eskmeaux were close by on that Road, but I determined upon taking the middle as it was a large piece of Water and running N. & S.

The middle channel of the Mackenzie River, which itself has many islands in it, giving the impression of multiple channels, is the largest and most obvious channel. The islands hid the confluence of the Peel River, coming in from the southwest, one of the very rivers flowing from the mountains that Mackenzie would have liked to know about. He took an observation at noon, when he determined his latitude to be 67° 47´, "farther North than I expected." (It was probably actually 68° 20´.)

Here we have from Mackenzie the first written indication that he was having doubts about ending up in the Pacific Ocean.

I am much at a loss here how to act being certain that my going further in this Direction will not answer the Purpose of which the Voyage was intended, as it is evident that these Waters must empty themselves into the Northern Ocean.

Mackenzie's book revised this text to eliminate any hint of doubt: "From hence it was evident that these waters emptied themselves into the Hyperborean Sea."

He was of the belief at this point that he would not be able to get back to "the Athabasca" that season, because of having to find food on the way upstream, which of course could be expected to take much longer than the trip downstream. "Therefore I determined," he wrote in his journal, "to go to the discharge of those Waters, as it would satisfy Peoples Curiousity tho' not their Intentions."

Now Mackenzie's guide was "quite discouraged and tired of his Situation" and revealed that

he never was at the Billhully Toe (which means Lake) that he only was at Eskmeaux lake, which is not far off, that he never has been at it this way, that he went to it overland from where we found him and to where the Eskmeaux pass their summer.

"Billhully Toe," "Benahulla Toe" in the book, is interpreted by Mackenzie to mean "White Man's Lake." The reference to "Eskmeaux lake" could be to a body of water which runs deep inland from Liverpool Bay, on the east side of the Mackenzie Delta, which is today called "Eskimo Lake." Mackenzie, though he had a guide, wasn't getting much help from him.

This information also discouraged the Chipewyans. "All this discouraged my Hunters and am confident were it in their power [they] would leave me, as they are quite disgusted with the Voyage." Now it sounds as though the natives thought they needed Mackenzie in order to get back to Lake Athabasca. Quite a reversal of roles! Mackenzie satisfied them a little by telling them

I would go on but 7 Days more, and that if I did not come to the Sea in that time I should return, and my scarcity of provisions will make me fulfil this promise, whether I will or not.

They had reached the Arctic for sure. The next day, 11 July, Mackenzie wrote: "I sat up last Night to observe at what time the Sun would set, but found that he did not set at all." Calling on one of his men to look at the midnight sun, his voyageur thought it was a signal to embark again, and could hardly believe that it was only half past midnight.

Later that day Mackenzie noted that the river was "very serpenting" as it meandered across the delta, a massive sinewy highway to the sea. They saw their first evidence of recent Inuvialuit (Mackenzie Inuit) settlement, with the remains of "upward of 30 Fires." Mackenzie noted that the fishing was very good here; at one point a fish jumped into his canoe.

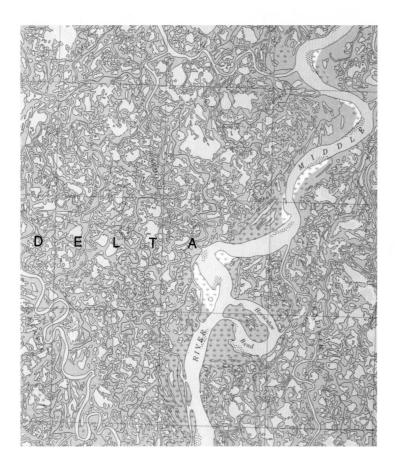

Above: This portion of a modern topographical map gives a good idea of the complexity of the channels of the Mackenzie Delta.

Right, top: The Middle Channel of the Mackenzie River in the delta. The smaller channel in the foreground leads to Shallow Bay, an unlikely route for Mackenzie given the sharp left turn here.

Right, below: Although Mackenzie never met any Inuvialuit, he did see plenty of evidence of them. This engraving of *Esquimaux Winter Houses* is from John Franklin's book about his 1825 second expedition, published in 1828.

At the point where the Middle Channel of the Mackenzie River splits into three more channels, it seems likely that they followed the most northerly channel. Although not the largest of the three, it would have been a continuation of the direction they were taking at the time. They camped that night on the east side of Langley Island. Their guide (even though he had previously purported not to know the way) told them that they would "see the lake tomorrow." He also told them "that he nor his Relations know nothing about it . . . only the Eskmeaux live about it that they kill a large Fish in it which they eat." Mackenzie thought this must be a whale.

Both his local guide and the English Chief were now fed up, and in order to keep them happy, Mackenzie gave one of his coats to the English Chief and a moose skin to the guide.

Next morning, 12 July, the party continued past more signs of recent habitation by Inuvialuit – wooden structures fabricated of driftwood that would be covered by earth and then snow and ice in winter, but no natives were seen. Mackenzie examined the detritus of the encampments and was fascinated by the bones of "two big heads, we don't know of what animal. I suppose the sea horses." He was referring to walrus, called sea horses in James Cook's book.

At this point we come to a significant passage in Mackenzie's journal.

After we had satisfied our Curiousity here, we embarked, tho' we did not know what course to steer, our Guide being as ignorant in this Country as any of ourselves. This appeared to be the Entrance of the Lake, tho' the Current was yet very strong, and set West, and we went with it for a high point about 8 miles distant,

The Middle Channel at the "Entrance of the Lake" where it widens and flows into Mackenzie Bay.

Opposite: Modern topographic map of the north part of the Mackenzie Delta.

which we took to be an Island separate from the plain, where we had last landed.

The Middle Channel of the Mackenzie River widens considerably on the southwest side of Niglintgak Island and then finally sheds its shield of low-lying islands either side as it enters Mackenzie Bay and the Beaufort Sea.

They paddled across the "lake" to an island. Mackenzie noted that "The Lake was quite open to us to the Westward," and that the water was very shallow. During the last 15 miles he noted that "5 feet was the deepest Water." On his map he recorded similar shallowness; "5 ft deepest Water in the Entrance of the Lake 12 July 1789." Shallow waters, of course, are a characteristic of deltas. Mackenzie's note about the lake being quite open to the westward is interesting in that a glance at the map confirms that it is to the west *only* that there is a view uninterrupted by islands, and so this seems to definitely confirm that this was the route he took. Though Mackenzie did not realize it, he had reached the Arctic Ocean.

MACKENZIE BAY

BELUGA BAY

Pelly
Island

Rae I

7   8   9   0

Kendall
Island

Garry

Island

100

Taglu

MN NN

Big
Lake

Seal Island

Big Horn
Pt

MM NM

10

KENDALL ISLAND BIRD SANCTUARY

Kimialuk
Lake

Island

Fish
Island

Niglintgak

REFUGE D'OISEAUX DE L'ÎLE KENDALL

Island

HARRY

M A C K E N Z I E

Old Trout L

55

Trench
Lake

MIDDLE

CHANNEL

HARRY

Grassy
Lake

MACKENZIE RIVER
(FLEUVE MACKENZIE)

Condition
Unknown

ARVOKNAR

D E L T A

CHANNEL

Hope
L

CHANNEL

ELLICE

Yaya

Another view of the "Entrance of the Lake," where the Middle Channel widens as it enters the Arctic Ocean.

From the end of the Middle Channel an island is visible immediately north and northwest, 8 to 16 km or 5 to 10 miles away. This is now called Garry Island. It is distinctively higher than all those Mackenzie had been passing for the past few days. Thus his comment that he thought it "an Island separate from the plain."

Reaching the island, Mackenzie's party "landed at the Limit of our Travels in this Direction." They pitched their tents and set nets, and then Mackenzie and the English Chief walked to the highest part of the island, which is only about 70 m or 225 feet high. From there they could see "Ice in a whole Body" (pack ice) extending from the southwest round to the east. To the southwest they could just see the Richardson Mountains, and to the east, many islands.

Mackenzie had reached Garry Island, but the island he thought he had reached, which he named Whale Island, remained on maps until the 1930s and the advent of aerial surveys. Only in the 1960s was it conclusively demonstrated that Garry Island was Mackenzie's Whale Island. Mackenzie was to stay on this island for three and a half days, the only time during his whole expedition that he stayed in one place.

The northern part of Mackenzie's map.

The central part of Garry Island, Mackenzie's Whale Island. Pelly Island is just visible in the distance, as is the white glow of the pack ice.

Garry Island, Mackenzie's Whale Island, viewed from the northwest. Mackenzie's first encampment here, at "the Limit of [his] Travels in this Direction," was on the beach at the right of this picture. Even in July, when this photograph was taken, ice remains in patches despite a 24-hour, 360° sun.

Southern end of Garry Island, where Mackenzie moved his camp after his failed foray to see the pack ice and near brush with a whale. It was here, camped on the beach in the foreground, that the rising tide finally convinced Mackenzie he must have reached an ocean.

At this point Mackenzie did not realize he had reached an ocean. He wrote in his journal:

My Men express much sorrow that they are obliged to return without seeing the Sea, in which I believe them sincere for we marched exceed[in]g hard coming down the River, and I never heard them grumble; but on the contrary in good Spirits, and in hopes every day that the next would bring them to the Mer d'Ouest, and declare themselves now and at any time ready to go with me wherever I choose to lead them.

Mackenzie then discovered that there was a tide, although he still did not attribute the rise in the water to a tide, but thought it due to the wind, which was so strong as to blow away one of the nets they set overnight to catch fish. On 13 July he wrote: "Soon after we went to bed last night" – adding in the book though not in his journal, "if I may use that expression, in a country where the sun never sinks beneath the horizon" – "some of them were obliged to get up and move the Baggage on account of the water rising."

The next day the wind blew strongly again. A number of whales, initially taken to be pieces of ice, were seen, and the men pursued some of them, only giving up when the wind became too strong. Probably just as well. In his book, Mackenzie added:

It was, indeed, a very wild and unreflecting enterprise, and it was a very fortunate circumstance that we failed in our attempt to overtake them, as a stroke from the tail of one of these enormous fish would have dashed the canoe to pieces.

This incident led Mackenzie to name the island they were camped upon "Whale Island." His map notes "A Number of Animals like pieces of Ice supposed to be Whales."

It seems that Mackenzie was still interested in the idea of searching for the Pacific Ocean by going westward along the coast, which of course would indeed have led them to that ocean, although given that they only had small canoes, a coastal voyage would have been hazardous. And it was a huge distance; at least 2 000 km or 1,300 miles even to the mouth of the Yukon River. Mackenzie wrote in his journal:

I intend to lose two or three Days to search for the Natives among the Islands, from whom perhaps I might get some interesting Intelligence tho' my Conductor assures me they are a very unaccotable [unaccountable] *set of Beings.*

That evening they camped at the eastern end of the island. Despite not having reached the Pacific Ocean, Mackenzie clearly felt he had achieved something, for, he says,

This Morning I fix'd a Post close by our Campm[en]*t* [when at the western end of the island] *on which I engraved the latitude of the Place, My own Name & the Number of Men with me & the time we had been there.*

The post has long since disappeared, but I judge that it must have read:

> 69° 14´
> Alex. Mackenzie
> & 5 Men
> July 14, 1789

Five men because he would have counted only those employed by the North West Company as "men."

Whale Island on Maps

Mackenzie's "Whale Island," the termination of his 1789 expedition, does not exist. It is Garry Island, which was named by John Franklin in 1825 in honor of Nicholas Garry, the Deputy Governor of the Hudson's Bay Company. This did not stop "Whale Island" from appearing on maps for more than the next hundred years, sometimes in different positions.

Sir John Franklin's map of 1825, drawn while he was in the Mackenzie delta or soon thereafter, shows Whale Island at Mackenzie's latitudes and at about 136° W. His published map three years later shows a better defined Whale Island now straddling 135° W. This map, which was of course the one that the world saw, noted the island "According to Sir A. Mackenzie." Copied by other mapmakers, the caveat was often omitted. Maps continued to show Whale Island until 1939–45, when aerial mapping techniques came into general use and it was noticed that Whale Island didn't exist. As late as the 1960s, the Bering Sea and Strait Pilot published by the British Admiralty still stated, "Whale Island lies with its north western extreme about twelve miles S.E. of Garry Island."

Like all mythical islands once created, Whale Island took a long time to disappear.

Even today it is easy to confuse the various islands in the delta. There are so many that look alike and so many channels that sorting out which is which without the help of an accurate map is difficult. And this is so even from the air, which gives a grand overview. On the ground or rather on the water, in a low canoe, the task would be insurmountable. It is easy to see how Mackenzie's specific route would loom large in his account, ignoring many other islands and channels he could not see. In 1789 Mackenzie also was unable to fix his position very accurately, particularly his longitude but also even his latitude. Small wonder Mackenzie's Whale Island took so long to be removed from maps.

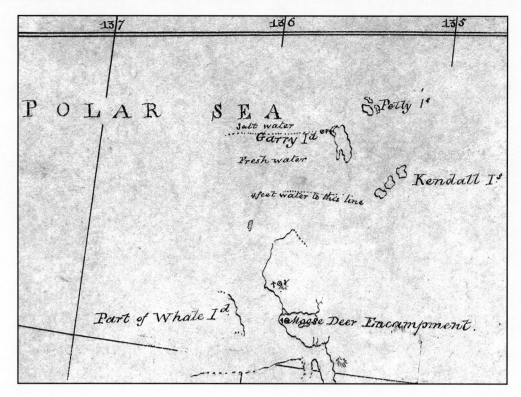

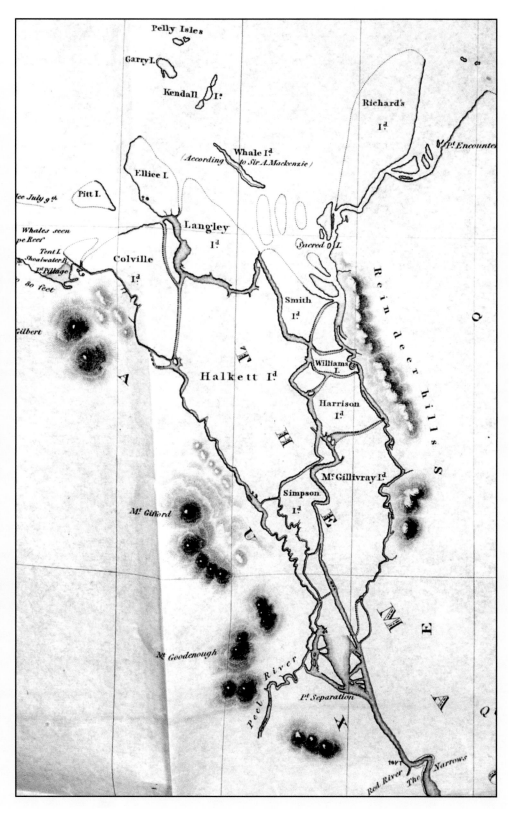

Sir John Franklin's maps of the Mackenzie Delta.

Left: The map he drew while on or near the scene in 1825.

Right: The map published in his book in 1828.

Franklin's first map, which shows the delineation of salt from fresh water at Garry Island, differs quite considerably from the details on the published map, probably the result of the confusing morass of islands and channels that confront the delta traveler. The published map shows Mackenzie's Whale Island in the position in which he reported it.

Where *Was* Whale Island?

Mackenzie named the island that was his most northerly point reached "Whale Island." How do we know where it is? A detailed study of Mackenzie's positions, carried out in the 1960s, revealed the answer. The study compared the stated latitudes of known locations according to Mackenzie with their actual positions as known today.

There were two sorts of errors that crept into Mackenzie's calculations: errors in latitude as he measured with his sextant, and errors of direction as measured by his compass. The latter were undoubtedly caused by, or at least significantly contributed to, by magnetic variation, the true extent of which was unknown at the time. Given these problems, Mackenzie did quite well.

Mackenzie's latitudes taken on Great Slave Lake were calculated all south of his actual position; the recurring error is six to sixteen minutes. After he left Great Slave Lake he only made four more observations, all in the Mackenzie Delta area, and all of which also have been shown to be south of their actual positions.

The positions that Mackenzie recorded on Whale Island were 69° 14´ N, at the northwestern tip of the island, and 69° 7´ N, near the southeastern end. The actual position of Garry Island is about 69° 30´ at the western tip and 69° 27´ N at the eastern. A degree of latitude is about 111 km or 69 miles. Thus it may be calculated that Mackenzie plotted his position about 30 km or 18½ miles too far south when he was at the western tip of the island, and about 37 km or 23 miles too far south when at the eastern end. This sixteen-minute and just under twenty-minute error is reasonably consistent with his errors farther south. Another position Mackenzie observed just before he got to Whale Island also displays this consistent error. The location of this position is reasonably certain, as it is where he recorded that he had traveled eight miles with a current "set West," which is true northwest, from the "Entrance to the Lake," almost certainly where the Middle Channel of the Mackenzie River begins to open up so that the broader expanse of the sea, the "Lake," is visible, but only to the west. Although this channel is today less significant than it was in Mackenzie's time, there is no evidence for the use of the West Channel, the other possibility. John Franklin, exploring the area thirty-six years later, was first to conclude that it was the Middle Channel Mackenzie took. From this point, Mackenzie recorded that he "continued the same Course [true northwest] for the Westernmost part of the high Island and the most Western land in S[igh]t distant 15 Miles. The Lake was quite open to us to the Westward [true northwestward]." Garry Island is the only island that even begins to answer to this description.

There is more corroborating evidence. Mackenzie records that he climbed a hill on the island and "as far as the eye could reach to the South-Westward, we could dimly perceive a chain of mountains, stretching further to the North than the edge of the ice." He also saw islands to the east. The only island in the vicinity that one can observe these features from is Garry Island. Mackenzie described the island as running west-east by compass, which is northwest-southeast true, and this is the trend of Garry Island. He also described the island as being seven leagues long and half a mile wide, but because Mackenzie used the term "league" very few times, it is likely that he meant "miles." And Garry Island is indeed seven miles long and half a mile wide.

There thus seems little doubt that Garry Island is Mackenzie's "Whale Island."

At his camp on the eastern end of Garry Island, early on 15 July, Mackenzie wrote that he was

surprised to observe the water had come under our Baggage as the Wind had not changed nor blew harder than when we went to Bed. I waken'd my Men to move the Baggage &c. We were all of Opinion that it was the Tide as we had observed at the other End of the Island, that the Water rose & fell, but we thot. that this had been occasioned by the Wind.

Mackenzie was unable to determine the amount of the tide, as the wind again "then began to blow very violently." So he resolved to stay until the next morning, and indeed by then he had made enough observations to be able to state: "As near as the inconstancy of the Weather would allow me to observe the Tide rises 16 or 18 Inches." Mackenzie had determined that he had reached at least a

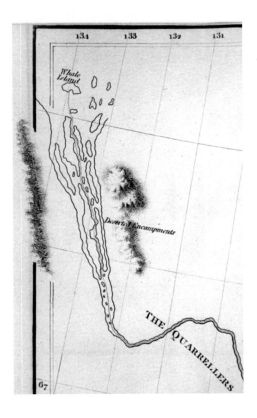

The Mackenzie Delta from the
hand-drawn pre-publication map,
above; and the published map,
below.

tidal estuary, though it is unclear whether at the time he still realized it was the Arctic Ocean. If he tasted the water to see if it was salt, he never recorded the fact; although it may not have not been salt anyway, due to the massive outflow of fresh water from the river. Franklin's map (page 114), drawn thirty-six years later, shows a line between salt and fresh water at the north end of Garry Island, Mackenzie's Whale Island.

The next European explorer to reach the Mackenzie River delta, John Franklin in 1825, had an interesting passage in his book, published in 1828, that addressed Mackenzie's failure to taste the water to see if it was salt:

Our enterprising precursor, Sir Alexander Mackenzie, has been blamed for asserting that he reached the sea, without having ascertained that the water was salt. He, in fact, clearly states that he never did reach the salt water. The danger to which his canoe was exposed in venturing two to three miles beyond Whale Island . . . at a time when the sea was covered with ice to the north, is a sufficient reason for his turning back; and we can abundantly testify that those frail vessels are totally unfitted to contend against such winds and seas as we experienced in advancing beyond the volume of fresh water poured out by the Mackenzie. It is probable, therefore, that even had the sea been free from ice at the time of his visit, he could not have gone far enough to prove its saltness, though the boundless horizon, the occurrence of a tide, and the sight of porpoises and whales, naturally induced him to say that he had arrived at the ocean.

It was now 16 July, and Mackenzie and his men began the long trip back to Lake Athabasca. Deliberately not taking the most direct route, they sailed

Inuvik

The major modern settlement in the Mackenzie Delta is Inuvik, created in the late fifties and early sixties to relocate the population of Aklavik, on the West Channel, which was subject to flooding and had no room to expand. Inuvik was deliberately created by the Canadian government as a town with modern amenities that would be a base for the rest of the delta region.

All buildings in Inuvik are on platforms above the ground, so that the permafrost does not thaw. Even large buildings such as the schools and the hospital are raised.

Today Sir Alexander Mackenzie has an ongoing presence in the town. The main street is Mackenzie Road, and the large elementary school is Sir Alexander Mackenzie School; interestingly, the other school in town is Samuel Hearne Secondary School. The modern library ("Remove your boots; no dogs") had four titles on Mackenzie when I visited, but no copy of Mackenzie's own book.

Inuvik's distinctive and famous landmark, the *iglu* church.

Sir Alexander Mackenzie School in Inuvik. The building is raised from the ground to prevent thawing of the permafrost.

among some islands "in hopes of meeting with some of the Natives but all to no purpose." Giving up, they made for the river, and "stemmed the curr[en]t at 2 oClk P.M." The journey upriver, now against the flow, had begun. The weather immediately became a lot warmer, but there was a trade-off: "We are much tormented by Musquittoes in consequence."

The weather in the delta at this time of the year can change frequently and rapidly, going from not much above freezing, sometimes with a biting wind, to quite hot and sultry, with mosquitoes to match. The temperature beyond the delta and out into the Arctic Ocean is also normally much colder, with the pack ice, acting like a giant icebox, being often near enough to be visible.

They camped that night on Richards Island and the next day passed many abandoned Inuit encampments, but still they met no natives. Then they came to a few small spruce trees, at the extreme northern extent of the treeline. Mackenzie noted, "It is surprizing that their should be any wood at all in a Country where the Ground does not thaw 6 Inches from the Surface." The wood used by the Inuvialuit was generally driftwood.

Although they were not able to catch fish, they did kill two reindeer, which must have given them much to eat, but Mackenzie was clearly concerned about their food supply. "Our pemmican has been mouldy this long time past, but in our Situation we must eat it & not loose [lose] a particle of it."

The next day, the guide ran off. Mackenzie was "surprized at the fellow's honesty, he left a Skin I had given him to cover himself, & went off in his Shirt, tho' the Weather is very cold" – it had become colder now. He probably thought Mackenzie meant to make him his slave, a common practise at the time among warring tribes.

Three days later, Mackenzie's party was reminded – if they needed to be reminded – that they were now going upriver. As they traversed the Lower Ramparts, at Arctic Red River, the current was so strong due to the narrowing of the channel that they had to tow the canoe from shore with a line. The same day they were back with the Gwich'in natives from whom their guide had come. They, naturally enough, were suspicious of the fact that Mackenzie had not brought their compatriot back again. Here the sun set below the horizon for the first time since they had passed this way going downstream.

On the Mackenzie at today's Tsiigehtchic (Arctic Red River) where the Dempster Highway crosses the river via a small ferry, you can see the power of the current. The surging silt-laden waters on a still mile-wide river give mute testament to the sheer volume of water passing beneath. One gets an appreciation for the physical achievement of Mackenzie's men when you realize they battled this opposing stream for the better part of 1 400 km or 850 miles just to Great Slave Lake.

Still towing the canoes, Mackenzie's party reached the upstream group of the same natives in three hours. Here they halted for two hours, and Mackenzie had the English Chief question them during that time. From this we learn again that this native group "[knew] nothing about the Lake in the Direction we were in." However, they were told an interesting story, learned in turn from the Inuit.

The Eskmeaux saw large Canoes full of White Men to the Westward 8 or 10 Winters since, from whom they got Iron of which they exchanged part with them for Leather. Where the big Canoes came to, they cal Belan howlay Tock (White Mens Lake).

What could this mean? It seems unlikely to be made up, since it is so realistic, but no Europeans left any record of such an encounter. The Inuit perhaps had traded iron with one or more middleman group, who had obtained it from Russians trading from their post at Unalaska into the Bering Sea. "Eight or ten winters hence" would mean about 1780. Since James Cook's expedition was in the Bering Sea in 1778 and 1779, very close to this date, it is tantalizing to consider the possibility that this iron was traded by his men, though no record exists of such an event.

John Franklin, some thirty-seven years later, in July 1826, confirmed that Inuit "procure the iron, knives, and beads . . . principally from a party of Esquimaux who reside a great distance to the westward," and he noted that the articles he saw were

not of British manufacture, and were very unlike those sold by the Hudson's Bay Company to the Indians, [so] it cannot be doubted that they are furnished by the Russian Fur Traders, who receive in return for them all the furs collected on this northern coast.

Again the next day, the current was too strong "to stem it with paddles." At an undetermined location that day Mackenzie noted among the stones of the bank "pieces of petrolium like pieces of Yellow Wax but more [friable]." The strata here are the same as those of the oil-bearing rocks of Norman Wells farther upstream, where today there is an oil refinery. The English Chief recognized the rocks as similar to those "that are about the Country where the Chippenwaems get Copper behind the Slaves Lake."

By 25 July, Mackenzie found that the current was not so strong, so

The Rapids on the Mackenzie River.
Engraving from John Franklin's
book, published in 1828.

that they could travel by paddling for most of the day. Sensing an oncoming storm, they landed and were making their camp when it struck. "We were obliged to throw ourselves flat upon the ground to escape being hurt by Stones that were hurled about by the Air like Sand," he wrote.

The following day, at about the location of today's Fort Good Hope, Mackenzie encountered "5 or 6 men here that we did not see before [on their way downstream], among which is a Dog Rib Indian who left his own Lands on acc[oun]t of some Quarrals." Since "the English Chief understood this Man as well as one of his own Nation," Mackenzie was able to gather some information that would have been extremely interesting to him.

He informed us that he understood from the People with whom he now lives (Hare Indians) that there is another large River on the other Side of the Mountains to the S.W. which falls into the Belhowlay Toe in comparison to which this [the Mackenzie River] is but a small River[,] that the Natives are Big and very wicked, kill Common Men with their Eyes, that they make Canoes larger than Ours[,] that those at the Entry kill a kind of large Beaver the Skin of which is almost Red, that there has been by Canoes say Ships there often, he knows of no Communication by water to the above River, those of the Natives who saw it went over the Mountains on Foot.

Could this be the river Mackenzie was looking for? In a way it was; the description seems to fit that of the Yukon River, of a comparable size to the Mackenzie, though not larger, which does flow to the Pacific. But the Yukon is over 3 000 km or 1,900 miles long, the fifth longest river in North America. It rises on the northern British Columbia boundary quite near to the Pacific, but then flows north and northwestward in a huge arc till it reaches the sea in Norton Sound, Bering Strait. It does not flow in the direction Mackenzie wanted to go, and wouldn't have been much help to him.

Russian Exploration of the Yukon River

The native report of a river west of the mountains flowing to the Pacific was probably the Yukon. The mouth of the Yukon had been found and mapped by A. K. Etolin and Mikhail Tebenkov in 1832, and the lower part of this immensely long river was explored by a Russian naval lieutenant at the request of the Russian-American Company the year after John Bell found its upper tributary, the Porcupine, for the Hudson's Bay Company in 1842.

Lavrentiy Alekseyevich Zagoskin left Fort Saint Michael, a Russian redoubt near the Yukon's mouth, at the end of 1842, and after wintering at Nulato, followed the river east in June 1843.

Zagoskin had read Mackenzie's book *Voyages from Montreal* and had been influenced by it. He wrote:

We ourselves did not know where we were going, but we entertained hopes of reaching the ridge that divides the British possessions from ours. I proposed that we undertake to prove Mackenzie's supposition about the true direction of the 'Great River' that flows westward from the Rocky Chain. I have no doubt that what he was told [by the natives] *concerned the Yukon.*

Unfortunately for Zagoskin and his men, his transportation was not a canoe but a skin-clad *umiak*. It was difficult to handle and was leaky, so that when he was faced with rapids swelled that season with an unusual amount of runoff, he found himself unable to proceed. Although he had intended to trace the Yukon to its source, he only got as far as the modern settlement of Ruby, Alaska, about 240 km or 150 miles from Nulato, and still 1 600 km or 1,000 miles from the river's source.

Zagoskin's expedition was not repeated; the Russian-American Company showed little interest in exploring or exploiting the interior.

The Hudson's Bay Company, successor to the North West Company, would take until 1840 to find any of the waters of the Yukon. That year Robert Campbell found the Pelly River by going up the Liard and Frances Rivers on the west side of the mountains. It would be 1842 before the Porcupine River, which flows into the upper Yukon, would be discovered by John Bell of the Hudson's Bay Company, who traversed the mountains westward from the Mackenzie. In 1844, on another attempt, he would reach the Yukon River itself. Even then the riverine geography remained unclear, and it would be 1851 before Robert Campbell, also working for the Hudson's Bay Company, would decipher the intricacies of the upper Yukon.

Up to that time the Yukon was confused with the Colville River, a relatively insignificant river flowing to the Beaufort Sea east of Barrow, Alaska, the mouth of which had been found by Peter Warren Dease and Thomas Simpson in 1837.

John Franklin, who was in this area in September 1826, concluded, probably correctly, that the native information given to Mackenzie referred to the Peel River, which Franklin had just found and named. This was the river that took the natives to the sea in five days. It could also have been a reference to Arctic Red River. Neither river is as large as the Mackenzie River, however.

The "large beaver" the native referred to may conceivably have been a reference to sea otters, which Mackenzie may have been aware of from Cook's voyage. At any rate, Mackenzie was clearly excited by this report and would spend considerable effort over the next few days to find out more.

The next day, 27 July, on meeting another native group, Mackenzie "endeavoured to get some further Intelligence respecting the River [he had] heard of yesterday." These natives, he wrote,

declared to us they knew nothing of it but from hearsay, that none of them were further than the Moutains on the other side of this River, that they were told it was a much larger River than this, that it ran towards the Midday Sun, and that there were People a little further up the River who inhabit the opposite Mountain and had lately come down from them to fish, and who knew the other River very well.

This was of great interest to Mackenzie, of course, who offered beads to one native if he would "describe the Country round upon the Land," that is, draw a map on the ground. This he did.

Without paying any regard to Courses, he drew a very long pr. [peninsula?] *of Land between the River running into the Great Lake* [the ocean], *at the Extremity of which he said there was a Belahoulay Cown white mens Fort that he did not see but was told of it by other Nations. This I take to be Unalaschka Fort & of course the River to the west to be Cooks River & this to fall into or join with Noxta*[Norton?] *Sound not a River but a Body of dead water.*

From this Mackenzie later deduced that the Mackenzie River "communicates with Norton Sound," and this is how it is written in his book; of course, he was still wrong.

Mackenzie asked the man who had given him this information if he would lead him across the mountains to this other river, but the man would not agree to this, "alledging that he did not know the Road & that he wou'd get some of the People close by to accompany me as they knew the Road very well," which Mackenzie judged just an excuse.

Buoyed by this information, which made sense to him in light of the perceptions of the geography of the Northwest he must by now have held, which would have been Peter Pond theories partially debunked, Mackenzie resolved to stay here the rest of the day to see if he could find out more. Given that he was by now concerned about the limited time he had to get back to Lake Athabasca, it is a measure of the importance Mackenzie gave to the acquiring of this information about a river flowing to the Pacific that he would spend yet more time here.

Mackenzie ordered the English Chief to "harangue them in Council" but derived very little further information, which simply became more fantastic and less believable. He concluded that "Its very certain that those People know more about the Country than thet chuse to tell me at least what comes to my ears." The English Chief, anxious to return home before winter, may well have concealed a lot of information from Mackenzie, in fear of him deciding to follow some perceived route to the west, when he himself wanted to go south, and home.

The next day, when Mackenzie was preparing to leave, he found most of the native group had already left, probably out of fear of being pressed into service to lead where they did not want to go.

Continuing upstream, Mackenzie wanted to keep to the west side of the river in order to see if there were any rivers of consequence flowing in from that direction, but, he wrote,

The No. of Sand banks & the Current being too strong obliges me to Traverse to the old Side where the Eddy Currents are very frequent [so that we can] *make much more headway.*

July turned into August. At Fort Norman, the point where the Great Bear River flows into the Mackenzie from the lake of the same name, Mackenzie found "that the whole Bank was on Fire for a considerable Distance." These were coal or lignite seams: John Franklin noted them burning in 1826, and they are still burning 200 years later.

By 10 August, all the time looking for natives who might be able to give him information about a river to the west, but finding none, he was back at Camsell Bend, where the river turns and flows north instead of northwest. As he would now leave the vicinity of the mountains, Mackenzie wanted to climb a mountain in order to perhaps see this elusive western river. He set off but did not make it even to the base of the mountain due to marshy ground, so he had to give up.

On 13 August they camped at the point where the Liard River flows into the Mackenzie, the site of Fort Simpson. Although Mackenzie noted this river in his journal on both the outward trip (1 July) and the return (calling it the "River of the Mountains"), he did not make anything of it, which is surprising in that it is a large river seemingly going in the direction he wanted. On the outward journey Mackenzie had described it as "a large River upwards of ½ Mile over, at the Entry."

It is perhaps just as well he did not follow the Liard, as it rises in the mountains of central Yukon, and he would have been hard-pressed to find a way through to a westward-flowing watershed. It would be 1840 before Robert Campbell, with the benefit of considerably more geographical knowledge than Mackenzie had in 1789 and building on initial exploration of the river by John McLeod in 1831, would

Sailing by canoe down the Mackenzie River. Engraving from Franklin's book.

ascend the Liard and find a way to the Pelly River, a tributary of the *eventually* westward-flowing Yukon River.

After eight days of hard paddling and towing, with occasional use of a sail, the party reached Great Slave Lake. The wind was too strong for them to attempt to travel the lake, but the next day they attempted it and nearly drowned as a result. "Hoisted half sail which drove us on at a great rate," Mackenzie recorded. "Took in much Water . . . went on with great Danger . . . Men continually Bailing out the Water which we took in on every side."

The next day, 24 August, the wind had died down to "Small breezes," and in the afternoon they saw a sail, which turned out to be Laurent Leroux, the man Mackenzie had left to trade at Great Slave Lake on his outward voyage. Leroux had been trading all summer and had made a trip to Lac La Martre, a large lake northwest of Great Slave Lake. Traveling again along the north shore of Great Slave Lake, Mackenzie made for the post that Leroux had established on Yellowknife Bay, this time cutting across the North Arm, a distance of about 40 km or 25 miles, taking advantage of a southwesterly breeze. Leroux was to winter here, so Mackenzie gave him all the trade goods he had left and said adieu to the English Chief and his hunters, who were also staying here.

Hopping across the islands in the middle of Great Slave Lake as he had done outbound, Mackenzie encountered difficult weather, nevertheless making it to the southern shore. They entered the Slave River again, where the canoe at one point hit a tree stump, filling it with water. Portaging up the rapids of that river, they took another nine days to reach Lake Athabasca, on 12 September. It was perhaps not too soon, for Mackenzie's journal entry for the second to last day of the expedition noted, "Froze hard last Night, cold weather throughout the Day, appearance of Snow." The short northern summer was at an end.

Mackenzie's last entry in his journal records the return to Fort Chipewyan in a matter-of-fact manner.

At 8 oClock entered the lake of the Hills, at 10 the Wind veered to the Westward, and strong as we could bear it with high sail, which wafted us to Fort Chipewean by 3 oClk P.M. Here we found Mr. [Alexander] McLeod with 5 Men busy building a new House. 102 Days since we had left this Place.

The title of the surviving journal of Alexander Mackenzie's voyage to the Arctic from which this account is derived makes it clear what his objective was, even though it was not reached. The *Journal of a Voyage . . . to the Pacific Ocean in Summer 1789* shows that in a very real sense the voyage to the Arctic was a part of the voyage to the Pacific that Mackenzie would finally complete four years later, even though at the time it was a monumental blind alley.

Clearly Mackenzie was not satisfied with his achievement. In a letter to Roderic dated 2 March 1791 he referred to the Mackenzie River as the "River Disappointment." This was the only reference Mackenzie ever made to this name for the river, although many writers have concluded this was what he named it.

In a memorandum probably written much later he recognized what had come out of his 1789 voyage. He wrote:

I went [on] this expedition in hopes of getting into Cook's River; tho' I was disappointed in this it proved without a doubt that there is not a North West passage below this latitude and I believe it will generally be allowed that no passage is practicable in a higher latitude the Sea being eternally covered with Ice.

A negative conclusion, it is true, but one that advanced geographical knowledge by its proof of the non-existence of the long-sought Northwest Passage south of the Arctic Ocean.

The Mackenzie Delta and Whale Island shown on a German map from Stieler's *Hand Atlas,* 1893.

The Fur Trade on the Mackenzie

After Mackenzie's exploration of 1789, fur traders slowly advanced down the Mackenzie River, setting up trading posts. Roderic McKenzie wintered on an island at the entrance to the river from Great Slave Lake in 1790, and in 1793 a post was built at Marten Lake. Another post was established in 1796 about 130 km or 80 miles below Great Slave Lake on the Mackenzie.

In 1799 a fort was built at Great Bear Lake, and one trader, Duncan Livingston, was killed with all his men in an attempt to establish trade with the Inuvialuit the same year. It was perhaps just as well for Mackenzie that the Inuvialuit had been away hunting when he was in the delta.

About 1804 a post called Fort of the Forks was built at the confluence with the Liard; it was renamed Fort Simpson in 1821, after the Hudson's Bay Company Governor George Simpson, when the North West Company merged with the Hudson's Bay Company that year.

In 1805 a post was established at Fort Good Hope, just below the Arctic Circle. Fort Liard was built on the Liard River, and Fort Nelson, also on the Liard, was constructed in 1805 and named after the British Admiral Horatio Nelson, who that year would defeat the French and Spanish fleets at Trafalgar.

Due to the long cold winters that produced furs of excellent quality, the region would in time become what Sir George Simpson, the Governor of the Hudson's Bay Company, the successor to Mackenzie's North West Company, would refer to as his "treasure house," the most valuable region in the company's empire. In 1823 he wrote:

The Trade of Mackenzie's River is so valuable and important and holds out such prospects of extension to advantage.

Mackenzie's Map of His Arctic Voyage

This map was originally found in the files of the British Colonial Office in 1918 and reported by Charles Davidson, a pioneer historian of the North West Company. It is today in the Public Record Office in London (the national archives of Britain), where it is referred to as "Chart called Mackenzie's Map." Davidson in 1918 found that Colonial Office officials were unable to state when the map came into their possession. The map is thought to be the only surviving copy of any maps actually made on either of Mackenzie's two expeditions. As such it is on a par with the only surviving copy of Mackenzie's journal, also of the Arctic expedition (see page 134). It is published here for the first time. Enlarged sections of this map are shown on pages 89, 95, 109, 151, and 159.

The theory that the map is a copy of one actually drawn during the expedition is supported by the immediacy of many of the notations. "5 ft deepest Water in the Entrance of the Lake 12 July 1789" is written at the point where Mackenzie's track is shown entering the Arctic Ocean, shown as a semicircular basin.

Mackenzie certainly initially thought that he had reached a lake, perhaps because of it being so described by his native guide, so would have noted this on his map. His journal noted the discovery of tides a few days later, although it does not specifically note the realization of having reached an ocean; this is just implied. Charles Davidson, based on the evidence of this map, concluded that it was by no means certain that Mackenzie realized while on his journey, or even soon after, how far north he had actually been, and noted that there is no definite statement in his manuscript journal or his book that he had reached the northern ocean. Thus, he wrote, "It would seem from this map that Mackenzie did not realize [at the time] that he had reached the Arctic Ocean."

But the map does note "A Number of Animals like pieces of Ice supposed to be Whales." They were first taken to be pieces of ice, although Mackenzie's journal notes, "I immediately knew them to be whales." How then a notation like this came to be written on his map is a bit of a mystery.

"Chart called Mackenzie's Map," western part. Almost certainly a contemporary copy of the map Mackenzie drew, now lost. Note the rendering of the Peace River, drawn from native report and seemingly approaching the Pacific. This was the route Mackenzie would take in 1793 when he finally achieved his goal of reaching the Pacific Ocean.

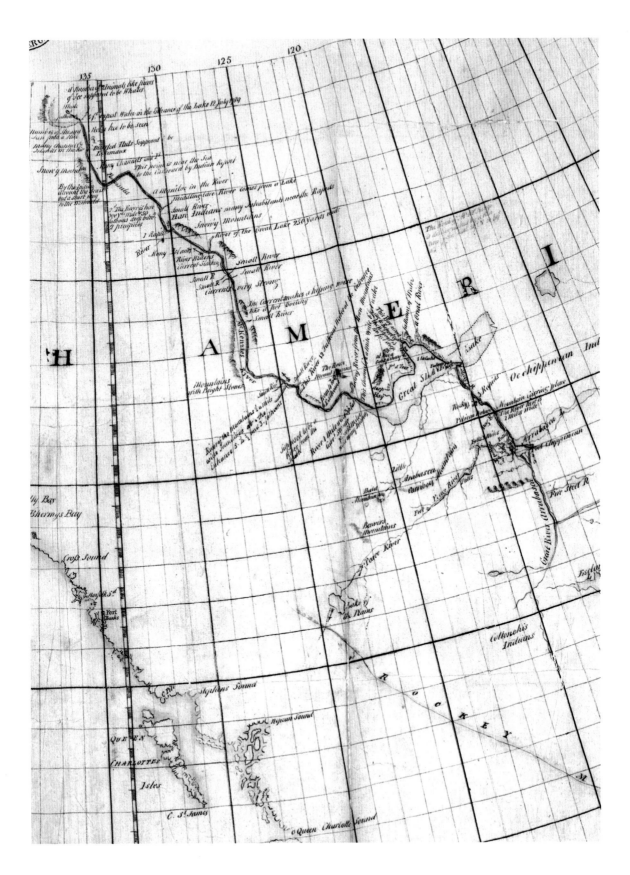

The Mackenzie River – The Question of a Name

The drainage basin of Alexander Mackenzie's eponymous river drains 1.8 million square km or 703,000 square miles, 22 percent of the surface of Canada. The river is 4 240 km or 2,650 miles long from its most remote source, the head of the Finlay River at Thutade Lake. As such, it is the second longest river in North America, second only to the Mississippi.

At least one modern native leader has derided the fact that the river is named after Mackenzie. Why should this be, he maintained, when all that Mackenzie did was to follow the river once, a river that had been traveled by native people from time immemorial? A Dene publication paraphrased the words of Franklin (below):

In justice to the memory of the thousands of Dene who have travelled on the Big River and lived on its shores for thousands of years, and have shown only love and affection for it, we hope the custom of calling this the Mackenzie, which has been in use by only a few people, and only in recent years, will be discontinued, and that the original name DEHCHO may be universally adopted.

The authors here have a point, of course, but at the same time let us critically examine why the river is called the Mackenzie today. The name is one for a unified whole; Alexander Mackenzie was the first to travel the whole, from source to mouth, and for the express purpose of determining where it went.

The Dene, at least before the opening of trading posts, never had to travel very far. More significantly, Mackenzie was the first to map the entire river from beginning to end, the first to place it on the map of the world, the first to notify the world of its existence.

The Dene name "Dehcho" was not applied to the whole river, but only to a part, approximately that south of Fort Good Hope. In other words, this Dene name was applied to the river where it flowed through Dene territory. Elsewhere, where it flowed through the territories of other groups, it had other names, such as "Dehoga" north of Fort Good Hope, a K'áshot'ine (Hare) name; "Nagwichoonnijk" toward the delta, a Gwich'in (Dinjii Zhuh or Loucheux) name; and "Kookpaic" in the delta, an Inuvialuit name. Farther south, as it flowed from Great Slave Lake, the Denesoliné (Chipewyan) called the river "Yuda Des Nedhé," and the Cree name of "Kis-Ca-Che-Wan" is what appeared on the first map to show the river at all (see map on page 34). "Mackenzie" is the only name, save for "Great River" or "Big River," that has *ever* been applied to the *whole*. For this reason it is perfectly fitting for the river to be named the Mackenzie.

Changes of language over sometimes short distances in the Mackenzie Valley had been noted by John Franklin in 1825. He noted one day "we found that the dialect of this party [of natives] was different from that we had seen yesterday," enough that his interpreter "did not understand their language."

The situation is reminiscent of that in India after the British withdrawal in 1947. Despite Indians' intense effort to rid themselves of British rule, the Indian constitution adopted English as an "associate" official language, for government business, as the only one that would not favor any particular Indian language and thus, perversely, would be the most acceptable to all.

Mackenzie himself referred to the river as "Mackenzie's River" in the summary of his book, published in 1801, though not in the body of his text, which surely shows he was not trying to promote that name.

The name did not come into use at that time, although in 1807 a supporter of the idea of naming some geographical feature after Meriwether Lewis, just returned from his expedition to the Pacific, wrote to President Thomas Jefferson:

The world has justly given the name Mackenzie to the great river of the north for the same obvious reason, the merit of discovery.

But the river was still referred to by fur traders as the "Great River" by the time of Sir John Franklin's expedition to the Arctic shore via the Mackenzie in 1825. In his book about his second expedition published in 1828, Franklin says:

In justice to the memory of Mackenzie, I hope the custom of calling this the Great River, which is in general use among the traders and voyageurs, will be discontinued, and that the name of its eminent discoverer may be universally adopted.

Map of the lower part of the Mackenzie, from Aaron Arrowsmith's 1802 edition of his map of North America. This copy of the published map, complete with pasted-on additions and pencil notations, belonged to the Hudson's Bay Company.

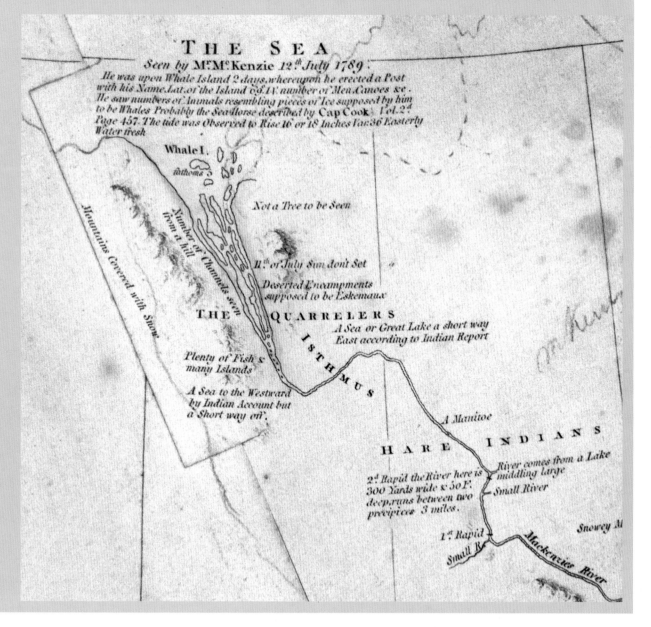

Mackenzie's Journal

The only surviving copy of a Mackenzie journal is one of the 1789 voyage to the Arctic, the text of which is that followed in this book. It is kept in the Manuscripts Department of the British Library in London, where it is known as Stowe 793, one of a series of manuscripts originally collected by the first Marquis of Buckingham at their family seat – Stowe, England. A catalog of the collection which was published in 1818 and 1819, when Mackenzie was still alive, states that the journal was presented to the marquis by him. The collection was acquired by the British Museum, now the British Library, in 1883.

Presented in a diminutive leather-bound volume about 18.5 cm high by 15.5 cm wide (7½ by 6¼ inches), its size would corroborate the idea that it could have been carried to the Canadian interior by canoe. At the time I examined it, everyone else in the bewooded and distinguished Manuscripts Reading Room was reading large, oversize, and thick medieval-looking documents, a considerable contrast to the tiny one I was reading. In pencil inside the front cover is the notation "This is the original journal in the handwriting of Mackenzie."

Unfortunately, however, it isn't. A twentieth-century note stuck in the front endpaper states: "Note – as this journal is written in two different hands, it does not seem possible to accept the statement that it is in Mackenzie's autograph." It may even be in three different hands. One may be that of Mackenzie, but none of it looks like his handwriting to me.

As an addendum to the journal at the end, there are three pages with "A few remarks to elucidate my tracks from Athabasca latitude 58. 38 North and longitude 110½ West from Greenwich to the North Sea and western ocean, as delineated on Mr. Arrowsmith's Map." Clearly a much later addition, this note is probably the original or a copy of an addendum published in Mackenzie's book in 1801.

The Mackenzie Delta and Whale Island on a Russian map, clearly copied from Mackenzie's own published map.

Right: This map is part of a world map by Aaron Arrowsmith. First published in 1790, this is from the first update, published in 1794. As can be seen, Arrowsmith has added the details of Mackenzie's 1789 expedition; in fact, there is so much correspondence between Mackenzie's own map (page 131) and these details that it is probably safe to assume that Arrowsmith was working from a copy of this map. This world map was the first widely available map to show Mackenzie's discoveries.

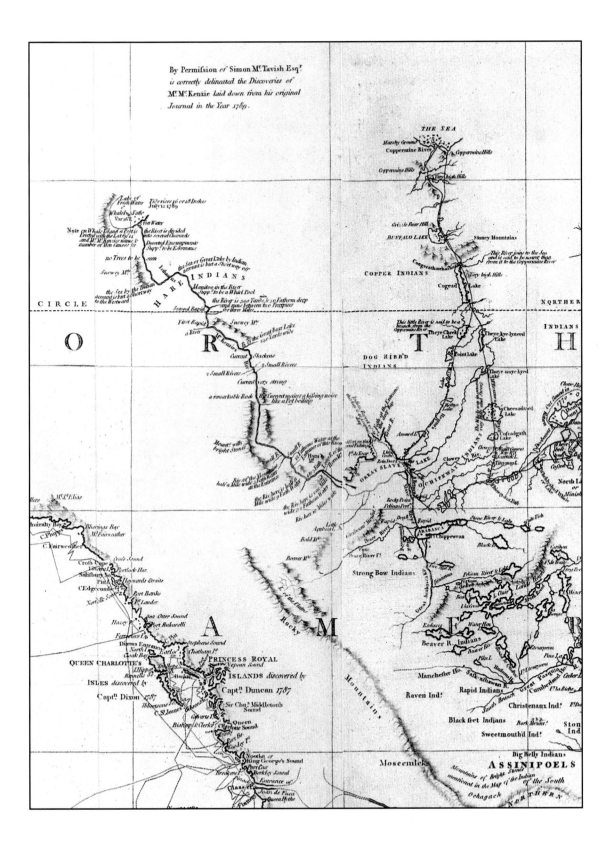

Dog

Ox Head

Provision Store
Moving Water..

Slave Fall 20 feet High 100 Yards
wide tremendous

Governe Weggs

cheboyne

River   White Earth

House   Little Rock

Lake Bonnet   Winnipeg R.

Yellow Earth

Island Portage Port

Dailles

Rat Portage

Great Flat Rocks

Lake of the
Woods

Back Road

Sable

la Pluie   Mapple R.   Lake
                                    la Pluie

                    Riv   Fort la
                                    Kni.... Fall

Rapid River

Long Falls

Maniton Rouestick

Great Forks

Little Forks

Cret

Flat

White W....
an....

48

My Expedition Is Hardly Spoken Of

He is not well convinced where he has been.

– Philip Turnor

I was not only without the necessary books and instruments, but also felt myself deficient in the sciences of astronomy and navigation: I did not hesitate, therefore, to undertake a winter's voyage in order to procure the one and acquire the other.

– Alexander Mackenzie

Previous page: The route to the North West Company's fort at Grand Portage (on Lake Superior) from Lake Winnipeg (top left), through Lake of the Woods and Rainy Lake (Lac La Pluie). This route into the Northwest was the route Mackenzie took in 1790. The map is a detail of *Canada and Nova Scotia,* drawn in 1814 by John Thomson.

Mackenzie spent the winter of 1789–90 at Fort Chipewyan. In the spring of 1790 he went to the annual meeting of the partners of the North West Company at Grand Portage, on Lake Superior. On his way there, at Cumberland House, where both the North West Company and the Hudson's Bay Company had posts, he met Philip Turnor, the surveyor for the latter, "appointed . . . for settling the Latitudes, Longitudes, Courses, and distances of the different Settlements Inland."

Turnor was a seasoned surveyor by this time, with the training, the instruments, and the experience to make reasonably accurate maps. No doubt the two had some interesting conversations; Turnor recorded in his journal for 23 June, the day Mackenzie arrived:

M^r McKensie says he has been at the Sea, but thinks it the Hyperborean Sea but he does not seem acquainted with Observations which makes me think he is not well convinced where he has been.

Mackenzie may have been unwilling to divulge all the details of his expedition to Turnor, who after all worked for a rival concern, but the meeting perhaps brought home to Mackenzie his need for more surveying skills.

Mackenzie arrived at Grand Portage on 13 July 1790 and "found every thing quiet." On the 16th, in a letter to Roderic, he wrote: "My Expedition is hardly spoken of but this is what I expected." Accustomed to making long journeys themselves, the North West Company partners probably saw little in Mackenzie's negative determination – that this

Beaten to It!

Peter Pond had presented his memorial to Henry Hamilton, the Lieutenant-Governor of Quebec, in 1785, urging British exploration of the Northwest, as had Alexander Henry the elder earlier. Pond had wanted private exploration rewarded with monopolies for the North West Company, but the British decided a government-sponsored expedition was the way to go. But, like most government operations in those days, things moved with glacial speed.

The scheme was partly that of Alexander Dalrymple, the hydrographer of the East India Company, who had had a hard time giving up the idea of a Northwest Passage and now hoped to prove that there was one using the river and lake systems from Hudson Bay west to the Pacific coast.

The government expedition was to be a two-pronged one. The first was to be a maritime survey to search for a strait from the west, or to prove its non-existence. This was the expedition which finally sailed from England in 1791 under the command of Captain George Vancouver, spending three seasons on the Northwest Coast and producing a magnificent survey that did indeed prove the non-existence of any strait. The second was to be an overland one, led by Captain John Frederick Holland.

Holland crossed to Quebec in the fall of 1790, only to receive the news, which had not yet reached England, of Mackenzie's trek to the Arctic the year before. Writing in Quebec on 10 November 1790, Holland records the news, and the motivations behind it.

The last accounts we have of the Slave Lake have been obtained through the medium of M. Mackenzie, a Person Employed by the Merchants of Montreal (self Entitled the North West Company) in Exploring one of the Outlets Issuing from that Lake and supposed by them, to have communicated with the Western Ocean, the contrary of which he has discovered . . . Their Views on taking these pains proceed from the hope that if they succeed in penetrating to the Ocean, Government may be induced to grant them a Charter and Exclusive Right in the Lucrative Furr trade to those parts.

A field compass of the early nineteenth century. This one belonged to William Clark, but Mackenzie's would likely have been exactly the same.

In February 1790, Holland had given the government a plan

for carrying into Effect the proposed Expedition for Discovering and Exploring the Interior parts of the Northern and Western Quarter of America: Lying between Lake Aurabusquie, or Arathpeskow [here he means Lake Athabasca], *and the Line of Coast discovered by Capt. Cook.*

He proposed a party of not less than sixteen persons, including a surveyor and assistant, with three years' supply of provisions transported to Lake Athabasca by another expedition from Fort Michilimackinac, in Lake Superior.

Holland outlined his proposed route from a base at "Aurabusquie,"

mounting the Slave River; thence North West Coasting the Slave Lake (which by information gained at Quebec from Persons who have been in that country) is not less than Ten Degrees of Longitude; that it Discharges itself into a River which takes its course NWest; and that its Distance from thence, to Prince William Sound or Cooks River does not Exceed Fifteen Degrees of Longitude. After Reaching the Mouth of Cooks River; or whatever other River, we may fall in with on the outset, It will be adviseable to stretch along the coast, to the South East, to observe the course of all such rivers as may appear of importance.

Holland then wanted to be picked up by a ship. He clearly expected to be able to walk along the coast.

Holland also submitted a large list of expenses and a list of surveying instruments that were the state of the art for the time. He must have been chagrined when he learned of Mackenzie's expedition, which had done what Holland would have likely done yet with far fewer men and no outside supplies other than what they could take with them.

Holland's list of instruments that he wanted to take with him is interesting in that it is exactly contemporary with Mackenzie, it was what a trained surveyor wanted to take on precisely the same expedition as Mackenzie's Arctic voyage, and it indicates what would have been available to Mackenzie when he went to London in 1791 to upgrade his skills and provide himself with better instruments for fixing his position. The list Holland submitted is shown below.

A Transit Instrument
A Time Piece

Telescopes   {*A Refractor*   } *Of sufficient Power to Observe*
        {*A Reflector*   } *the Eclipses of Jupiter Sattilites*

A Thermometer graduated considerably below the Freezing Point
A Barometer constructed for measuring Heights
A Theodolite Azimuth, and Hadley

was *not* the way to the Pacific Ocean – to get excited about. In addition, the partners were negotiating a new partnership agreement, which they undoubtedly saw as much more important; however, Mackenzie was awarded two out of the twenty shares in the concern, an indication that his work was still considered of importance to the partnership, for he had held only one share previously.

On his return from Grand Portage, Mackenzie again met Philip Turnor at Cumberland House, on 25 and 26 August. Turnor's comments in his journal are interesting for the light they throw on the size of fur trade operations in the Athabasca country and the provisioning of fur trade posts, but nothing was recorded about the unfolding geography of the Northwest. On 25 August Turnor wrote:

8½ PM two Canoes of Canadians arrived, on their way to the Athapiscow Country, they left ten more in Saskashawan River which are to follow.

And the next day Turnor recorded:

10 AM the Canadians embarked for the Athepiscow Lake, before M^r McKensie embarked he presented me a Promissory Note given him . . . in 1787 for 150 lb^s of Fatt which this House stands indebted for, but I could not pay it, not having 50 pounds of Fatt in the House.

The following winter Mackenzie spent at Fort Chipewyan, and the following spring the trip to Grand Portage was made again.

On his way there, at Buffalo Lake, now Peter Pond Lake, Saskatchewan, Mackenzie met Philip Turnor a third time, with Peter Fidler, Turnor's assistant surveyor. Turnor had been assigned to fix the position of Fort Chipewyan and Great Slave Lake. "[O]ur sole motive for going to the Athapescow is for Mr. Turnor to survey these parts in order to settle some dubious points," wrote Fidler in his journal. Both Hearne and Pond, he wrote, "fixes these places on their respective maps far more West than there is good reason to think them."

Turnor was to calculate these positions in order to satisfy a challenge to Samuel Hearne's fixing of the position of the ocean at the mouth of the Coppermine River, the accuracy of which had been questioned by Alexander Dalrymple, the hydrographer for the East India

Company and a man of some influence with the British government. Dalrymple thought the position wrong because it blew holes in his theories about the existence of a Northwest Passage. (Hearne did indeed place the Coppermine River's mouth too far north, but only by about 440 km or 275 miles, not enough to make a difference to Dalrymple.) Of course, Mackenzie's voyage also blew independent holes in Dalrymple's theories, but Dalrymple had not yet heard of his exploits. The idea was that fixing the position of Great Slave Lake would allow Hearne's work to be checked because Hearne returned via that lake.

Turnor recorded the meeting with Mackenzie in his journal for 1 June 1791:

At 7 PM Mr Alex Mackensie the Master of the Athapiscow Lake settlement and its dependances arrived with one Canoe in which he had 20 Packs of furrs besides his own things which is not common for a Canadian Master to have as they mostly keep their own Canoe for their own things [and] *he informed me that he had Fourteen Canoes more following him deeply loaded.*

Mackenzie in turn wrote a letter to Roderic, whom he had left in charge of Fort Chipewyan, to be delivered by Turnor. "I met Mr. Turner &c. here this Evening. I find their only intention is Discoveries. I also find they [are] very ill prepared." The latter was a reference to the Turnor party's small amount of provisions.

Turnor and Mackenzie likely discussed further the results of the latter's voyage, but it is typical of the period that both thought it more significant to record information about the fur trade, including Mackenzie's establishment of a

new Settlement up the Peace River near the Stony [Rocky] *Mountain*[s] *and* [where they] *got Sixty Packs of Beaver from Indians that never traded with Europeans or Canadians before.*

Mackenzie's expedition had been discussed, then or previously, for Turnor knew some details about it, as is shown from a later description he made of Great Slave Lake. Turnor wrote in his journal on 26 July 1791:

A large River runs out on West side of the Lake which Mr Alex^r Mackensie *went down to the Sea which is the only river which I hear of that runs* *out of it.*

Nearer to Grand Portage, perhaps as a result of further ruminations after meeting the skilled Philip Turnor, Mackenzie had formulated in his mind the idea of making a quick trip to England to learn surveying skills and buy new instruments. "I have some idea of crossing the Sea," he wrote in a letter to Roderic dated 10 August 1791.

This of course in turn shows that Mackenzie's intention was to try again to find a route to the Pacific Ocean. By the time he reached Grand Portage, he had made up his mind, and he continued eastward to Montreal, and thence sailed for England, where he spent the winter of 1791–92.

In his later book, his intentions to go to England appear much more determined and earlier formulated, but this is with descriptive hindsight, not to mention the help of his editor:

In this voyage [of 1789], I was not only without the necessary books *and instruments, but also felt myself deficient in the sciences of as-* *tronomy and navigation: I did not hesitate, therefore, to undertake a* *winter's voyage to [England], in order to procure the one and acquire* *the other.*

Mackenzie was particularly in need of the ability to determine longitude. In a later letter he explained:

Not having been furnished with proper Instruments to ascertain my *Longitude in my first Expedition, I made myself but little known during* *my residence in London the Winter 1791/92, but to prevent the like* *Inconvenience I then purchased the proper ones, in case I should make* *a second attempt.*

There were some newly available books that Mackenzie likely saw and perhaps purchased copies of, in addition to the practical treatises on navigation and astronomy. It is reasonable to assume that since he had determined to attempt another expedition to find the Pacific, he would have been keenly interested in any books from which he might glean information that would be of possible use to him.

One such book, published just the year before, was John Meares' *Voyages Made in the Years 1788 and 1789 from China to the North West Coast of America,* which contained some maps in which speculation was mixed with survey. We know that Mackenzie did in fact read this book, because he later refers to it during his expedition to the Pacific (see page 186). One map in this book (below) shows Samuel Hearne's discoveries, including "Arathapescow Lake," which is Great Slave Lake,

Part of one of John Meares' maps showing Great Slave Lake ("Arathapescow Lake") too far west. *Chart of the N.W. Coast of America and N.E. Coast of Asia, Explored in the Years 1778 & 1779, by Capn Cook; and further Explored, in 1788, and 1789.*

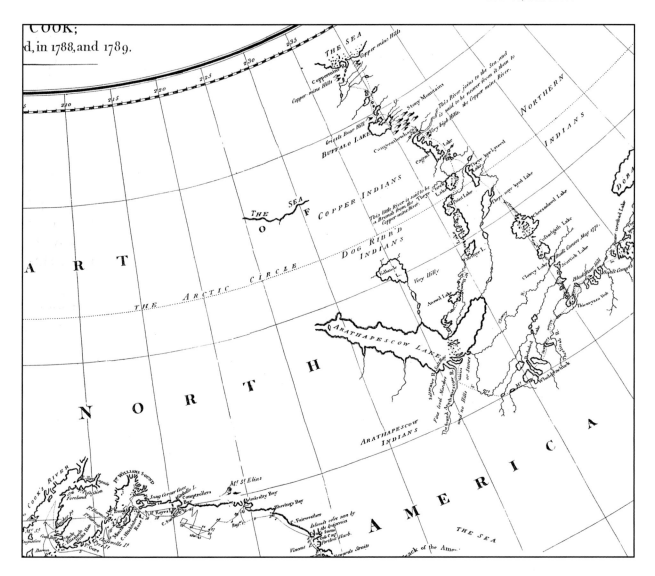

with an opening at its western end, and a river flowing out of the lake at about 226° E, which is 134° W. The lake and river system is placed too far west and too far north, making the distance from Great Slave Lake to the Pacific (or the Arctic) Ocean look invitingly short. The map shows "The Sea" a short distance to the north of the lake at about 68° N, as well as Hearne's depiction of the mouth of the Coppermine River, placed where Hearne put it at about 72° N, too far north. One wonders whether Mackenzie realized at this time that his placing of the sea at about 69° N was more accurate.

On another map in Meares' book (and shown at left), this coast is shown to be a misplaced version of the "Sea seen by Mr. Hearn agreeable to Mr. Arrowsmith's Chart," whereas the mouth of the Coppermine River is labeled "Sea seen by Mr. Hearn agreeable to Capᵗ Cook's Chart."

On yet another map (shown on page 187), Great Slave Lake – here just "Slave Lake" – is shown as another lake altogether, connected to "Arathapescow L.," the western end of which is now relegated to about 244° W, which is 116° W, ironically almost correct for Great Slave Lake; its real location is at 117° W. But it also shows a river flowing out of "Slave Lake" to connect with the Pacific both at Cook's River and Prince William's Sound. Mackenzie, of course, by now knew some of this to be false, yet some of it could still be correct. These maps illustrate the plethora of confusing information Mackenzie had to contend with. It is also no wonder that Great Slave Lake and Lake Athabasca were confused by mapmakers for many years after.

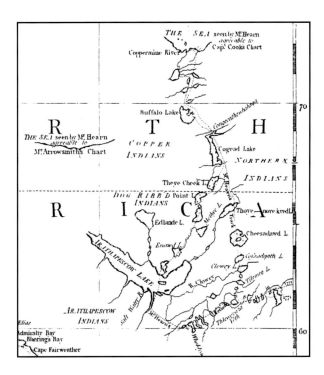

Part of a map which appeared in John Meares' book: *A Chart of the Northern Pacific Ocean, Containing the N. Coast of Asia & N.W. Coast of America, Explored in 1778 & 1779, by Captain Cook, and further Explored in 1788 & 1789, by John Meares.* Now Hearne's sea has two locations.

Mackenzie would probably have also seen books published two years before, in 1789, by two of James Cook's officers who returned to the Northwest in search of sea otter furs. These books, by George Dixon and Nathaniel Portlock, showed somewhat different details and interpretations of the Northwest coastline, filling in the simple dotted trendline that Cook had drawn for the coast north of Nootka Sound until he resumed surveying the coast in Alaska. Both books would have served to reinforce Mackenzie's determination of the position of the coast as being between about 138° W at the latitude of Fort Chipewyan and considerably less than that farther south. Neither, of course, was any help with details of the interior.

Mackenzie may have purchased a copy of Aaron Arrowsmith's new map of the world, which was by far the best available at this time. Published on 1 April 1790, the map was the Arrowsmith firm's first commercially published map and was meticulously constructed from all the latest information available. Arrowsmith himself soon developed a relationship with the Hudson's Bay Company, which gave him access to their information often long before it was available to any other mapmaker.

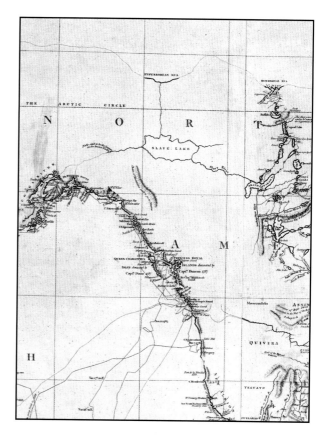

Part of Aaron Arrowsmith's world map of 1790. Obviously predating any of Mackenzie's information, this map was the most advanced map available at the time it was published. Nevertheless, one can imagine Mackenzie having a hearty laugh about its representation of the region he had so recently explored. On Arrowsmith's map, Lake Athabasca is shown as "Arathapeskow L." and the Slave River connects it, correctly, with (Great) Slave Lake. Peter Pond's presumed river flowing to Cook's River (Cook Inlet) flows out of Slave Lake, and "Falls said to be the largest in the known world" are marked on this river. This was information Pond had received from native sources and probably misinterpreted. A line of mountains parallel to the coast is labeled "Chain of mountains said to go to Mexico" – the Rocky Mountains. This map graphically illustrates how little was known about the western part of North America at the time.

Returning to Canada in the spring of 1792, Mackenzie immediately traveled back to Fort Chipewyan, intent on preparations for another attempt to find a route to the Pacific. He gave instructions for the construction of another post farther up the Peace River than the existing settlement, with the intention of making this his jumping-off place; after all, it would make sense to start from as far west as possible.

By this time Mackenzie had resolved that a possible route to the Pacific lay up the Peace, or Unjigah River, and he had given up on finding any route via a tributary to the Mackenzie River itself, which he had gone to so much trouble to find out about during his previous expedition. When he got back to Fort Chipewyan, if not before, he would have learned of Philip Turnor's reasonably accurate fixing of the position of that location, and in any case we can be certain that he would have now fixed the fort's position himself. He now had a chronometer, and he also now knew of the methodology of astronomical observations, using the moons of Jupiter, required to determine longitude. This time, Mackenzie was determined not only to find a route to the western ocean but also to be able to reliably fix his position so that he could prove where he had been.

Fixing the Position of Fort Chipewyan – and Its Significance for Mackenzie

It was not until 1791 that the longitudinal position of Fort Chipewyan was reasonably accurately fixed, and not until 1792, on his return from England, that Mackenzie knew that position. Finally he knew quite accurately the distance to the west that he would have to traverse to reach the Pacific Ocean – and it was a great deal farther than he had originally thought.

It was Philip Turnor, together with his assistant Peter Fidler, working for the rival concern, the Hudson's Bay Company, who found the position of Fort Chipewyan. On 28 June 1791, they

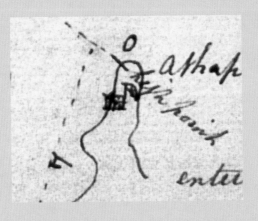

came to the Canadian Settlement called Fort Chepawyan . . . the House stands upon a heigh sandy point with but little woods around it.

Turnor wrote in his journal:

We were very kindly received by Mr Roderick Mackensie who is head clerk in these parts and stays as summer Master of all these parts.

On 29 June 1791 and the next day Turnor entered in his journal two latitudes for the fort that he had observed and calculated, 58° 37´ 34´´ and 58° 37´ 30´´ N. His latitudes were quite accurate, the true latitude of (old) Fort Chipewyan being 58° 40´ N, so that Turnor was only about 5 km or 3 miles too far south. His longitudes are not recorded in his journal, but from his map, drawn the next year, we know he calculated the longitude of the fort to be 110° 23´ W.

The correct longitude is 110° 28´ W, so Turnor was very close, about 5 km or 3 miles too far east – insignificant in terms of the distance to the Pacific Ocean, the distance that Mackenzie now knew he would have to cover. When he returned from England in the spring of 1792, Mackenzie could determine the westward distance that he would need to travel, for by that time he himself knew how to observe and calculate his longitude.

James Cook, with chronometers to help him, had established the position of Ship Cove in Nootka Sound, at 49° 36´ N, as 233° 18´ E, that is, 126° 42´ W. It was not known at this time that Vancouver Island was an island. However, Cook's maps showed the Northwest coastline trending southeast-northwest, with the result that at the latitude of Fort Chipewyan, the ocean would not have been reached until 138° W, at Cape Fairweather in Alaska.

Thus Mackenzie would have been able to calculate that he would have to cover about 28° of longitude, which is about 1 500 km or 950 miles at that latitude, if he were to trace a solely westward path to the ocean, and about the same if he were to head for Nootka, due to the distance to the south as well as the east-west distance. The straight-line distance from Fort Chipewyan to North Bentinck Arm, where he was to in fact reach the Pacific, was about 1 250 km or 780 miles. Although he would have to follow rivers or other existing routes, knowing the coast's directional trend he would probably have realized that there was more likely to be a distance advantage if he kept toward the south rather than to the north. It is conceivable that when he had to make the choice between the northern branch of the Peace, the Finlay River, and the southern one, the Parsnip (see page 173), this knowledge may also have added weight to his decision to follow the latter southward.

Above, top: Peter Fidler's sketch map of the location of Fort Chipewyan ("Athapescow House") on Lake Athabasca, Mackenzie's starting point for both his expeditions. The map is one of sixteen Fidler drew in his journal, detailing much of the shoreline of the lake.

Left: Detail from same map.

Also shown is an example from Fidler's notebook of the immense amount of observation and calculation that went into every fix of position.

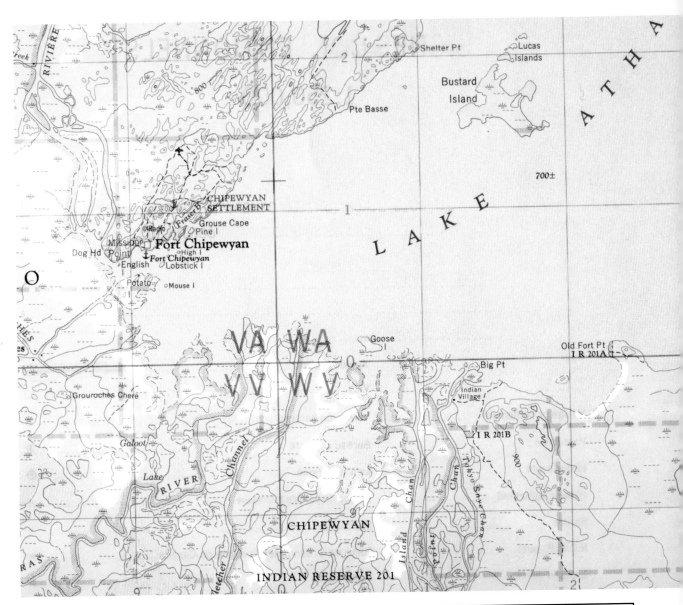

Creek

RIVIÈRE

2

Shelter Pt

Lucas
Islands

Bustard
Island

Pte Basse

700±

CHIPEWYAN
SETTLEMENT

1

LAKE

ATHA

Grouse Cape
Radio
Pine I

Mission
Dog Hd Point
English
Potato

Fort Chipewyan
High I
Fort Chipewyan
Lobstick I
Mouse I

VA WA
VV WV

Goose
I

Big Pt

Old Fort Pt
I R 201A

Grouroches Chere

Indian
Village

I R 201B

Galoot

900

Lake
RIVER

Channel I

Island

Point

Tokyo Stive Chan

Chan

CHIPEWYAN

RAS

Fletcher

INDIAN RESERVE 201

2

O

A Plan or Rough Sketch
of
Fort Chipewyan Depot
N.W. Indian Territories.
Lat 58.38 N. Long: 110.28 W.

References

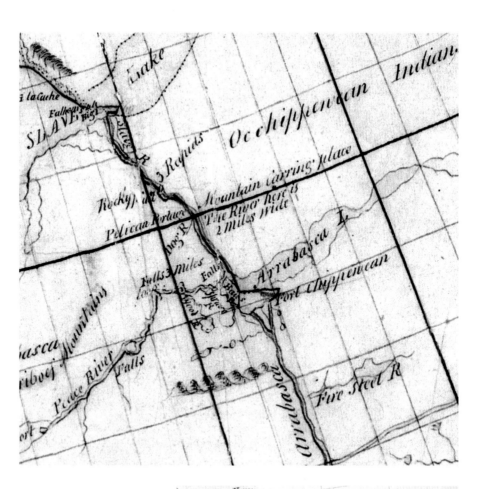

Above left: Modern topographic map of the southern end of Lake Athabasca. Old Fort Point is the site of the first Fort Chipewyan; Fort Chipewyan is the "new" site.

Above right: Mackenzie's map of the Lake Athabasca ("Arrabasca L.") and Slave River region.

Right: Fort Chipewyan and Lake Athabasca on Mackenzie's published map.

Left: A Plan or Rough Sketch of Fort Chipewyan Depot, drawn about 1820, and a photograph taken at the end of the nineteenth century. Both of these illustrations are of the "new" Fort Chipewyan, in its present location. It was moved to the north shore of Lake Athabasca in 1803.

To Traffick with the Russians

FORT FORK

Another very large river to the westward of this river
at a distance of two days march,
but to find, if there be such, is the difficulty.

I send you a couple of Guineas.
The rest I take with me
to traffick with the Russians.

– Alexander Mackenzie

Above: Sign at Fort Fork, near the town of Peace River, Alberta.

Previous page: The site of Fort Fork on the banks of the Peace River, and commemorative cairn.
The cairn is on the opposite side of the river from the site of the fort.

By October 1792, Mackenzie was ready to begin the first stage of operations for his "voyage" to the Pacific Ocean, moving from Fort Chipewyan to a new post being built some distance up the Unjigah, the Peace River, near its confluence with the Smoky River; by reason of location this site has usually been referred to as Fort Fork. It is called Fork Fort on Mackenzie's map.

On Wednesday, 10 October 1792, Mackenzie recorded the first entry in his journal of his expedition to the Pacific:

1792.
October 10.

Having made every necessary preparation, I left Fort Chepewyan, to proceed up the Peace River. I had resolved to go as far as our most distant settlement, which would occupy the remaining part of the season, it being the route by which I proposed to attempt my next discovery, across the mountains from the source of that river; for whatever distance I could reach this fall, would be a proportionate advancement of my voyage.

Leaving the fort in the hands of Roderic, Mackenzie, with three canoes, made for what he referred to as the Pine River, which is probably today's Claire River, leading to the Peace through a somewhat confused mess of lakes and channels at the western end of Lake Athabasca where the flow of the water changes from season to season.

Due to the lateness of the season, Mackenzie found the upstream journey to be less strenuous than expected, but it was getter colder. "The weather was cold and raw, so as to render our progress unpleasant," he recorded. By 17 October they had reached Vermilion Falls, and snow during the night was "several inches deep." On 19 October they arrived at what they called the "Old Establishment," a post originally established in 1787 near today's Fort Vermilion, Alberta, and marked on Mackenzie's map. Overnight, there must have been careless smoking or tending of a fire, for one of the buildings burned down. Mackenzie records that a garden had been sown there in the summer of 1788, with turnips, carrots, parsnips, potatoes, and cabbages, all of which, except the last, had done well. He noted that "there is not the least doubt but the soil would be very productive, if a proper attention was given to its preparation," the first reference ever to the potential of what is now an important agricultural area, the Peace River Valley.

The next day they reached the "New Establishment," a post built at some later, undetermined date, as the fur trade area tributary to Fort Chipewyan had been expanded. Here Mackenzie addressed a group of forty-two native hunters, encouraging them to continue to supply the post with their furs and strengthening his "admonition with a nine gallon cask of reduced rum and a quantity of tobacco." Here they dropped off James Finlay, one of their traders, who was going to winter at the post.

It continued to get colder, and on 21 October Mackenzie sent two canoes loaded with supplies ahead. He himself left on 23 October. "The thickness of the ice in the morning was sufficient notice for me to proceed," he recorded, for he feared that the ice would freeze solid and make canoeing impossible. A few days later he passed what was up to that year the westernmost post ever built, marked "McLoeds Fort" (sic) on his map, a temporary fort built in 1790 or 1791 by Alexander McLeod. Then, on 1 November, he passed the confluence of the Peace River and the Smoky River, and about 10 km or 6 miles farther up the Peace, as he recorded, he "landed at the place which was designed to be my winter residence," Fort Fork. His men were exhausted from paddling hard to beat the freeze-up.

No buildings had yet been completed, but the squaring of timbers for the buildings and the cutting of stakes for a palisade were well advanced. Here Mackenzie and his men were to spend the winter of 1792–93.

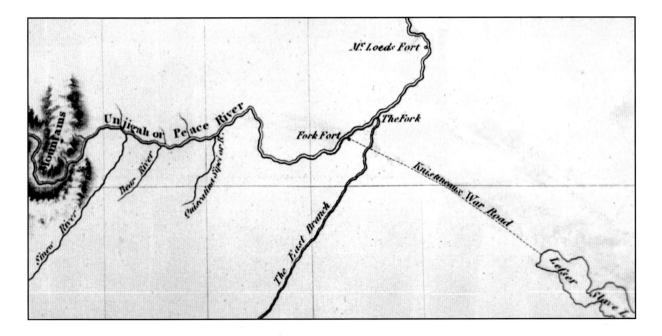

The location of Fort Fork, from the map published in Mackenzie's book. "The East Branch" is today's Smoky River.

After spending a week equipping the natives of the area for their winter hunting, the business of the fur trade still being of primary importance, everyone was put to work building the fort, a house, store-houses, and the palisades. On 22 November the river finally froze solidly, although ice had been running since the 6th, and by 27 November "the frost was so severe that the axes of the workmen became almost as brittle as glass." In a period of four days, from 25 to 28 November, Mackenzie recorded temperatures as low as –4° F (–20° C) as part of what must be the first record of weather in the region, but on 2 December, he broke his thermometer, so his weather recording ended. He was, however, later to record the occurrence of a chinook wind, warm winds that acquire their heat from adiabatic warming during descent from the Rocky Mountains, when "the atmosphere became so warm that it dissolved all the snow on the ground; even the ice was covered with water, and had the same appearance as when it is breaking up in the spring."

During the stay at Fort Fork, Mackenzie also had to use all his skills of first aid to cure several natives of injuries, and his success enhanced his reputation. In the new year he managed to deal with a particularly distressful case caused by the bursting of a gun in a man's hands; here he was also successful, and the native person involved was very grateful to him.

On 23 December, Mackenzie's house was ready and he moved into it, but the houses for the rest of the men still had to be built. In his book Mackenzie felt he had to defend his action to a British audience, for he writes: "It would be considered by the inhabitants of a milder climate, as a great evil, to be exposed to the weather at this rigourous season of the year, but these people are inured to it." Presumably the rest of the shelter was completed in record time!

On the first day of the new year, 1793, Mackenzie recorded:

Model of Fort Fork, reconstructed from archeological evidence, and now in the Peace River Museum. The fort is viewed here from the southwest; the river is on the far side.

My people, in conformity to the usual custom, awoke me at the break of day with the discharge of fire-arms, with which they congratulated the appearance of the new year. In return, they were treated with plenty of spirits, and when there is any flour, cakes are always added to their regale, which was the case on the present occasion.

On 5 January they experienced another chinook wind. Mackenzie, noting the wind's direction, from the southwest, thought he knew the reason for the warmth.

These warm winds come off the Pacific Ocean, which cannot, in a straight line, be very far from us; the distance being so short, that though they pass over mountains covered with snow, there is not time for them to cool.

What encouraging but totally erroneous reasoning! It was still 800 km or 500 miles in a straight line to the nearest salt water. The modern road distance from Peace River to Bella Coola is a stunning 1 750 km, or more than 1,000 miles, and this is no shorter than the distance via rivers.

But Mackenzie must have known the approximate distance he had to go, for now he had the instruments and the knowledge to find his longitude himself. He determined that Fort Fork was at 117° 35′ 15 ″ W (later "corrected" to 117° 43′ W) and the latitude was 56° 9′ N. The actual longitude of Fort Fork is 117° 27′ W, and its

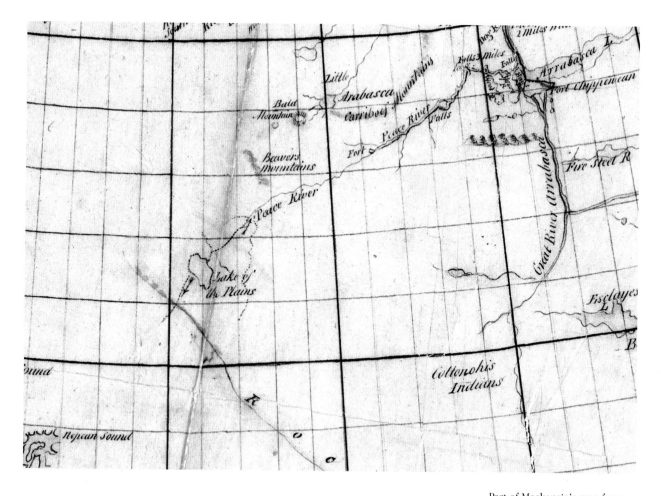

latitude 56° 8´ N. His first longitude was only about 8 km or 5 miles out, too far west, and his latitude was almost spot-on. But then 500 miles was perhaps not much in Mackenzie's estimation; like all fur traders, he was used to traveling vast distances, and he was already more than 2,000 miles west of Montreal. What matter another 500? He probably didn't at this point realize the roughness of the mountainous terrain he was going to have to traverse for that apparently little extra distance.

On 10 January Mackenzie penned a letter to his cousin Roderic at Fort Chipewyan in which he asked to be sent two books he had forgotten in the fall, "Atkinson's *Epitome of Navigation* [and] Marcurus['] *Chemistry* 2 vols." The first was an edition of *An Epitome of Navigation* by Henry Gellibrand, revised by J. Atkinson, but the book on chemistry has not been identified, nor the reason why he might have needed it. He also asked for "what Quick Silver you have (with the Sextant) as

Part of Mackenzie's map from his 1789 voyage to the Arctic shows what was known of the Peace River toward the Rocky Mountains at that time. The "fort" marked is not Fort Fork, since it was not built by Mackenzie until 1792, but the "Old Establishment," a post built in 1787 near Fort Vermilion, Alberta. On this map the position of the Rocky Mountains is shown reasonably correctly, but the course of the Peace River is known only from native reports, and includes a fictitious "Lake of the Plains."

All that was left above-ground when Fort Fork was rediscovered in the 1920s was that essential piece of northern equipment, the fireplace. The photo on the left shows it as it was found, and the other as it is today, reconstructed outside the Peace River Museum.

Below: The plaque on the cairn across the river from the site of Fort Fork, just west of the town of Peace River, Alberta.

FORT FORK

The remains across the river are those of Fort Fork, built by the North West Company in 1792 as a western base for Alexander Mackenzie's search for a route to the Pacific. The explorer wintered here before setting out in May 1793, on his historic journey to the Pacific. Fort Fork was subsequently abandoned for McLeod's Fort on the north bank, but was reoccupied about 1800. Until it was replaced by Fort Dunvegan in 1805, this was the North West Company's uppermost post on the Peace River.

De l'autre côté de la rivière se trouvent les vestiges du fort Fork, construit en 1792 par la Compagnie du Nord-Ouest pour servir de base à Alexander Mackenzie qui cherchait un passage vers le Pacifique. L'explorateur hiverna ici avant d'entreprendre son expédition historique vers le Pacifique en mai 1793. Le fort Fork fut plus tard abandonné quand on occupa le fort McLeod sur la rive nord, mais on le réintégra vers 1800. Jusqu'à son remplacement par le fort Dunvegan, en 1805, le fort Fork demeura le poste le plus à l'ouest sur la rivière de la Paix.

Historic Sites and Monuments Board of Canada.
Commission des lieux et monuments historiques du Canada.

Government of Canada · 1929 · Gouvernement du Canada

I have lost all mine." This was mercury, to provide an artificial horizon for observations.

Mackenzie had not been able to obtain any information from native sources about the region farther up the Peace River, for he wrote, "I have not been able to get any certain information respecting the country beyond this." He also asked for Alexander Mackay, who was at Fort Chipewyan, to join him at Fort Fork if he could be spared, as "he would be of great service to me should I undertake any expedition." This suggests that Mackenzie had not yet made up his mind for sure to attempt his expedition to the Pacific.

Yet about this time Mackenzie did gain some new information. Two natives from farther afield had now joined the natives gathered around the fort. From them, Mackenzie learned that the course of the Peace River upstream was "interrupted, near, and in the mountains, by successive rapids and considerable falls," a correct description. But he also recorded:

These men also informed me that there is another great river towards the mid-day sun, whose current runs in that direction, and that the distance from it is not great across the mountains.

This was the first hint of the existence of the Fraser River on the other side of the watershed of the Rocky Mountains, and it would guide Mackenzie later to take the southern branch at the point where the Peace divided into the Parsnip and Finlay Rivers.

By 20 April spring was in the air, and "the change in the appearance of nature was as sudden as it was pleasing." But there was a downside. "We were now visited by our summer companions the gnats and the mosquitoes," wrote Mackenzie.

Mackenzie had clearly made up his mind by now to attempt the journey. The month of April was spent busily trading for furs, and at the beginning of May the canoes were repaired, new ones were built, and six canoes were loaded with furs and sent back to Fort Chipewyan on 8 May. Two men were left at Fort Fork to look after it and supply the natives with ammunition that summer.

Lantern found at the site of Fort Fork, photographed on the reconstructed fireplace.

Six voyageurs agreed to accompany Mackenzie on his "projected voyage of discovery": Joseph Landry and Charles Ducette, who had been with Mackenzie on his voyage to the Arctic Ocean in 1789, and François Courtois, Baptist Bisson, Jacques Beauchamp, and François Beaulieux, together with Alexander Mackay as his second-in-command. There were also two Beaver natives as hunters and interpreters, one of whom was called Cancre, from a French term meaning duffer, which he had inherited from childhood. With Mackenzie, too, was his dog; as with many fur traders, his dog was an indispensable aid and companion in the wilderness, performing the useful task of warning of the approach of enemies – man or beast.

Mackenzie had had trouble finding any "volunteers" from among the natives. Some who had previously agreed to go with him, who actually seemed to have some first-hand knowledge, had deserted. Mackenzie wrote on 8 May 1793 in a last letter to Roderic to be sent with the furs leaving that day:

There is no dependence to be put on the promises of any of these people – and without Indians I have very little hopes of succeeding. I mean getting out of the River.

Anyway, with or without guides, Mackenzie meant to try. Again in the letter to Roderic he wrote:

The Indian who has deserted me has been on another very large River to the westward of this river at a distance of two days march, but to find, if there be such, is the difficulty. At any rate we are too far advanced now not to make some attempt.

They had built a new canoe, "twenty-five foot long within, exclusive of the curves of stem and stern, twenty-six inches hold, and four foot nine inches beam." The canoe was loaded with "provisions, goods for presents, arms, ammunition, and baggage, to the weight of three thousand pounds," plus the ten men, and Mackenzie's dog. Small wonder the day after they left it started to leak!

Mackenzie checked his chronometer, which he refers to as an "acrometer," and at seven in the evening on 9 May 1793 they pushed off up the Peace River for parts unknown.

Mackenzie knew where he wanted to go, even if he was unsure of how to get there. He finished his last letter to Roderic with a telling sentence, for he had read Cook's account of his meetings with Russian chief Gerasim Ismailov on the island of Unalaska: "I send you a couple of Guineas. The rest I take with me to traffick with the Russians."

The first Russian settlement in North America, at Three Saints Bay on Kodiak Island.

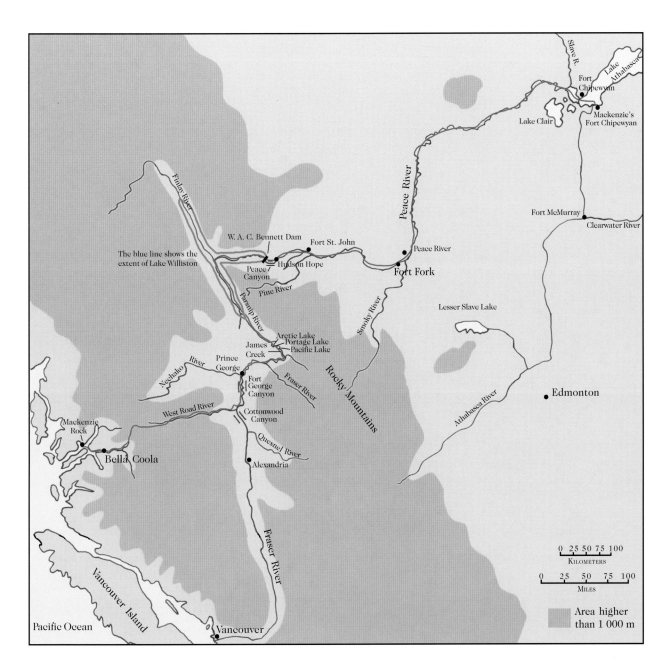

The blue line shows the extent of Lake Williston

Mackenzie's route from Fort Chipewyan to the Pacific Ocean shown on a modern map.

Area higher than 1 000 m

From Canada by Land

JOURNAL

OF A

SECOND VOYAGE, &c.

Previous page: This remarkable photograph could almost have been taken by Mackenzie just prior to setting off for the Pacific. It is actually a photograph of a surveying party taken about a hundred years later. But the canoe is birchbark, about the right size, and there are the correct number of men – nine: seven pipe-smoking voyageurs (including Alexander Mackay, Mackenzie's second-in-command), and two who could have been the native guides, a total of nine, plus Mackenzie, who of course would have been taking the photograph.

Alexander Mackenzie and his party left Fort Fork late on 9 May 1793, a Thursday, traveling only an hour before camping for the night. It was considered bad luck to begin a trip on a Friday, thus the late Thursday departure.

They had not progressed very far the next day when the canoe, so heavily laden, began to literally burst apart at the seams. A birchbark canoe of the type Mackenzie was using was sealed at the seams with pine or spruce resin or gum. Ideal to portage because even this large one was light enough that two men could carry it some considerable distance without resting, it needed frequent ongoing maintenance to keep it watertight. And only the voyageurs' skill would prevent it from being dashed to pieces in rapids.

They paddled westward along the magificent Peace Valley, its abrupt sides preventing any view from the water of the country beyond, and on 11 May, near the site of Fort Dunvegan, a North West Company post

View upstream on the Peace River. The photograph was taken a few miles from Fort Fork, from the middle of the river where a ferry crosses.

which would be established in 1805, they met with a group of natives who told Mackenzie that "according to our mode of proceeding, we should, in ten days, get as far as the rocky mountains."

By 13 May they were in a part of the river beyond where their guides had been. They saw a den of a "kind of bear, which is called the grisly bear" on an island, heard of its massive size and power, and later saw some, but did not (unlike Lewis and Clark)

The Peace River near Taylor, B.C.

Peace River east of Hudson Hope, B.C. From a canoe on the river, the Rocky Mountains would have just become visible to Mackenzie at this location.

have an encounter with one. They progressed along the river, gumming their canoe from time to time and noting fur resources, surrounded by increasingly higher cliffs each side. Here the river had carved itself deeper into the plateau land either side – today's fertile Peace River country of northwest Alberta and northeast British Columbia. They passed close to the site of modern Fort St. John, and continued, ever westward. Then, about halfway between modern Fort St. John and Hudson's Hope, the tops of the mountains came into view.

Before he met the Peace River Canyon, as he was about to do, it must have appeared to Mackenzie that he had, this time, hit the jackpot. Here he was, cruising serenely along in a broad and beautiful river valley, headed in the right direction and with what now appeared to be relatively low mountains ahead. Surely this must be the way at last!

In fact Mackenzie was headed for the only place where a river crosses the chain of Rocky Mountains, that area of the Peace, Parsnip, and Finlay Rivers now submerged behind the W.A.C. Bennett Dam in Lake Williston.

But getting there was not to be easy. Approaching the Peace River Canyon, Mackenzie noticed that the current was getting much stronger, and stones fell from the banks into the river, increasing the hazard. The last natives Mackenzie had encountered had told him there was a "considerable succession of rapids, cascades, and falls, which they never attempted to ascend; and where they always passed over land the length of a day's march." Although they found the native portage trail, Mackenzie judged that the canoe could make it if some of the men walked, thus lightening it. But they only made it partway through the canyon, and perilously at that. After one portage of 120 paces over a rocky point to avoid a particularly dangerous rapid, Mackenzie then walked, watching the canoe when he could. "Here I could not but reflect, with infinite anxiety, on the hazard of my enterprize," he wrote.

One false step of those who were attached to the line, or the breaking of the line itself, would have at once consigned the canoe, and everything it contained, to instant destruction: it, however, ascended the rapid in perfect security, but new dangers immediately presented themselves, for stones, both small and great, were continually rolling from the bank, so as to render the situation of those who were dragging the canoe beneath it extremely perilous; besides, they were at every step in danger, from the steepness of the ground, of falling into the water.

Now the canoe needed repair, and a convenient site presented itself, so they stopped for the night.

The next day, 20 May, it got worse. They progressed slowly upstream by pole and line (see photograph on page 181), at one point stripping to the waist to cross from one bank to the other. At noon, when they

stopped to take an altitude – a fix for latitude – the canoe was not secured properly and was only prevented from being dragged to destruction by one man hanging desperately onto the line. The rapidity of the current increased again, so that, recorded Mackenzie:

In the distance of two miles we were obliged to unload four times, and carry everything but the canoe: indeed, in many places it was with the utmost difficulty that we could prevent her from being dashed to pieces against the rocks by the violence of the eddies.

Then, near tragedy. As they were towing the canoe, a particularly violent wave broke the line and "filled us with inexpressible dismay, as it appeared impossible that the vessel could escape from being dashed to pieces, and those who were in her from perishing." They were lucky. Another wave drove the canoe out of the tumbling water, so that the men still in her were able to scramble out and bring the canoe to the shore. The canoe, miraculously, was not damaged. But they could go no farther. "The river above us, as far as we could see, was one white sheet of foaming water."

The Peace River Canyon. The photograph opposite was taken by B.C. Hydro prior to the building of the dam. Bottom left is a view from the ground, taken in 1891, and bottom right is the view today; the rapids have become a lake.

Hudson's Bay Company Archives, James McDougall (1987/13/139).

Some of Mackenzie's men now thought that the voyage should be abandoned, but Mackenzie was having none of it. The next day was spent reconnoitering a portage around the rapids, and the next three days cutting a path and manhandling the canoe and all it contained up a mountain and toward the point where the river again became navigable, a distance of perhaps 13 km, about 9 miles. Mackenzie expressed the opinion that perhaps it would have been a better idea to have taken the native portage trail in the first place. He thought it could not be more than 10 miles; it is 12.

The next day, 25 May, was spent putting things in order and preparing again for travel by water, embarking only at five in the afternoon. They were out of the Peace River Canyon and on that part of the Peace River that is now Lake Williston. They continued upstream, sometimes paddling, sometimes poling against the still strong current. On 29 May it rained so hard that they could make no progress; since "this being a day which allowed of no active employment," Mackenzie entertained himself by writing an account of their trip through the canyon. He put it in a rum keg they had emptied that day, and "consigned this epistolatory cargo to the mercy of the current." It was never found.

Mackenzie's dog proved its worth on 30 May; by continual barking and running back and forth it alerted them to the presence of a wolf nearby.

The Finlay Rapids, which, despite their name, were on the Peace River near the Finlay River.

The next day Mackenzie arrived at the point where the Peace became two rivers, the Finlay River flowing from the north, and the Parsnip from the south. Mackenzie recorded his decision as to which branch to take:

The Parsnip River flowing from the south (bottom) and the Finlay River (left side) join to form the Peace River (flowing off the top) in this 1949 aerial photograph, taken before the waters behind the W.A.C. Bennett Dam flooded the entire area. The bulk of the sediment (here colored white) is flowing down the Finlay and gives the distinct impression that the Finlay-Peace is the main stream. Yet Mackenzie turned southward, up the Parsnip.

If I had been governed by my own judgement, I should have taken the [Finlay], *as it appeared to me to be the most likely to bring us nearest to the part where I wished to fall on the Pacific Ocean* [nearest to the Russian fort?], *but the old man whom I have already mentioned* [his first potential guide back at Fort Fork] *. . . had warned me not, on any account, to follow it, as it was soon lost in various branches among the mountains, and that there was no great river that ran in any direction near it; but by following the* [southern branch, the Parsnip], *he said, we should arrive at a carrying-place to another large river, that did not exceed a day's march, where the inhabitants build houses, and live upon islands. There was so much apparent truth in the old man's narrative, that I determined to be governed by it; for I did not entertain the least doubt, if I could get into the other river, that I should reach the ocean.*

And so they took the Parsnip River southward.

It is interesting to note that if Mackenzie had chosen the northern branch of the river, and followed the Finlay upstream, he would likely have crossed over into the valley of the Kechika River, which is a tributary of the Liard, and would have ended up in the same position as he would have if, on 13 August 1789, he had turned up the Liard at its confluence with the Mackenzie in search of the westward-leading river he was so keenly seeking (see page 126). Then, as now, he would have had a hard time finding a route to a river that led to the Pacific. It is true that had he continued to the lake regarded as the source of the Finlay, Thutade Lake, which would have only been achieved by turning almost due south again, he could have come within 30 km or 20 miles of the Skeena River, which would have taken him to the sea

Finlay Forks, the joining of the
Parsnip (right) and Finlay (left)
Rivers to form the Peace (flowing
to the east, away from the
camera). This was the decision
point for Mackenzie; his men
wanted to take the north branch,
the Finlay, but, acting on native
information received, Mackenzie
correctly took the south branch,
the Parsnip. The country shown in
this photograph, taken by B.C.
Hydro about 1964, no longer
exists; it is under Lake Williston,
the lake behind the massive W.A.C.
Bennett Dam. The courses of the
three rivers, shown also on this
1959 map, are likewise now
obliterated by the lake.

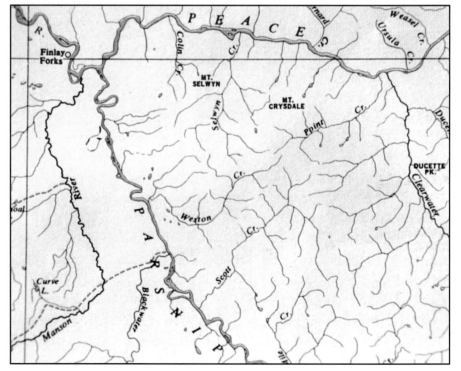

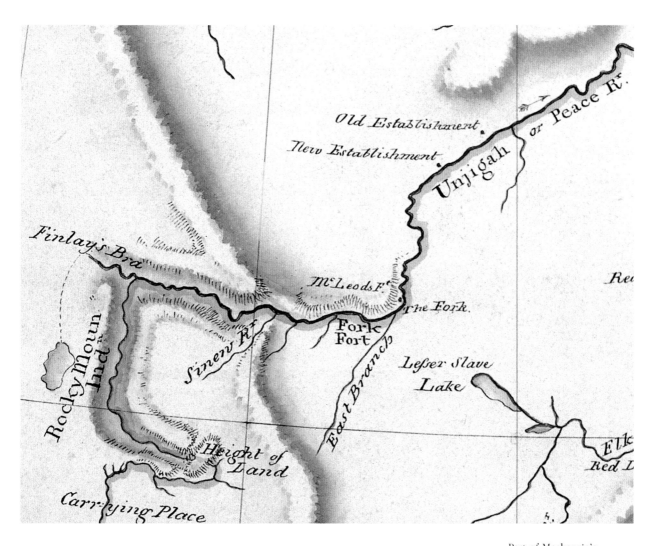

The following labels appear on the map:

Old Establishment

New Establishment

Unjigah or Peace R.

Finlay's Bra

McLeods F.

rne Fork

Fork Fort

Re

Sinew R

Rocky Mountain Ind

Lesser Slave Lake

East Branch

Height of Land

Elk

Red L

Carrying Place

Part of Mackenzie's prototype map prepared for publication in his book, showing his track from Fort Fork to the Continental Divide.

near modern Prince Rupert. But this course is tortuous and often involves going in an opposite direction from that to the sea, so whether he would have found his way by this route is doubtful. The route might have been easier than the one he eventually took, as he probably could have stayed with his canoe the whole way. Or he might have found the Stikine River, as the Hudson's Bay Company's Samuel Black would do in 1824.

It was Mackenzie's decision to take the southern branch; his men protested that they should take the northern, which was broader and slower-flowing. The current on the Parsnip was very strong, so that it took them "the greatest part of the afternoon in getting two or three miles – a very tardy and mortifying progress." Mackenzie had to use his not inconsiderable powers of persuasion to convince his men that they were going the right way. "I delivered my sentiments in such a manner as to convince them that I was determined to proceed," he wrote.

Exploration of the Northern Branch

Mackenzie decided to follow the "southern branch" of the Peace River, the Parsnip, at Finlay Forks on 31 May 1793.

The "northern branch," the Finlay River, was named after John Finlay, another Nor'Wester, who carried out the first tentative exploration of that river four years later, in 1797. But he did not get very far. After the amalgamation of the North West Company with the Hudson's Bay Company in 1821, the governor, George Simpson, thought that this northern area was potentially a rich fur region like the Mackenzie Valley on the other side of the mountains. He was even of the opinion that there would be another large river paralleling the Mackenzie to the Arctic.

In 1823 Simpson appointed former Nor'Wester Peter Warren Dease to explore from the Finlay northward, but Dease delayed because he didn't relish the job, and the following year Simpson assigned Samuel Black, another former North West Company man, with specific instructions to find the river he supposed to be flowing to the north.

During 1824, Black led an expedition to the source of the Finlay, Thutade Lake, then struck out overland looking for Simpson's river. Of course, he didn't find it, but he did find the Stikine River – he called it the Schadzue – which flows to the Pacific in the Alaska panhandle, then Russian territory. Because of Simpson's instructions, Black did not follow the Stikine to the sea. If he had done so, the Hudson's Bay Company probably would have been able to establish a post near the coast, but still in British territory, to cut off the fur trade to the Russian-American Company, their rival on the coast, and Black's name would likely have been remembered by history along with those of Mackenzie, Fraser, and Thompson.

Ironically, in 1834 Simpson sent Peter Skene Ogden by ship to establish just such a Stikine post. He was thwarted by the Russians, who went on to build their own fort at the mouth of the Stikine.

1793.
June.

Continuing upstream against a strong current with rising water volumes, with the men walking some of the time to lighten the canoe, they passed by the vicinity of the modern town named after our explorer – Mackenzie, B.C.

On 5 June they passed the Pack River, flowing in from their right, but it went unnoticed or at least unrecorded. This was unfortunate, as following that river would have afforded a very much easier route across the watershed, water flowing as it does so gently from Summit Lake, along the Crooked River to McLeod Lake, and through the Pack to beautiful Tudyah Lake and then to the Parsnip. (Now the original confluence of the Pack and the Parsnip is submerged under the Parsnip Reach of Lake Williston. See the map on page 300.) This route, plus the Salmon River, and later with the Giscombe Portage between Summit Lake and the Fraser River, was used as the route to the Fraser for many years.

A few years later Simon Fraser would pen a scornful comment at Mackenzie's missing of the route Fraser found and took, ironically on the very same day of the year that Mackenzie was passing. On 5 June 1806 Simon Fraser, camped a short distance up the Pack River, wrote:

Notwithstanding the [Pack] *River that leads to this place, Trout Lake* [McLeod Lake], *is a considerable large and navigable River in all seasons, it does not appear to have been noticed by Sir A.M.K.* [Sir Alexander Mackenzie]. *As he used to indulge himself sometimes with a little sleep, likely he did not see it, and I can account for many other omissions in no other manner than his being asleep at the time he pretends to have been very exact, but was qualified to make observations and* [if I were] *inclined to find fault with him, I could prove that he seldom or ever paid the attention he pretends to have done, and that many of his remarks were not made by himself but communicated by his men. It is certainly difficult to stem the current of the east branch* [the Parsnip] *during the high water, but not near so much as he makes it.*

It is indeed possible that Mackenzie was dozing when he passed the Pack River. The day before Mackenzie reached here, he lost the notebook with his courses from 27 May to 4 June. In explanation he admitted, "I was in the habit of sometimes indulging myself with a short doze in the canoe, and I imagine that the branches of the trees brushed my book from me, when I was in such a situation."

However, the criticism of Mackenzie by Fraser was unwarranted, for Fraser admitted that he had learned of the Pack River route from natives whom Mackenzie did not meet.

Apart from the exciting bits we tend to concentrate on in an account such as this, traveling by canoe often involved much unrelenting tedium. The traveler was low on the water, sometimes unable to see much beyond the river's banks, and progress was slow. Mackenzie was often up later than the others trying to take astronomical observations. It is not at all surprising, nor is it any indictment, that he took a nap now and then. If he had thought it at all injurious to his reputation, it is doubtful the admission would have found its way into print eight years later.

On 6 June, at about the point where the modern highway crosses the river, the current was too strong to use paddles, too deep to use

The town of Mackenzie sits on the banks of Lake Williston, formed by the damming of the Peace River above the Peace River Canyon by the W.A.C. Bennett Dam. It was an "instant town," created in 1968 as the result of the building of a pulp mill. The site of the town is close by the Parsnip River, which Mackenzie passed by in June 1793. The town's first mayor, A. M. Sheppard, wrote:

In our search for a name for our instant town, it became our knowledge that while there was a river and a district named after this very famous explorer of our country, there had not been a town or city named in his honour. Once this was known the choice became simple.

The Parsnip River, looking upstream (south) from the modern highway bridge.

poles, and the banks so tree-lined as to make it impossible to use a line, so they had to pull themselves upstream close to the bank from branch to branch. The next day they began to hope that they would soon find the carrying place to another river.

Mackenzie hoped to find more natives who could guide him, but he found none. "All that remained for us to do," he wrote, "was to push forwards till the river should no longer be navigable." They did find "plenty of wild parsneps," which would later give the river their name, which they boiled and had with their pemmican for supper.

Then, suddenly, on 9 June they came across a group of Sekani natives. It took a while for them to realize that Mackenzie meant no harm, but was "desirous of demonstrating every mark of kindness and friendship." But, Mackenzie found, "They did not, however, seem disposed to confide in our declarations, and actually threatened . . . that they would discharge their arrows at us."

Mackenzie here reveals that his intentions were to trek overland in several directions in order to try to find the other river, and if this didn't work, to go up the Parsnip as far as possible and find natives to tell them which way to go; if this didn't work either, he intended to go back to the northern branch of the Peace, the Finlay, and try that. As it was, the second option was the one he carried out, for he did get the information he wanted from the Sekani.

It was here also that Mackenzie noted that the natives possessed iron implements that had come to them through trade routes from European traders "in vessels as big as islands" on the Pacific coast or, as the Sekani referred to it, the "stinking lake" – that is, salt water.

After a number of false reports, or at least reports that were unintelligible to Mackenzie, the next morning a native who stayed at his campfire after the others had left told Mackenzie through the interpreters that

he knew of a large river that runs towards the midday sun, a branch of which flowed near the source of that which we were now navigating; and that there were only three small lakes, and as many carrying-places, leading to a small river, which discharges itself into the great river, but that the latter did not empty itself into the sea.

Mackenzie got him to draw a map.

I desired him to describe the road to the other river, by delineating it with a piece of coal, on a strip of bark, which he accomplished to my satisfaction. The opinion that the river did not discharge itself into the sea, I very confidently imputed to his ignorance of the country.

Mackenzie's hopes were now renewed, and with presents he persuaded one of the natives to guide him to the lakes. While they were making ready, Mackenzie wrote an ethnographic-type description of the Sekani.

On 10 June, they were off again. The river became narrower and more meandering. The next day, they left the Parsnip proper, which at this point flows from its source in the mountains to the east and north. They continued in the same general southwesterly direction as the Parsnip had taken up to then, up a small stream to Arctic Lake. Here Mackenzie thought he had found the source of the Peace, and it is one of them. On 12 June, after paddling the length of the lake, about 4 km or 2½ miles, they "landed and unloaded, where [they] found a beaten path leading over a low ridge of land of eight hundred and seventeen paces in length to another small lake." They had at this point crossed the Continental Divide; the waters they would henceforth travel upon would flow to the Pacific Ocean.

They were now on Portage Lake, half the length of Arctic Lake. Native canoes and baskets containing various implements had been left here; Mackenzie helped himself to some items, but left some trade goods as payment. Paddling down the lake, they again portaged, over a shorter distance than before, 175 paces, to a farther lake about the same length as Portage Lake. This was Pacific Lake, which they crossed. They then entered a small river flowing from it, in which they sometimes had to force their way across

The maps on this page are the modern 1:250 000 topographic map and the same area depicted on Mackenzie's published map of 1801. The topographic map shows the four lakes traversed across the watershed, the southernmost of which remains unnamed to this day. The Continental Divide, between waters flowing to the Arctic and the Pacific, is between Arctic Lake and Portage Lake. Note the modern map refers to the Bad River. This watershed is shown on Mackenzie's published map some 24 km or 15 miles east of where it would have been placed following the observation noted in his text. The observation was itself 40 km or 25 miles too far east, so the adjustment he chose to make, presumably from a consideration of his dead reckoning, only made his error worse.

gravel bars or cut their way through fallen trees. Then they traversed a fourth lake, so small that it is still unnamed. Again entering the river, they found that it "soon ran with great rapidity," a precursor of things to come. Stopped by two large trees that had fallen right across the river, they camped for the night.

That evening, Mackenzie sent some of his men ahead to check the state of the river they were about to descend. This was James Creek; Mackenzie was to name it the "Bad River" from his experiences; for now his men "brought back a fearful detail of rapid currents, fallen trees, and large stones." From the fourth lake to Herrick Creek and reasonably flat water, James Creek descends 60 m in 9 km, or more than 200 ft in 5½ miles.

Mackenzie's Sekani guide got cold feet; he wanted no more of this. But Mackenzie needed him and would not let him go. However, it was going to become increasingly difficult to keep him.

It was the nature of exploration in this part of the world during Mackenzie's time and for a long time after that if you wanted to travel a long distance – and, hopefully, return – in a single season, you had to start as early as the weather and river ice would allow. What this often meant, however, was that much of the travel on the steeper parts of the route occurred when the rivers were at or near freshet. This was the situation Mackenzie faced now; the creek was at or near its highest water volume of the year.

The next day, the men cut a path to portage around what they thought were the worst of the rapids. But they soon ran into more. The current suddenly increased in speed, the canoe struck rocks, and Mackenzie and his men were in the water trying desperately to save themselves and their canoe with all its vital life support. Alexander Mackay grabbed a tree branch to try to arrest the runaway canoe but was jerked clean out of it onto the bank. The canoe, now badly holed, partially sank, but in so doing it gave the men something to hold onto so they were not swept away. "This alarming scene," Mackenzie wrote afterwards, "with all its terrors and dangers, occupied only a few minutes." The natives seemed unable to help; "when they saw our deplorable situation, instead of making the least effort to help us, sat down and gave vent to their tears."

They were safe, just, but their canoe was essentially wrecked, and they had lost their entire stock of balls – ammunition for the guns. Mackenzie's leadership skills were now forced into play, for most of his

Poling a canoe down a rapid. Where the current is too fast, paddles become useless and better control can be achieved by the use of poles, which (with luck) gain some traction on the riverbed and can at least be used to fend off obstacles and keep the canoe pointed as near downstream as possible.

men wanted to call a halt and retrace their steps. With the help of a little rum he persuaded them that they should go on. "I brought to their recollection . . . that they were made acquainted with the difficulties and dangers they must expect to encounter, before they engaged to accompany me." He appealed to their sense of honor and pride:

I also urged the honour of conquering disasters, and the disgrace that would attend them on their return home, without having attained the object of the expedition. Nor did I fail to mention the courage and resolution which was the peculiar boast of the North men [the voyageurs who paddled north canoes, that is, the smaller ones operating north and west of Grand Portage on Lake Superior], *and that I depended on them, at that moment, for the maintenance of their character.*

The canoe had to be repaired as much as was possible until they could find more appropriately sized pieces of birchbark to fashion another. The vital gunpowder was spread out to dry; another near miss was recorded as one of the voyageurs walked by smoking his pipe; "one spark might have put a period to all my anxiety and ambition," Mackenzie wryly observed. They took several days to repair the canoe, dry their goods, make some more bullets, and cut some paths to use as a portage. When it was time to continue their journey, one of the voyageurs, Jacques Beauchamp, refused to embark, so again Mackenzie had to bring his powers of persuasion to bear.

By a continuing process of cutting paths, carrying goods, and carrying or lining the canoe, they reached what Mackenzie refers to as "the great river," but which was in fact only Herrick Creek, into which James Creek flowed. But it must have seemed like a major advance just getting out of James Creek, which Mackenzie named and marked on his map as "Bad River" on account of their experiences in it. It is still called by this name on some maps today (see page 180).

It was 17 June. It had taken them five days from when they first entered James Creek to go about 14 km or 9 miles. The night before they arrived at Herrick Creek, their Sekani guide deserted; he'd had enough. This despite the fact that Mackenzie and Mackay had been taking turns sitting up at night to watch him. With a palpable sense of relief, Mackenzie wrote:

At length we enjoyed, after all our toil and anxiety, the inexpressible satisfaction of finding ourselves on the bank of a navigable river, on the West side on the first great range of mountains.

Herrick Creek flows into the McGregor River only a short distance farther downstream, and the next day Mackenzie and his crew passed first into the McGregor and then into the Fraser,

the great fork, of which our guide had informed us, and it appeared to be the largest branch from the South-East. It is about half a mile in breadth, and assumes the form of a lake. The current was very slack.

Now moving much faster, they descended the Giscome Rapids, which must have seemed like nothing at all after James Creek. The next day they passed the Nechako River, though Mackenzie does not mention it, and the site on which Simon Fraser was in 1807 to establish Fort George, today's city of Prince George.

Going almost due south, they passed through the Fort George Canyon, where they portaged a short distance around a rapid; the canoe was now so heavy from all the repairs made to her that portaging was now a more difficult proposition. "The labour and fatigue of this undertaking, from eight till twelve, beggars all description," Mackenzie recorded. After another minor portage in the canyon, they were out of it and on a fine wide river once more.

Seeing rising smoke, Mackenzie sent his two guides in search of local natives, but they returned after being shot at with bows and arrows. The next day, 20 June, started so foggy that they "could not see the length of our canoe, which rendered our progress dangerous, as we might have come suddenly upon a cascade or violent rapid." That day they passed the West Road River on their right, which Mackenzie noted without comment; it would assume more significance later.

The canoe was almost falling to bits. "Our canoe was now become so crazy, that it was a matter of absolute necessity to construct another," Mackenzie wrote, and he dispatched men to search for sufficient quantity of birchbark to make another. Finding enough, they carried it with them rather than making a new canoe there and then. They ran the Cottonwood Canyon rapids rather than carry the heavy canoe.

The next day they buried a cache of "ninety pounds weight of pemmican" under a campfire site as was the custom, to "guard against any possibility of distress . . . on our return." They passed the Quesnel River and the site of modern Quesnel, and near the mouth of Narcosli Creek they encountered local natives. Mackenzie made contact with the wary natives by walking along the shore alone, covered from a hiding place by one of his native guides. Having made contact, it seemed that the natives with Mackenzie could communicate easily with the locals.

From these local natives, through his interpreter, Mackenzie was able to gain a significant account of the course of the Fraser River, recording that

this river, whose course is very extensive, runs towards the mid-day sun; and that at its mouth, as they had been informed, white people were building houses. They represented its current to be uniformly strong, and that in three places it was altogether impassable, from the falls and rapids, which poured along between perpendicular rocks that were much higher, and more rugged, than any we had yet seen, and would not admit of any passage over them.

Didn't sound good. But there was more.

Besides the dangers and difficulties of the navigation, they added, that we should have to encounter the inhabitants of the country, who were very numerous. They also represented their immediate neighbours [Shuswap] as a very malignant race . . . and when they were made to understand that it was our design to proceed to the sea, they dissuaded us from prosecuting our intention, as we should certainly become a sacrifice to the savage spirit of the natives. These people they described as possessing iron, arms, and utensils, which they procured from their neighbours to the Westward, and were obtained by a commercial progress from people like ourselves, who brought them in great canoes.

Relatives of these natives, who were of Carrier tribes, now arrived, and advised Mackenzie to wait until the entire group, currently downstream, had arrived too, as they had been alerted to Mackenzie's canoe but did not yet know they were friendly. So Mackenzie stayed until the following morning. During this time Mackenzie tried to acquire more knowledge of the Fraser, in the form of a map.

My first application to the native whom I have already particularly mentioned was to obtain from him such a plan of the river as he should be enabled to give me; and he complied with this request with a degree of readiness and intelligence that evidently proved it was by no means a new business to him.

Accompanied now by three of the local natives, two in their own canoe and one with Mackenzie, they paddled downstream next morning. They soon met another native group, and then another. The presence of a woman, a prisoner who had learned the Cree language, and another who was a Sekani, meant that communication with Mackenzie's interpreters was good. Mackenzie was able to obtain more information – information so significant that it was to change his plans. Selecting an older man as most likely to know, Mackenzie wrote:

I now proceeded to request the native, whom I had particularly selected, to commence his information, by drawing a sketch of the country upon a large piece of bark, and he immediately entered on the work, frequently appealing to, and sometimes asking the advice of, those around him. He described the river as running East of South, receiving many rivers, and every six or eight leagues encumbered with falls and rapids, some of which were very dangerous, and six of them impracti-cable. The carrying-places he represented as of great length, and passing over hills and mountains. He depicted the lands of three other tribes, in succession, who spoke different languages. Beyond them he knew nothing of either the river or country, only that it was still a long way to the sea; and that, as he had heard, there was a lake, before they reached the water, which the natives did not drink [presumably because it was salt water].

Another old man reported that he had long known of white people to the south, and although he was not sure of the accuracy of the report, he had heard that one of them had tried to come up the river, but had been destroyed. This is an intriguing report, as there is no record of any attempt at an ascent of the Fraser from the coast. How-ever, if such a venture met with total disaster, it is quite possible that no written record would survive.

In short, Mackenzie was advised that the way would be long, diffi-cult, and dangerous if he continued south on the Fraser, the truth of which would be borne out by Simon Fraser when he attempted to do just this in 1808. Mackenzie, for the *second* time in his exploring ca-reer, found himself on a river flowing in a different direction from that which he wished to go. This time the river flowed south when he wanted to go west. And here the wrong direction was apparently fraught with difficulties. He was by now used to native reports telling him of impos-sible difficulties ahead, but this time it was different. Not only were the natives telling him of the difficulties of continuing down the Fraser, they also held out the notion of a much easier, shorter, and more direct route overland to the west of their present location. Perhaps most significantly, this agreed with Mackenzie's own concepts.

"These people describe the distance across the country as very short to the Western ocean;" he wrote, "and according to my idea, it cannot be above five or six degrees." This means that Mackenzie thought the straight-line distance at this latitude to be 330 to 400 km or 200 to 250 miles.

Showing he had read John Meares' book *Voyages . . . from China to the North West Coast of America*, Mackenzie continued, "If the asser-tion of Mr. Mears be correct, it cannot be so far, as the inland sea which he mentions within Nootka, must come as far East as 126 West

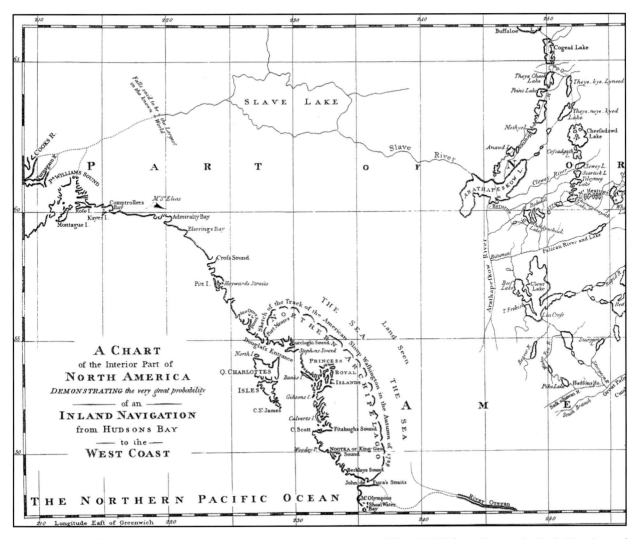

A map from John Meares' book with the long title *Voyages Made in the years 1788 and 1789 from China to the North West Coast of America to which are prefixed An Introductory Narrative of a Voyage performed in 1786, from Bengal in the Ship Nootka; observations on the probable existence of a Northwest Passage and some account of the Trade Between the North West Coast of America & China, and the latter country & Great Britain,* 1790.

longitude." This was a reference to an inland sea Meares had fabricated in his book, saying it had been discovered by the American captain Robert Gray; unknown to Mackenzie, Gray had already met George Vancouver, on his way to begin his coastal survey in 1792, and told him of its complete falsehood. When Mackenzie published his book in 1801, he would add a footnote about Meares' assertion of an inland sea and note he had been informed by "Captain Grey" that he gave Meares no such information. Nevertheless, at this point in his expedition it was yet another incentive for Mackenzie to strike west.

The "inland navigation" this map purports to show is from Hearne's "Arathapeskow L." to Cook Inlet or Prince William Sound on the Alaskan coast, through Slave River, Slave Lake, and "Cook's River." As such it mirrors the ideas of Peter Pond. A huge inland sea is shown from the Strait of Juan de Fuca to Dixon Entrance (shown here as "Douglas['] Entrance") north of the Queen Charlottes. If this inland sea had been correct, Mackenzie would have reached the sea sooner than expected.

The natives assured Mackenzie

that the road [to the west that they used for trade] *was not difficult, as they avoided the mountains, keeping the low lands between them, many parts of which are entirely free of wood . . .* [and that] *this way is so often travelled by them, that their path is visible throughout the entire journey, which lies along small lakes and rivers.*

Not only did this route promise to be easy, it promised to be fast: "It occupied them, they said, no more than six nights, to go where they meet the people who barter iron, brass, copper, beads, &c. with them." These "people" were the Nuxalk, or Bella Coola, who acted as middlemen between the coast and inland tribes. Further, this route would seem to be on track to meet the Russian traders Mackenzie felt must be on the coast.

They had been informed by those whom they meet to trade with, that the white people, from whom these articles are obtained, were building houses at the distance of three days or two nights journey from the place where they met last fall.

It seems that this could only be a reference to a Spanish post at Nootka Sound on Vancouver Island, rather than a Russian post at Unalaska or Kodiak Island, but none really fits the description.

Mackenzie also tried to find the female prisoner he had met the previous day, in order to try to question her about an easier way across the mountain divide they had crossed ten days before. But she could not be found; her captors evidently thought Mackenzie might help her escape, which could have been a correct assumption.

Mackenzie's voyageurs thought it madness to attempt to strike out westward; it went against their entire experience, which was to follow the rivers, portaging when necessary but staying with the river. But they were running low on supplies, especially their critical ammunition. Mackenzie was now having doubts about the Fraser River, which he assumed was a branch of the "River of the West," or the Columbia. He wrote:

Such being the discouraging circumstances of my situation, which were now heightened by the discontents of my people, I could not but be alarmed at the idea of attempting to get to the discharge of such a rapid river, especially [and perhaps more importantly] when I reflected on the tardy progress of my return up it, even if I should meet with no obstruction from the natives; a circumstance not very probable . . . At all events, I must give up every expectation of returning this season to Athabasca.

But Mackenzie was coming to a decision in his own mind.

I determined to proceed with resolution. At the same time I suffered myself to nourish the hope that I might be able to penetrate with more safety, and in a shorter period, to the ocean by the inland, western communication.

Despite the reports of the dangers that lay ahead if they continued down the Fraser, Mackenzie was later to write:

I have not the least doubt of this Great River being Navigable with Canoe and Boats to its mouth[.] I have mentioned above the Causes of my not putting this to the proof . . . [for] the distance to the Mouth of [the Fraser] would be too great for me to go and come back in the Course of the Seasons.

It was, retrospectively at least, the lure of an easier and shorter route rather than the difficulty of the present one, the carrot not the stick that made up Mackenzie's mind.

Simon Fraser would no doubt have read this with great interest, but it was written in a statement of explanation for Mackenzie's map published by Aaron Arrowsmith and is not in Mackenzie's book, so although Fraser did have a copy of the book with him, he might still not have been aware of Mackenzie's contention.

A serious negative aspect of the plan to go overland was the fact that they would all have to retrace their steps upriver again, "a retrograde motion [that] could not fail to cool the ardour, slacken the zeal, and weaken the confidence of those who have no greater inducement in the undertaking, than to follow the conductor of it." As a good leader, Mackenzie recognized the psychological effect this could have on his men.

The next day, 23 June, Mackenzie tried to obtain more information about this proposed westward route, as he felt it was becoming critical that he come to a decision before too much time was wasted. Not only did he get the same information as he had the day before, always an encouraging sign, but he obtained yet more details. Describing their trade route, known today as a "grease trail" after the transportation of fish oil from the coast to the interior, the Carrier natives told Mackenzie

that where they left this river, a small one from the Westward falls into it, which was navigable for their canoes during four days, and from thence they slept but two nights, to get to the people with whom they trade, and have wooden canoes much larger than ours, in which they go down a river to the sea.

They told him he would have to leave his own canoe behind, but thought it probable that the coastal natives, the Nuxalk, would lend him another.

From thence, they continued . . . the distance [was] *only one day's voyage with the current to the lake whose water is nauseous* [salt water], *and where they had heard that great canoes came two winters ago, and that the people belonging to them, brought great quantities of goods and built houses.*

Could this be a reference to European maritime fur traders, who had swarmed to the Northwest Coast following the discovery of the sea otter and its magnificent, highly valuable fur by James Cook's men on the latter's third voyage, in 1778?

One of the natives had a question for Mackenzie which caught him off guard. "What can be the reason," he demanded to know, "that you are so particular and anxious in your inquiries of us respecting a knowledge of this country: do not you white men know everything in the world?" After some hesitation, Mackenzie cleverly replied that he was acquainted with the "principal circumstances of every part of the world," and that he knew where the sea was, and where he was, but that he "did not exactly understand what obstacles might interrupt me in getting to it." Amazingly, this was not very far from the truth, for Mackenzie, like most European explorers of this period, did indeed know the general outline of the world; he did know where the coast was, approximately. He even knew, perhaps even more approximately, where he was, at least in relation to his known world over the mountains. And he had that global perspective that the natives, however detailed their knowledge of their immediate environment, did not at this time possess.

Mackenzie had to make up his mind: continue downstream or strike out overland. His decision was made: "No long interval of reflection was employed, before I preferred to go over land: the comparative shortness and security of such a journey, were alone sufficient to determine me." He managed to get two of the Carrier natives to agree to accompany him as guides.

Now Mackenzie had a sales job to do on his men. After "passing a warm eulogium on their fortitude, patience, and perseverance," he compared the pros and cons of each route and told them of his decision to go west. He recorded his sales pitch: "At all events, I declared, in the most solemn manner, that I would not abandon my design of

The Fraser River near Alexandria, B.C. This was as far south on the Fraser as Mackenzie reached.

reaching the sea, if I made the attempt alone, and that I did not despair of returning in safety to my friends." But he need not have worried; his men readily agreed to continue with him. They

unanimously assured me, that they were as willing now as they had ever been, to abide by my resolutions, whatever they might be, and to follow me whereever I should go.

And so they prepared to depart upstream again. As this was a turning point and as far south as he would get on the Fraser, Mackenzie asked Alexander Mackay to carve on a tree

Alex. Mackenzie
1793

an unenduring record of his southernmost point reached. It was 23 June 1793. The tree was never found, and the precise location is unknown,

Alexander Mackay – Mackenzie's Overlooked Lieutenant

Not much is known about Mackenzie's second-in-command on his expedition to the Pacific. He was considered very reliable, but Mackenzie did not give him much credit. There is one footnote in his book, referring to their trip back up the strong current of the Bella Coola River on 23 July 1793, where Mackenzie says, "It is but common justice to him, to mention . . . that I had every reason to be satisfied with [Mackay's] conduct." But then, Mackenzie did not give much written credit to any of his men.

Mackay became a partner in the North West Company in 1799 and retired in 1808. Then, in 1810, he was persuaded to join John Jacob Astor's Pacific Fur Company. Astor liked to hire Canadian fur trade men; he once said that he reckoned one Canadian voyageur to be worth three American rivermen. Mackay became one of the men from Astor's company who beat David Thompson to the mouth of the Columbia. They established the first Northwest Coast post at Fort Astoria in the spring of 1811, arriving on the *Tonquin* after a voyage around Cape Horn from New York. Thus did Mackenzie's overlooked lieutenant become the first to carry out part of his long-advocated policy of having trading posts on the Pacific shore. But certainly not the way Mackenzie had foreseen it!

But this accomplishment didn't do Alexander Mackay much good. He was killed later that same year on board the *Tonquin*, on a first cruise northward to gather furs for the new post. In Clayoquot Sound on the west coast of Vancouver Island in June 1811, Mackay was one of the first killed during a native attack apparently in revenge for poor treatment by the captain of a previous fur-trading ship. The ship was blown up as a last resort, killing all aboard – by all accounts some 200 people. The story was related in the journal of Gabriel Franchère, whom Mackay had signed up for the Astorian venture. Rumor of the tragedy first circulated among natives from the Strait of Juan de Fuca who had come to the Columbia to fish, and it was later confirmed by an individual from the Gray's Harbor area who had sailed with the ship and was the sole survivor.

That Mackay was a key person in the enterprise, as he had been when he was with Mackenzie, is shown by Franchère's comment that "the death of Mr. Alexander McKay was an irreparable loss to the [Pacific Fur] company, which would probably have been dissolved then but for the arrival of Mr. [Wilson Price] Hunt [leader of Astor's overland party]."

It seems that Mackay's only memorial today is a street name in Bella Coola, Mackay Street; Cape McKay near Mackenzie Rock is named after somebody else.

but it was certainly close to present-day Alexandria. This is the place where the North West Company established Fort Alexandria, named appropriately enough after our intrepid explorer, in 1821. John Stuart, Simon Fraser's associate, in 1813 had solved the riddle of how to transport furs around the difficult stretch of the Fraser below here, and the fort was built at the northern end of a brigade route to the Columbia via Kamloops and the Okanagan River.

Repairing a north canoe. This old photograph from the archives of the Hudson's Bay Company shows what must have been a familiar sight to voyageurs. The resins used to gum canoes did not last long, and constant attention was required to ensure a canoe stayed relatively watertight.

Hudson's Bay Company Archives (1987/363-C-11A/19).

Mackenzie's men were to reverse their willingness to accompany him in the next day or two, which Mackenzie this time would deal with by setting an example of quiet determination to go on. A newly acquired guide, who had agreed to go overland to a rendezvous point, appeared to have deserted already, and the natives upstream had deserted their encampments through some sort of general alarm the reason for which Mackenzie was unable to determine. The men expected to be attacked at any moment.

Discovering an old man who had been too infirm to run away, Mackenzie found that the natives were alarmed because another group from farther upstream had arrived and told them that Mackenzie was an enemy, and his unexpected return upriver had confirmed this feeling. Commandeering the old man for his ability to introduce them to hostile natives they might meet, Mackenzie had to have him carried to the canoe, for he did not want to go. This was the first act during the voyage, Mackenzie noted, "that had the semblance of violent dealing." Two days later they would prevent him from trying to escape, though soon after, they let him go.

For three days Mackenzie and his men stayed in one spot, tormented by flies on an island in the Fraser they called Canoe Island, finally building a replacement canoe, long after they should have replaced the old one so grievously damaged since the descent of James Creek. On 1 July it was complete, though only with the help of gum taken from the old one. On that day two natives appeared, telling Mackenzie that they had just returned from a meeting with "the natives of the sea coast," further reinforcing the idea that the ocean was not that far overland.

Because of the prolonged halt, Mackenzie was able to make an observation of Jupiter's first satellite, which allowed him to calculate, with the help of his chronometer, that the longitude was now 122° 48′ W, close to the actual longitude of 122° 33′ W.

Embarking northward again in the new canoe on 2 July, they traversed up the Cottonwood Rapids, and the next day they arrived at the stream Mackenzie was to name the West Road River. Here they expected to rendezvous with their Carrier guide, but he was nowhere to be found. Finding the river navigable only for very small canoes, they continued upstream and found the guide they thought had deserted paddling downstream to meet them.

Knowing that they were to leave the river, they needed to cache some of their supplies, which they did at two hiding places nearby. Then they landed "at the entrance to a small rivulet, where our friends were waiting for us." The location was about 4 km or 2½ miles upstream from the mouth of the West Road River.

They cached more goods – all they did not want to carry – and hid

Building a cache in the woods. Raised from the ground on a makeshift platform to protect it from wild animals, this cache, made by surveyors in Alberta, is similar to that made by Mackenzie's men prior to leaving the Fraser and starting their overland trek.

the canoe in the trees. This trek was to be even more physically demanding than heretofore, and certainly no lightweight hike. Mackenzie recorded the loads:

We carried on our backs four bags and a half of pemmican, weighing from eighty-five to ninety pounds each, a case with my instruments, a parcel of goods for presents, weighing ninety pounds, and a parcel containing ammunition of the same weight. Each of the Canadians had a burden of about ninety pounds, with a gun, and some ammunition. The Indians had about forty-five pounds weight of pemmican to carry, besides their gun, &c. with which they were very much dissatisfied, and if they had dared they would have instantly left us. They had hitherto been very much indulged, but the moment was now arrived when indulgence was no longer practicable. My own load, and that of Mr. Mackay, consisted of twenty-two pounds of pemmican, some rice, a little sugar, &c. amounting in the whole to about seventy pounds each, besides our arms and ammunition. I also had the tube of my telescope swung across my shoulder, which was a troublesome addition to my burthen.

Thus they began their overland journey west. It was midday on 3 July 1793. They climbed out of the valley of the Fraser on a steep beaten path; most of the time now they would be following existing native trade trails. That night they camped at beautiful Punchaw Lake,

Punchaw Lake.

and Mackenzie met another native who had some sort of a lance that he said he had traded from "the natives of the Sea-Coast, who procured it from the white men." Another had a sea otter skin, which Mackenzie purchased. This must have given Mackenzie early encouragement that his decision to come this way was the correct one. The next day he bartered for "two halfpence, one of his present Majesty, and the other

The trail marker at the western end of the trail.

of the State of Massachuset's Bay, coined in 1787." They hung as ornaments in children's ears. What clearer evidence of the visits of British and American ships to the Northwest Coast could there be?

For the next twelve days Mackenzie and his men trekked westward, generally following an established native "grease trail." There were in fact at this time some seven trails which left the coast to go toward the Fraser River. They were native trade routes, named from the transportation of oolichan grease, prized by the Carrier. The oil protected them from the cold and was used in the tanning of moose, deer, and caribou hides, in particular to produce a soft smoked leather known as buckskin, which could be traded back to the natives of the coast. The oolichan oil was carried in sealed cedar boxes but inevitably there were leaks, so on the the trail there were often oil drip marks – literally a grease trail.

The distance from Punchaw Lake to the Bella Coola Valley overland on the route that Mackenzie was taking is about 285 km or 180 miles. The twelve days he took, and the almost unbelievable eight days on his return, compares with about fifteen days that it takes an *expert* hiker today. Of course, one of the reasons Mackenzie was able to travel so far so fast was that he demanded a very long day, typically starting out at five in the morning, sometimes earlier, and continuing late, sometimes as late as nine. Thus he could get up to sixteen hours of travel in each day. And this in country that is by no means flat. A blistering pace indeed!

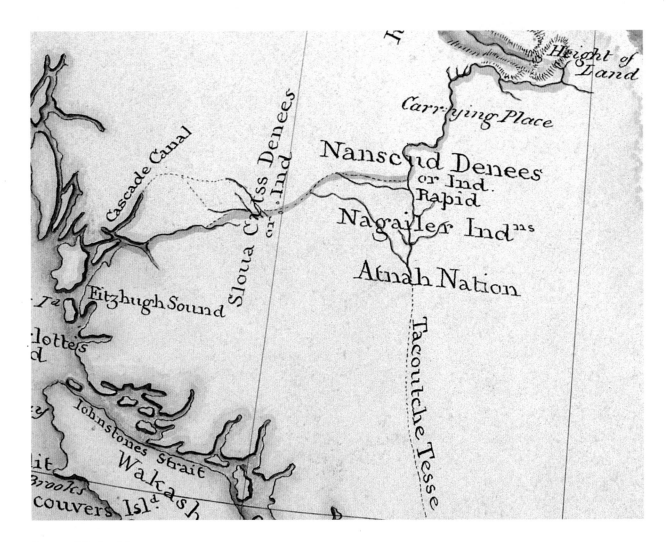

Portion of Mackenzie's map showing the route from the Fraser to the Pacific Ocean. This map was the prototype for the published map.

Mackenzie found that the trail was well defined most of the time. It was well used, too, if we judge by the number of native groups Mackenzie met on his way. As early as 6 July they met a native of the coast, a Nuxalk (Bella Coola) woman who was the wife in a native family they met. Another family provided the information that they were "approaching a river, which was neither large or long, but whose banks are inhabited; and that in the bay which the sea forms at the mouth of it, a great wooden canoe, with white people, arrives about the time leaves start to grow." This seems to be a fairly clear reference to the Bella Coola River and North Bentinck Arm, and was certainly the sort of thing Mackenzie wanted to hear.

They progressed rapidly west, along lake and stream, following the valley of the West Road River, cutting across to the Euchiniko Lakes, back to the West Road, on to Tsacha Lake, into the valley of the Dean River, southwest to Tanya Lakes, past the mountain today named Mount Mackenzie, and finally south to the Bella Coola Valley. On his way Mackenzie lost his guides but managed to procure others to take up the task.

On 11 July they came in view of the snow-topped ranges of the Coast Mountains, which could not have been encouraging. On 13 July they came across three native families who were much relieved when they discovered Mackenzie's men were not going to massacre them. From one woman, they learned that the sea was visible from the mountains ahead. On 15 July they met a small native group and Mackenzie reveals that "they must have been told that we were white, as our faces no longer indicated that distinguishing complexion."

At Tanya Lakes they were expecting to continue westward, which would have taken them down the Dean River to the sea in Dean Channel and probably to the Nuxalk village of Kimsquit, but the native group with whom they were traveling at the time decided to take another route, and so they turned directly southward. Now they had to cross the coastal range, which they did by way of a high pass now called Mackenzie Pass, which is at at about 1 800 m or 6,000 feet.

Mackenzie's route from the Fraser to tidewater and Mackenzie Rock shown on a modern map, the aeronautical 1:1 000 000 chart. This type of map has the advantage of showing relief very well, though unfortunately while also showing much information of interest only to pilots.

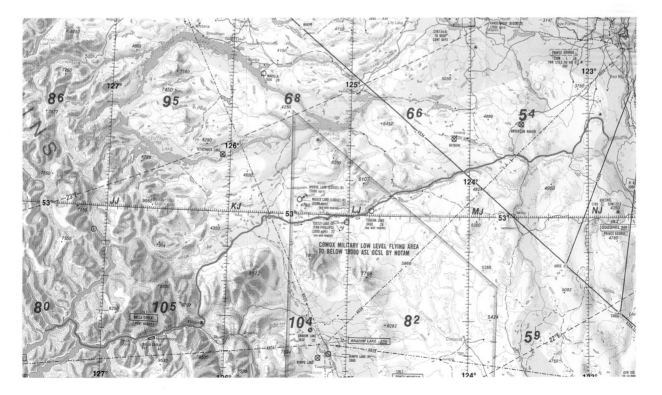

"We now gained the summit of the mountain, and found ourselves surrounded by snow," Mackenzie recorded, "but this circumstance is caused rather by the quantity of snow drifted in the pass, than the real height of the spot, as the surrounding mountains rise to a much higher degree of elevation."

At this, the highest elevation that Mackenzie was to reach anywhere between Montreal and the Pacific Ocean, "The wind rose into a tempest, and the weather was as distressing as any I had ever experienced," he wrote.

But they were almost to the valley of the Bella Coola River. "Before us appeared a stupendous mountain, whose snow-clad summit was lost in the clouds; between it and our immediate course, flowed the river to which we were going." The mountain Mackenzie saw is today named Stupendous Mountain. Now steeply descending about 900 m or 3,000 feet into the valley – a gorge, really – they arrived in the valley at the point where today Burnt Bridge Creek joins the Bella Coola. Finally and belatedly they were once again on a river flowing west to the Pacific Ocean, only this time the ocean – or at least a long arm of it – was only 40 km or 25 miles away!

Today a road descends precipitously into the Bella Coola Valley, descending that same 900 m or 3,000 feet near where Mackenzie descended. Even now, the road is narrow and unpaved and is a hair-raising switchback in places. After 19 km or 12 miles of steep descent there is a certain sense of relief on reaching the valley floor. The building of this road, which was completed in 1954 by the citizens of the valley when the provincial government said it couldn't be done, is a story unto itself.

At least it was now warmer. "We were now sensible of an entire change in the climate, and the berries are quite ripe," noted Mackenzie.

Stupendous Mountain, Bella Coola Valley, with Burnt Bridge Creek in the foreground.

Mount Mackenzie.

Here Mackenzie emerged from the dense stands of trees and walked into a Nuxalk (Bella Coola) native village unceremoniously, shaking hands with everybody much as he might have done if he had arrived 200 years later, though there is no settlement there today. This was the encampment Mackenzie was to name "Friendly Village," and with good reason. Their new hosts presented them with dishes of salmon roe, the "luxury" of boards for their beds, and Mackenzie was able to record, "I never enjoyed a more sound and refreshing rest, though I had a board for my bed and a billet for my pillow." It was 17 July.

The next day Mackenzie and his men awoke to more food – berries and roasted salmon. He was to note the abundance of salmon and the way it had become a complete way of life to the Nuxalk. "These people indulge an extreme superstition respecting their fish, as it is apparently their only animal food," he noted. When one of his men threw a bone into the river, a native promptly dove in and retrieved it, burnt it in the fire, and washed his hands afterwards.

With the sea within reach, one of Mackenzie's guides persuaded the Nuxalk to lend him two canoes, which were only given on the understanding that no meat would be carried in them.

From the Fraser to the Pacific – Today

Today the road to Bella Coola leaves the Fraser River at Williams Lake, B.C., 140 km or 90 miles south of the point Mackenzie left the river to strike out overland. But it is the same distance to the sea, still a long 456.8 km away *exactly* – about 290 miles. And even the road is not easy. The double-lane highway leading west out of Williams Lake gives no hint of the trials to come, for there are still 100 km or 60 miles of rough road in the link to Bella Coola. A sign halfway up the first hill warns of Heckman Pass – closed when lights flashing – yet it is still 350 km or 220 miles away.

The difficulty in getting to Bella Coola is shown by the fact that the road was not completed until 1954, and even then only because local residents took matters – and bulldozers – into their own hands. The British Columbia government thought it impractical to build such a road. Only when the residents had used up all their money doing it themselves did the flamboyant Highways minister, Phil Gaglardi – "Flying Phil," he was called – impressed by their efforts, give them the money they needed to complete the road. Today, as it was christened in 1954, it is the "Freedom Road."

The Bella Coola River cascades
through its misty gorge on its way
to the sea early one morning, just
below the site of Mackenzie's
Friendly Village.

Nuxalk "spoon" canoes are shown drawn up on the bank of the Bella Coola River in this photograph, taken before 1912.

Below: The Bella Coola River at the site of the "Great Village" (on the right bank). Mackenzie noted the whiteness of the river's water, recording: "The water of this river is of the colour of asses milk, which I attributed in part to the limestone that in many places forms the bed of the river." In fact the color is due to the glacial origins of the water, as the rock is granite, not limestone.

At noon, they embarked in the canoes for the final westward leg of their trip, accompanied by seven of the natives. They traveled fast, with the current of this fast-flowing river, the Bella Coola River. Mackenzie commented that he had thought his voyageurs incomparable in handling a canoe on a river such as this, but acknowledged that they were "very inferior to these people."

In only two and a half hours they arrived at Nooskulst, the major native settlement in the valley, at the mouth of the Noosgulch River. This Mackenzie was later to name the "Great Village." Here they stayed for twenty-four hours; Mackenzie made considerable notes on the structures in the settlement and the customs of the natives, which are significant as the first written European record of the Nuxalk (see page 206). The natives were interested in Mackenzie's instruments, which he showed them. The chief insisted that Mackenzie spend the night with his "bed-companion," but Mackenzie, "notwithstanding his repeated entreaties . . . resisted this offering of hospitality." Mackenzie was assumed to have great powers of healing, which in fact were limited to giving out some doses of Turlington's Balsam, a cure-all of the day. He had to leave one particularly gruesome scene, where a man afflicted with what he referred to as a "violent ulcer" was being "treated" with fire and knife, "the cruel pain of which operation the patient bore with incredible resolution."

Here also Mackenzie records that he lost his dog. He would find him again, but not until he passed through on his return journey.

At noon the next day, after recovering a pilfered axe, they were again ready to depart. Now the chief supplied them with a much larger, seagoing canoe and four natives to propel it. It was of the type typical of the Northwest Coast; built of western red cedar, it was, Mackenzie measured, some 13.5 m or 45 feet long, 1.25 m or 4 feet wide, and 1 m or 3 feet deep. He described it as "painted black and decorated with white figures of fish of different kinds. The gunwale, fore and aft, was inlaid with the teeth of the sea-otter."

The chief told Mackenzie that about ten winters ago he went "a considerable distance towards the mid-day sun, with forty of his people, when he saw two large vessels full of such men as myself, by whom he was kindly received." Mackenzie was of the opinion that this must have been Captain Cook, but unless the natives had gone on a considerable trip down the west coast of Vancouver Island, where Cook stayed for a month in Nootka Sound, this seems unlikely. More likely they met fur-trading vessels, which became increasingly common on the coast of the Northwest after 1785. Nevertheless, this remains an intriguing reference.

They continued toward the sea. At this point you can begin to smell the salt in the air, and it seems that the sea must be round the next corner. The river, Mackenzie observed, was "almost one continued rapid." They stopped briefly at three smaller settlements, and at each of these were received in a friendly manner. At the first, the chief produced many European articles, including "at least forty

Nuxalk owl mask.

A photograph of the Nuxalk native Potlas in 1885. The photograph originally showed Potlas with feathers in his hair, as the German photographer wanted to make his subjects conform to European stereotypical ideals and was prepared to doctor his photographs to achieve this. The archival photograph is marked "remove feathers," and thus I have removed them.

Mackenzie's Description of a Nuxalk Village

Even native people who may dispute the significance of Mackenzie's trek today agree that his observations were important because they describe their settlements and customs before any major contact with Europeans. Here are some extracts from Mackenzie's description of the Nuxalk village of Nooskulst, the settlement he called the Great Village.

[The village] *consisted of four elevated houses, and seven built on the ground, besides a considerable number of other buildings or sheds, which are used only as kitchens, and places for curing their fish. The former are constructed by fixing a certain number of posts in the earth, on some of which are laid, and to others are fastened, the supporters of the floor, at about twelve feet above the surface of the ground . . . Along the centre are built three, four, or five hearths, for the two-fold purpose of giving warmth, and dressing their fish. The whole length of the building on either side is divided by cedar planks, into partitions or apartments of seven feet square, in the front of which there are boards, about three feet wide, over which, though they are not immovably fixed, the inmates of these recesses generally pass, when they go to rest . . . On poles that run along the beams, hang roasted fish, and the whole building is covered with boards and bark, except within a few inches of the ridge pole; where open spaces are left on each side to let in light and emit the smoke. At the end of the house that fronts the river, is a narrow scaffolding . . . at each corner of this erection there are openings, for the inhabitants to ease nature. As it does not appear to be a custom among them to remove these heaps of excremental filth, it may be supposed that the effluvia does not annoy them.*

Near the house of the chief I observed several oblong squares, of about twenty feet by eight. They were made of thick cedar boards, which were joined with so much neatness, that I at first thought they were one piece. They were painted with hieroglyphics, and figures of different animals, and with a degree of correctness that was not to be expected. [There was] a large building in the middle of the village . . . fifty feet by forty-five; each end is formed by four stout posts, fixed perpendicularly in the ground. The corner ones are plain, and support a beam of the whole length, having three intermediate props on each side, but of a larger size, and eight or nine feet in height. The two centre posts, at each end, are two and a half feet in diameter, and carved into human figures, supporting two ridge poles on their heads, at twelve feet from the ground . . . The posts, poles and figures, were painted red and black; but the sculpture of these people is superior to their painting.

Above: Nuxalk village, about 1885.

Left: Roasting salmon.

Far left: Nuxalk seagoing dugout canoe.

Right: Nuxalk wolf mask.

pounds weight of old copper stills." Copper was a favorite trading item on the coast at this time, as it could be fashioned into many useful articles and was not otherwise available. Many a trading ship loaded up on sheets of copper before sailing for the Northwest Coast. The chief came with Mackenzie in the canoe. At the second, smaller settlement, they were presented with a trough of berries. The river now divided into many channels, although the current did not seem to slacken.

The village of Qomq'-ts (Bella Coola). At left is a street scene, from an 1897 photograph. Above is Qomq'-ts in 1873. The occasion was the visit of the provincial government Indian Commissioner, and the photograph, by Richard Maynard, provides a rare early record of the village.

Far right: Nuxalk bear of heaven mask.

After the third brief stop at a small settlement, they arrived at a village consisting of six large houses "erected on pallisades, rising twenty-five feet from the ground, at the time containing only four men and their families"; the rest of the inhabitants were at the settlements Mackenzie had already visited or now with him in the canoe. This was Qomq'-ts, the place Mackenzie would later dub "Rascal's Village," at the location of the modern village of Bella Coola.

Mackenzie later found out that this village had been visited by James Johnstone on 1 June 1793, in a surveying boat from *Chatham,* which

Above: North Bentinck Arm at Bella Coola.

Left: The Bella Coola River, Bella Coola village, and North Bentinck Arm. The Pacific at last!

accompanied George Vancouver in *Discovery* on the latter's major survey of the Northwest Coast between 1792 and 1794.

For Mackenzie, this was a location of extreme significance, for, as he mildly reported: "From these houses I could perceive the termination of the river, and its discharge into a narrow arm of the sea." This was North Bentinck Arm, at the head of Burke Channel.

The following morning, with only two of his four Nuxalk natives agreeing to accompany him any farther, "as they imagined that [he] should be satisfied with having come within sight of the sea," Mackenzie acquired an even larger canoe, though one that apparently leaked. It was 20 July 1793. "At about eight," he was able to record, "we got out of the river, which discharges itself by various channels into an arm of the sea." This was an amazingly restrained comment, due to the fact that although he had reached salt water, he had not in his own mind reached the ocean. But it did in reality mark the success of a more than five-year quest to attain the Pacific Ocean. He had traveled 1 350 km or 850 miles in 72 days since leaving Fort Fork on the banks of the Peace River on 9 May (not including the distance from the West Road River to Alexandria and back again, which was a dead end in terms of the distance to the Pacific).

Now began a different sort of odyssey, that of a canoe on an ocean, for although the waters Mackenzie was now to traverse were protected, they can still get very rough at all times of the year. However, they had a large seagoing Nuxalk cedar canoe, not the more fragile birchbark

Bella Coola is today still the main settlement for the Nuxalk Nation. While many of the streets have native names and there is a sprinkling of Scandinavian names, reflecting the immigrants to the valley in the late nineteenth century, there is also Mackenzie Street and Mackay Street. The secondary school for the entire valley, in Hagensborg, is Sir Alexander Mackenzie Secondary School, coexisting with the native-named Nusatsum Elementary.

Green Bay, Mackenzie's Porcupine Cove.

one, and in addition were used to traveling the large lakes of the interior, where the conditions, as we have seen from Mackenzie's experiences on Great Slave Lake in 1789 (see pages 85–88), can be just as bad.

The very first comment Mackenzie made about this saltwater body was that the tide was out – an interesting contrast to his experience when he reached the Arctic Ocean, when it took him several days to realize there was a rise and fall in the water level at all. Almost immediately he saw sea otters, then the staple of the west coast fur trade. The sea was difficult; by two that afternoon, Mackenzie says, "the swell was so high, and the wind, which was against us, so boisterous, that we could not proceed with our leaky vessel," and they landed in a small bay, today called Green Bay, from its color, but which Mackenzie named Porcupine Cove, after a porcupine the natives and some of Mackenzie's men ate that evening for supper.

Mackenzie had hoped to be able to get a look at the sky that night, in order to fix his longitude, so that he could prove to the world where he had been. He did not want a repetition of his inadequacies on the shores of the Arctic Ocean in this regard; he had gone to a lot of trouble and to England to ensure he had the required skills and instruments for this moment. But the sky was cloudy that night. He wrote:

I had flattered myself with the hope of getting a distance of the moon and stars, but the cloudy weather continually disappointed me, and I began to fear I should fail in this important object.

One of the two Nuxalk escaped that evening, and although he was recaptured, Mackenzie let him go, partly because their food was getting low.

Our stock was . . . reduced to twenty pounds of pemmican, fifteen pounds of rice, and six pounds of flour, among ten half-starved men, in a leaky vessel, and on a barbarous coast.

The next morning Mackenzie and Mackay ate a breakfast of small mussels the latter had collected, but the voyageurs, being unused to such food, would "not partake of this regale." Then they embarked, and rounded Masachi Head into Labouchere Channel. Mackenzie was looking for a suitable place for his all-important astronomical observations. He wrote:

As I could not ascertain the distance from the open sea, and being uncertain whether we were in a bay or among inlets and channels of islands, I confined my search to a proper place for taking an observation.

This probably meant that he needed to find a place with an uninterrupted view over water for some distance, so that he could check

Captain R. P. Bishop's map of Mackenzie's track west of Bella Coola. This map was included in his publication of the determination of the location of "Mackenzie Rock."

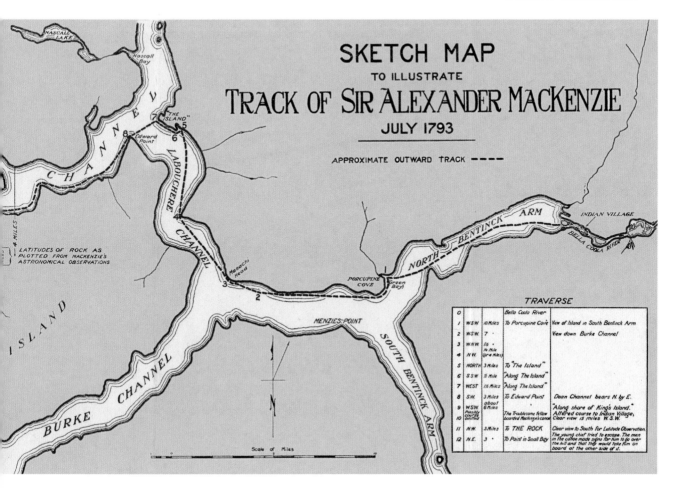

his artificial horizon against the natural one. They proceeded north up Labouchere Channel toward what Mackenzie thought was an island but which turned out to be a promontory.

Crossing westward to Edward Point at the northern end of King Island they now met Heiltsuk (Bella Bella) natives, who were to prove less friendly than the Nuxalk. There were fifteen men in three canoes, who "examined every thing we had in our canoe, with an air of indifference and disdain." One of them made Mackenzie understand,

with an air of insolence, that a large canoe had lately been in this bay, with people in her like [Mackenzie], and that one of them, whom he called "Macubah" had fired on him and his friends, and that "Bensins" had struck him on the back, with the flat part of his sword.

"Macubah" is thought to mean George Vancouver, who in a historical "near miss" was in this location in the yawl of his ship *Discovery* on 31 May and 1 June of the same year, only fifty days before. It has been suggested that "Bensins" is a reference to Archibald Menzies, Vancouver's surgeon and naturalist, but Menzies was not with Vancouver on this particular boat excursion. There is no record of any such incident in Vancouver's journal, or in Menzies', or in anybody else's, for that matter. It may perhaps have been considered unnewsworthy by these European explorers, or perhaps the incident referred to others, such as coastal fur traders.

Mackenzie now paddled southwest along the northern shore of King Island, westward along Dean Channel. The natives decided to accompany them, much to Mackenzie's chagrin. The "troublesome fellow" now forced his way into Mackenzie's canoe and insisted that they go to Elcho Harbour, at the head of which was a native village. Mackenzie ordered this, but the native's "importunities now became very irksome"; he tried on Mackenzie's hat and rifled through his belongings. When they were in the middle of Dean Channel, Mackenzie saw what looked like some sheds or remains of old buildings and, thinking that they might be European in origin, steered for that location. They turned out to be the ruins of a native village, overgrown with weeds (as it is today), but "in a situation calculated for defence." Mackenzie landed here, at what was destined to be the most westerly point he would reach.

This site had been used as a native village for a long time even though it now was not; timbers of a prehistoric house have been found deep below the surface, and trading items have been found nearer the surface: metal that was perhaps a knife, blue glass beads, and a finger ring, possibly even originating with Mackenzie.

Ten canoes then arrived, each with three to six men, from the village of the "troublesome fellow," and Mackenzie became apprehensive about their intentions. "From their general deportment I was very apprehensive that some hostile design was meditated against us," he wrote, "and for the first time I acknowledged my apprehensions to my people."

Luckily, they were at a very good spot from the point of view of being able to defend it if necessary.

We no sooner had landed, than we took possession of a rock, where there was not space for more than twice our number, and which admitted of our defending ourselves with advantage, in case we should be attacked.

This was "Mackenzie Rock," now the focal point of Sir Alexander Mackenzie Provincial Park, where a commemorative obelisk now stands.

Mackenzie Rock from the air.

Mackenzie Rock, on Dean Channel. The obelisk was erected in 1927. The re-creation of Mackenzie's inscription is on the exposed rock below the bush on the right of the main rock mass.

More natives arrived, but they wanted to trade, a sure sign of previous European contact. The natives drove a hard bargain, refusing much of what was offered to them, which, said Mackenzie, "proves the unreflecting improvidence of our European traders."

That night, the natives left. It was, Mackenzie recorded, "a fine moonlight night." Why Mackenzie did not then and there take the astronomical observations he was so desperate to acquire is a total mystery. Perhaps something happened that prevented him; perhaps he was too tired, but it seems incomprehensible that a driven man like Mackenzie would not have found the time to take his vital observations. More likely he forgot to record the fact that he did so, though even this explanation seems unlikely in light of the extensive record of his observations the following night. The following morning he did take five altitudes to work out the local time and notes that his "achrometer" (chronometer) was slow. But nowhere did he record his

View from Mackenzie Rock, looking southwest. This was the "view of the Pacific" as seen by Mackenzie. See also the title page.

Mackenzie Rock from the air, with Elcho Harbour to the left. The coast here is very steep and inaccessible, with "the rock" providing an unusual small flat area.

longitude while at Mackenzie Rock. He even at this point wrote that he "was determined not to leave this place, except I was absolutely compelled to it, till I had ascertained its situation." Why then did he not do so on the night of 21 July?

What thoughts must have gone through Mackenzie's head as he stood upon this remote rock in its superbly beautiful setting on Dean Channel? An immense sense of satisfaction and achievement, one would imagine, on finally making it to the Pacific Ocean, that goal that had eluded overland explorers from the east for centuries. Unfortunately, at that precise moment he was probably too preoccupied with the survival of himself and his men to allow himself much self-congratulation. After all, if they did not return to tell the tale, the world would know nothing.

On the morning of 22 July, more canoes came up Dean Channel, and their remaining Nuxalk guide, who understood what was going on, "renewed his entreaties for our departure," for he thought that this was the beginning of a massing for an attack. Mackenzie by this time was very concerned, and his "people were panic struck." He consented to having them load up the canoe in readiness for a speedy getaway should this become necessary. He took a latitude with his sextant and calculated it to be 52° 21´ 33´´ N with an artificial horizon, and 52° 20´ 48´´ N with a natural one. The true latitude of Mackenzie Rock is 52° 22´ 30´´ N.

Mackenzie finally agreed that they should move farther away from the native village (at the head of Elcho Harbour), but before they did he resolved to mark the location of this, his most westerly point. He had come prepared.

I now mixed up some vermilion in melted grease, and inscribed, in large characters, on the South-East face of the rock on which we had slept last night, this brief memorial –

> *Alexander Mackenzie,*
> *from Canada, by land,*
> *the twenty-second of July,*
> *one thousand seven hundred and ninety-three.*

These words had long been erased when in 1926 the Historic Sites and Monuments Board of Canada had these words chiselled into the same rock and filled with red cement, to make more permanent Mackenzie's record. This record is still there, athough the red cement has fared little better than Mackenzie's vermilion. The rock itself is now covered with thimbleberries, interspersed with stinging nettles, making a visit to the monument a painful experience for the unwary!

Mackenzie moved a short distance east, to a cove near Cape McKay. His Nuxalk guide had been induced to attempt to escape by the Heiltsuk natives, and Mackenzie had to watch him, for his men refused, while he finally obtained his positional fixes. That afternoon he took more altitudes to calibrate his chronometer and that evening "observed an emersion of Jupiter's third satellite" and then "an emersion of Jupiter's first satellite" to calculate his longitude as 128° 20´ W. The correct position of the cove is 127° 27´ W, so Mackenzie placed his position about 40 km or 25 miles too far west – only a 3 percent error on the total straight-line distance from Fort Chipewyan. Near enough!

Right: The inscription on Mackenzie Rock today, as re-created in 1926. The original inscription was painted onto the rock by Mackenzie using a mixture of vermilion and bear grease. Vermilion is a brilliant red pigment made by grinding cinnabar, a mineral form of mercuric sulfide, from which mercury is obtained, and was used in the fur trade to mark bales of furs. That Mackenzie had bothered to carry this with him may indicate that its use here was premeditated.

FIRST CROSSING OF NORTH AMERICA
LA PREMIÈRE TRAVERSÉE DE
L'AMÉRIQUE DU NORD

On 22 July 1793, Alexander Mackenzie of the North West Company wrote his name on this rock, signalling the end of an epic journey which had begun with his departure from Montreal in the spring of 1792. Although the route he travelled was not the practical trade route he sought, he had become the first man to cross the continent north of Mexico, completing an enterprise which had begun with the voyages of Cabot and Cartier almost three centuries before.

Le 22 juillet 1793, Alexander Mackenzie, de la Compagnie du Nord-Ouest, inscrivit son nom sur cette pierre, marquant la fin de son voyage épique entrepris de Montréal au printemps de 1792. Même s'il ne trouva pas la route commerciale qu'il cherchait, il fut le premier à traverser le continent au nord du Mexique, terminant ainsi la recherche commencée par Cabot et Cartier près de trois cents ans auparavant.

Historic Sites and Monuments Board of Canada.
Commission des lieux et monuments historiques du Canada.

Government of Canada - 1926 - Gouvernement du Canada

This obelisk commemorating the place where Mackenzie reached the Pacific was unveiled in September 1927 by Robert Bruce, Lieutenant-Governor of British Columbia. The ceremony was attended by many dignitaries and many native people. "May it in future years," Bruce said, "become a shrine where thousands will come to pay worshipful respect to the memory of a remarkable man." But few people visit the overgrown site today. It remains strangely unpromoted by tourist bodies, and the large provincial park that surrounds it is undeveloped forest. The rock is seen from a ferry on one B.C. Ferries route from Bella Coola a couple of times a week in the summer.

Above: Cape McKay and the cove. At this cove, Mackenzie's Nuxalk guide was urged by the Heiltsuk to escape over the ridge, where they would pick him up on the other side.

Above left: The commemorative metal plaque shown is a replacement for the original one, shown on page 13.

Bottom left: Mackenzie Rock and Cape McKay. The cove where Mackenzie finally fixed his position is shown in the middle of the photograph.

"I had now determined my situation," Mackenzie recorded, "which is the most fortunate circumstance of my long, painful, and perilous journey, as a few cloudy days would have prevented me from ascertaining the final longitude of it."

It was now ten in the evening of 22 July. Wasting no more time now that he had his precious observations, Mackenzie and his men left in a hurry. This point marks the beginning of the return journey. "We proceeded at a considerable rate, as my people were very anxious to get out of the reach of the inhabitants of this coast," wrote Mackenzie. They paddled all night and reached Qomq'-ts, the native village from which they had embarked on their excursion to the Pacific Ocean. Here they faced another problem; the "troublesome fellow" was here with some associates, who made attempts to attack Mackenzie. They were fended off, not least because the natives knew

Finding Mackenzie Rock

The exact location of Mackenzie Rock, the most westerly point reached and where the explorer inscribed the now famous words noted in his book, "Alexander Mackenzie, from Canada, by land, the twenty-second of July, one thousand seven hundred and ninety-three," was unknown before 1923. In that year, a B.C. land surveyor named Captain R. P. Bishop conducted an extensive and detailed study of Mackenzie's courses and distances with a view to determining the exact location of the rock. Most but not all of these courses and distances are recorded in his book, the only evidence we have, since no journal of the Pacific voyage survives.

After considering the possible errors in Mackenzie's latitude and longitude, Bishop traced the hour-to-hour movements of Mackenzie, comparing them with what is seen on the ground or, rather, on the water. His reference to an island at the junction of Dean Channel and Labouchere Channel, for instance, is understandable, because although it is not an island, this peninsula is so shaped as to appear so from certain angles to the southward.

From all this, Bishop settled on Mackenzie Rock as the correct location. It has the required distance to the horizon, and its description, plus that of what can be seen from it, as well as its relationship to the cove near Cape McKay where Mackenzie moved to be farther away from the native village, all agree with what our explorer wrote in his book.

I have followed Mackenzie's words and Bishop's map particularly looking to see if any other locational interpretation was possible, and particularly another penininsula, but I have become convinced that Bishop was correct in his interpretations; his location of the rock is the only possible one that satisfies the evidence available.

Captain Bishop's work was published by the Canadian government in 1924, and three years later, accepting Bishop's work as conclusive, the Historical Sites and Monuments Board erected an obelisk and plaque on the site. The plaque was later changed to include an inscription in French, but the obelisk remains.

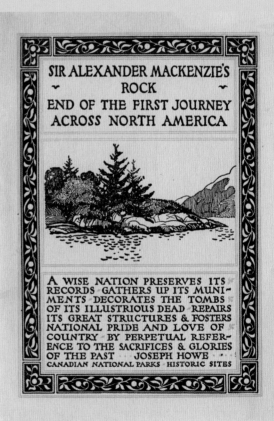

SIR ALEXANDER MACKENZIE'S ROCK END OF THE FIRST JOURNEY ACROSS NORTH AMERICA

A WISE NATION PRESERVES ITS RECORDS GATHERS UP ITS MUNIMENTS DECORATES THE TOMBS OF ITS ILLUSTRIOUS DEAD REPAIRS ITS GREAT STRUCTURES & FOSTERS NATIONAL PRIDE AND LOVE OF COUNTRY BY PERPETUAL REFERENCE TO THE SACRIFICES & GLORIES OF THE PAST · JOSEPH HOWE · · CANADIAN NATIONAL PARKS · HISTORIC SITES

Title page of Captain R. P. Bishop's book.

the effect of firearms. Mackenzie found that the attack had been oc-casioned by the "troublesome fellow" telling the others that Mackenzie had killed four of his companions. After the necessary explanations, assisted by the young chief from the Great Village who had been their guide, "a reconciliation now took place." Mackenzie took a final lati-tude, which was 52° 23´ 43´´ N. (The correct latitude is 52° 22´ 30´´ N, so he was very close.) Canoes and poles (for going upstream) were supplied, Mackenzie paid for everything, including the loan of the ca-noe, and they were off, eastbound. Their guide, however, took off ahead of them, as did the "rascals."

In a quasi-humorous commemoration of the village having been the place where the natives who had attacked him had been waiting, and their lying to the others in the settlement, Mackenzie gave the place the moniker "Rascal's Village." It is the modern town of Bella Coola. This name has been held up by some to be the epitome of all that was wrong in European explorers' attitudes toward native people, but clearly anyone who would advance such a theory has not read Mackenzie's book properly; he named it for the few *individuals* who attacked him, not *all* the inhabitants of the village. On the whole, calling one's attack-ers "rascals" is remarkably restrained, don't you think?

Nuxalk sea monster mask.

I sat in a restaurant in Bella Coola on 27 August 1999, having recently returned from Mackenzie Rock, and drank a toast to Alexander Mackenzie – congratulations on covering all that *distance*.

After the drive to Bella Coola and the flight from there to "the rock," *I* felt a sense of achieve-ment – and it had only taken me four days from Peace River and the site of Fort Fork to the Pacific by car and floatplane. Mackenzie took sixty-two days outbound (not counting the diversion down the Fraser, with which it would total seventy-four days) and only thirty-three days back, a magnificent achievement in such rough country.

By sheer coincidence, my wife happened to be in Montreal when I visited Mackenzie Rock. That evening I phoned her in Montreal from Bella Coola – a personal act the symbolism of which was not lost on me. What a difference two hundred years makes!

There is a surprising lack of interest, or perhaps enterprise in developing that interest, in Mackenzie Rock, now in a provincial park and marked with an impressive monument, placed there in the 1920s. Bruce, the pilot of the floatplane that flew me out to Mackenzie Rock, told me that since he had been flying out of Bella Coola – about two years – only five or six people had asked to fly by the rock "just to see it" while on other business, and no one had asked to be taken to see it. I was his first such customer.

The Native View

Because native history is generally oral, it is often difficult to assess what the view of an event such as the coming of Mackenzie to Pacific waters was from the point of view of the local inhabitants at the time. In an unidentified newspaper clipping from 1934 now held in the British Columbia Archives, there is a story told to B. Fillip Jacobsen, a Norwegian who in the 1880s collected native art on behalf of German museums, and who returned to Bella Coola about 1900 to live. The story was told by Au Kvalla, a Heiltsuk who, Jacobsen says, must have been nearly a hundred at the time. Au Kvalla claimed his grandfather saw Mackenzie and told him about it. The account could be perfectly authentic but somewhat garbled. Nevertheless it is an interesting alternative view. Here is Au Kvalla's story retold.

"Mackenzie came as far as Eastam before the [Heiltsuk] noticed him [Eastam was the site of Mackenzie Rock; this account says there was a village there *at the time*]. As the canoe came closer to shore the natives hid, ready to attack if necessary. But the canoe did not stop and continued to *Waa Pilot,* a distance of about 4 miles [6 km]. Here was another small village. Again the natives hid, fearing that it was a party of Haidas or Fort Ruperts. As the canoe approached they saw a man in the middle who looked like a goat [Jacobsen offered the explanation that it could have been Mackenzie with a beard]. The native thought that this man must have white paint on his face, because he was so pale. Because of his strange appearance they thought that this man must be a spirit.

The canoe stopped for a while, and this spirit stood up in the boat and looked at the sky. He moved his arms about and at times stars, or eyes, seemed to shine from his person. [Jacobsen thought this was Mackenzie using his sextant, with light being reflected from parts of the instrument.] The natives went to Eastam to report to their chief. On their way back they noticed writing on the rocks. They thought Mackenzie must have done this, but it looked like crows' claws. The figures did not resemble any animals as their own characters did. Their chief advised them to stay away from this thing for fear of displeasing the gods.

Mackenzie returned to [Qomq'-ts]. Sears Killa, the chief, decided he would give a reception for Mackenzie, including a peace dance. The natives dressed for the dance, and when they approached Mackenzie to invite him they were waving their spears and wearing masks, giving the appearance (Au Kvalla's words) "of savages thirsting for blood." Their intended guest of honor took their approach as a sign of hostility and left. The chief was upset about this."

Were the natives surprised by the appearance of "white" men? It is unlikely that either Mackenzie or his men looked anything but plain dirty by this time. In addition, we know that some trading with European ship-borne traders had occurred before Mackenzie's arrival, and the boats of George Vancouver and James Johnstone had arrived just before; Mackenzie himself referred to the natives using the English word "no," which I should think is just about incontrovertible proof of contact with English sailors. Thus is it likely that the appearance of Mackenzie's men would have been that novel?

One difficulty with the last part of this story is that Mackenzie specifically stated that among the would-be attackers he "recognized the man whom [he] had already mentioned as being so troublesome to [them]"; and the men did not have masks, for Mackenzie noted the "fury in their aspect." Nonetheless, it could conceivably be that a general reconciliation was planned; who knows? Interesting for its opposing view, Au Kvalla's account is also unique, and valuable for that reason.

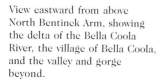
View eastward from above North Bentinck Arm, showing the delta of the Bella Coola River, the village of Bella Coola, and the valley and gorge beyond.

The return to Fort Fork, like most return journeys, was an anticlimax. It was accomplished in only thirty-three days, the party spurred on by knowing the route and by wanting to get back to reveal the achievement.

First there was the strong current of the Bella Coola River to be overcome. Most of his men decided it would be better to travel by land so as to avoid contact with any more natives, for it was assumed that the "rascals" would make similar trouble for them at the villages upriver; however, there was no more trouble of that sort. All except Mackay and two others went on foot as far as the first settlement, and after that Mackenzie divided his men so that some continued on foot in order to lighten the canoe and make it easier to pull, pole, or drag upstream in the turbulent and fast-flowing river. Just before they arrived at the Great Village, out of curiosity they went into two deserted houses, then quickly wished they had not. The houses were full of hungry fleas, and, as Mackenzie relates, "We were immediately in the same condition, for which we had no remedy but to take to the water."

Now they walked. The trail they were taking had a fine stand of western red cedar trees; Mackenzie measured several of them and found them "twenty-four feet in girth and of a proportionate height."

At the Great Village they heard that Mackenzie's dog had been seen, but they could not find him; later, as they were leaving, the dog appeared, and after some inducement he rejoined the party. Then they reached Friendly Village, which still deserved its name. Mackenzie here recorded more ethnological observations, noting in particular an apparently exclusive right of certain individuals to salmon weirs that had been built by them with considerable effort to trap salmon, the principal food source. Nevertheless, the chief had an unlimited power over everyone.

At eleven in the morning on 26 July they left Friendly Village to begin the overland trek back to the Fraser River. They arrived at the point where their canoe had been hidden on the banks of that river at two in the afternoon on 4 August. In just over nine days they had walked about 275 km or 170 miles, a speed of 30 km or 19 miles per day – a blistering speed over such country, kept up for a nine-day period.

The canoe was untouched, as were most of the goods and food they had cached. They retraced their route now, up the Fraser, up the McGregor, up Herrick Creek; on 14 August they camped on the banks of the lower part of James Creek, Mackenzie's "Bad River." The water in this creek that had given Mackenzie so much trouble on his outward trip was luckily now much reduced in volume, so that the canoe could be dragged upstream by men standing in the water, albeit leg-numbing, icy cold water. They portaged around many *embarras*, tangles of fallen tree branches and undergrowth. They searched for the ammunition they had lost on the way down, a search possible now because of the lower water level, but without success. On 16 August they arrived at the Continental Divide between Portage Lake and Arctic Lake, then once more were in the drainage basin of the Mackenzie River.

Ever the schemer, Mackenzie noted that he would have liked to have transported some salmon alive across the Divide so as to colonize them in the Peace River, but by now his ankles had swollen to the point where he had difficulty walking, and they were in a hurry, so he did not do this.

On 17 August they "began to glide along with the current of the Peace [Parsnip] River," a significant moment because from now on they would be going with the flow of the river all the way back. Aided almost everywhere by much lower water levels, due to the time of year, they progressed quickly. They portaged around the Peace River Canyon, which had given them so much trouble on the outward voyage.

Finally, on 23 August, they arrived back at Fort Fork.

At length, as we rounded a point, and came in view of the Fort, we threw out our flag, and accompanied it with a general discharge of our fire-arms; while the men were in such high spirits, and made such an active use of their paddles, that we arrived before the two men whom we left here in the spring, could recover their senses to answer us. Thus we landed at four in the afternoon, at the place we left on the ninth of May. Here my voyages of discovery terminate. Their toils and their dangers, their solicitudes and sufferings, have not been exaggerated in my description. On the contrary, in many instances, language has failed me in the attempt to describe them. I received, however, the reward of my labours, for they were crowned with success.

A little later that season, Mackenzie traveled back to Fort Chipewyan, on Lake Athabasca. He had been away eleven months. There, having "resumed the character of a trader," his great account of his travels ends, and he remained at Fort Chipewyan "for the purposes of trade, during the succeeding winter."

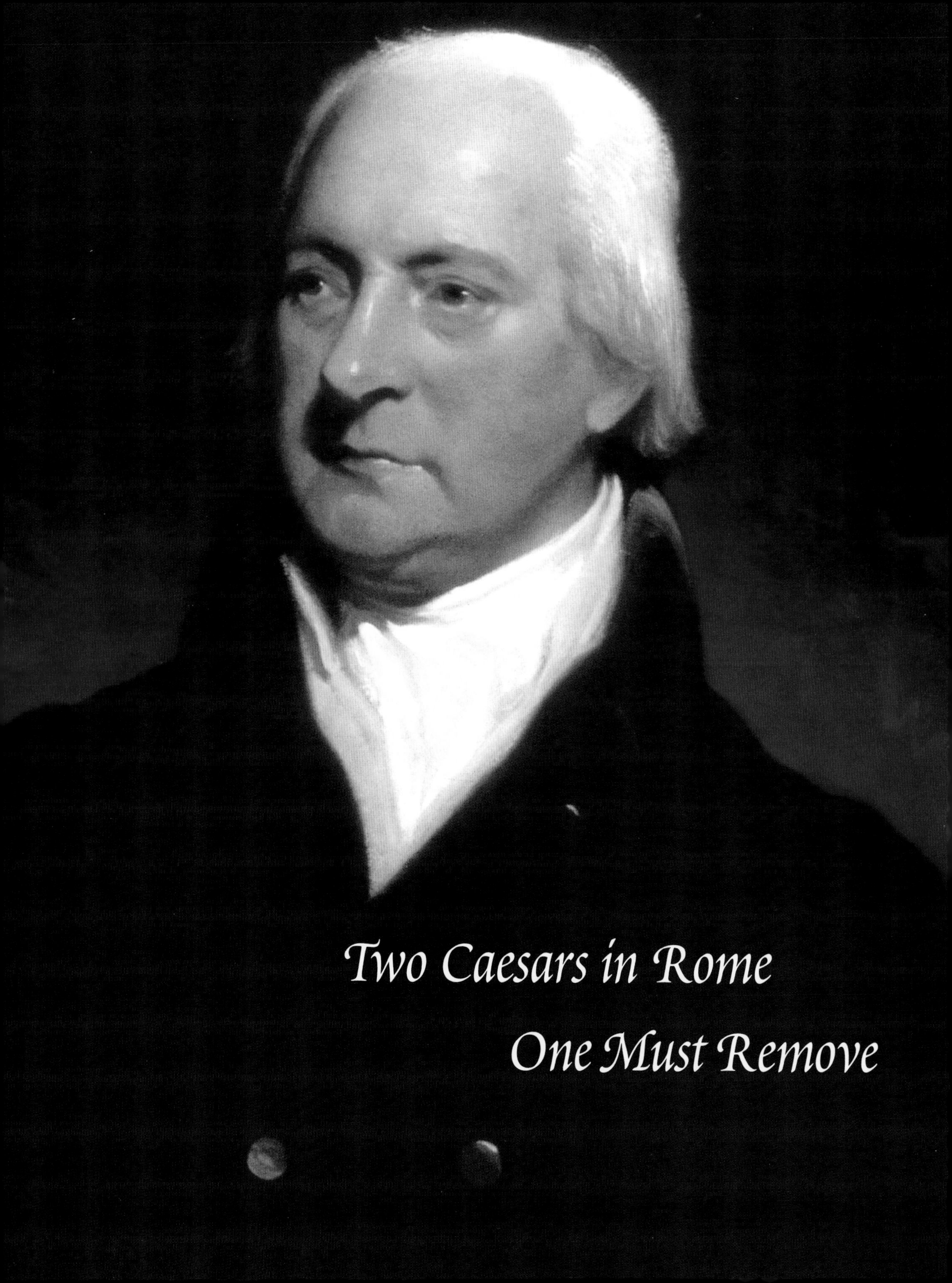

Two Caesars in Rome

One Must Remove

*He has made a journey which is the most astonishing
that has ever been undertaken, having crossed the
whole breadth of the immense continent of North America.*

– Julian Niemcewicz

*Our A McKenzie is determined to leave our
Concern & the Country for ever.*

– William McGillivray

Previous page: Alexander Mackenzie (left) and Simon McTavish (right).
Mackenzie's portrait was painted by René Quentin in 1893–95, in Victoria, B.C.,
and the painting was later acquired by the British Columbia Archives.
McTavish's portrait, by an unknown artist, is in the National Archives of Canada.

The winter following his Pacific voyage must have been quite an anticlimax for Mackenzie, and the evidence is that during the winter he became quite depressed, suddenly forced to stay in one place, not doing anything he perceived as *useful*. A letter he wrote to his cousin Roderic dated at Fort Chipewyan on 13 January 1794 expressed his resolve to leave the Athabasca country.

I think it unpardonable in any man to remain in this country who can afford to leave it. What a pretty situation I am in this winter. Starving and alone, without the power of doing myself or any body else any Service. The Boy at Lac La Loche, or even my own Servant, is equal to the performance of my Winter employment.

He became depressed on finding himself unable to speedily make a fair copy of his journal, which from the first he no doubt intended to publish. In another letter to Roderic he wrote:

Last fall I was to begin copying it but the greatest part of my time was taken up in vain Speculations. I got into such a habit of thinking that I was often lost in thoughts nor could I ever write to the purpose.

He was learning, as writers know, that it takes a lot longer to complete something than one would think. And it would be this same problem that, many years later, would finally lead Mackenzie to hire a ghostwriter to finish and polish his work.

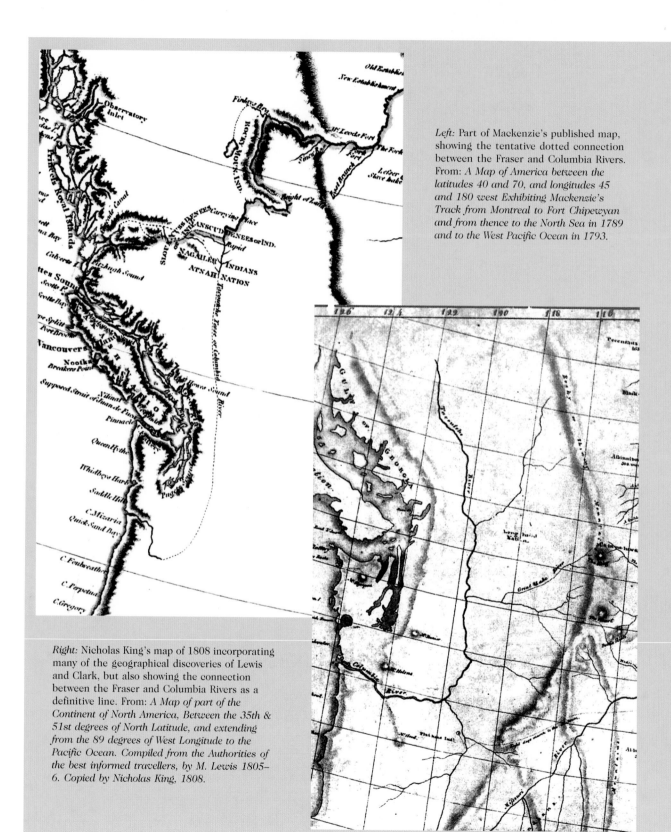

Left: Part of Mackenzie's published map, showing the tentative dotted connection between the Fraser and Columbia Rivers. From: *A Map of America between the latitudes 40 and 70, and longitudes 45 and 180 west Exhibiting Mackenzie's Track from Montreal to Fort Chipewyan and from thence to the North Sea in 1789 and to the West Pacific Ocean in 1793.*

Right: Nicholas King's map of 1808 incorporating many of the geographical discoveries of Lewis and Clark, but also showing the connection between the Fraser and Columbia Rivers as a definitive line. From: *A Map of part of the Continent of North America, Between the 35th & 51st degrees of North Latitude, and extending from the 89 degrees of West Longitude to the Pacific Ocean. Compiled from the Authorities of the best informed travellers, by M. Lewis 1805– 6. Copied by Nicholas King, 1808.*

Columbia or Fraser?

When Mackenzie reached the Fraser River near where it begins its big curve westward and then southward, he thought he had reached the Columbia, the large river often referred to as the River of the West, or River Oregon. For the better part of the century it had been considered as the river which must flow to the Pacific Ocean from the Rocky or Stony Mountains to somehow "balance" the Mississippi-Missouri flowing to the east.

He named the river "Tacoutche-Tesse," following the native name for it, because the Columbia had only just been named, by American captain Robert Gray after his ship the *Columbia Rediva,* in 1792, information that Mackenzie did not have at the time. Gray was the first to sail into the river's mouth, across the treacherous sandbars that had kept it hidden from so many for so long.

But Mackenzie did think his river was the same river as the Columbia, and by the time he came to write his book, he had decided:

It is the extension of [the Rocky Mountains] *so far South on the sea coast, that prevents the Columbia from finding a more direct course to the sea, as it runs obliquely with the coast upwards of eight degrees of latitude before it mingles with the ocean.*

A glance at the map shows immediately to modern eyes the improbability of the Columbia undergoing such geographical contortions as are required to link the upper Fraser with the lower Columbia, which, of course, accounts for Mackenzie's need to explain his theory. But it is true that both the Fraser and the Columbia do take unlikely paths in their upper reaches, both caused by the northwest to southeast trend of the mountains, and it is easy to see how the two could have been confused.

The great English mapmaker Aaron Arrowsmith showed the linking of the Fraser and the Columbia, although as was his habit, he did not usually show features until their position had been reported by actual exploration. It was he who drew the map for Mackenzie's book; it shows the two rivers linked only by a dotted line (left, top), as does his map of North America of 1802. These enormously influential maps were widely copied, so that the same features show up on the maps of many contemporary mapmakers. The second 1802 version of the latter map was the one carried by Lewis and Clark when they arrived on the lower Columbia in 1805, and so may be said to reflect their perception of the river geography at that time. A similar map by the American mapmaker Nicholas King, drawn in 1803 for the Lewis and Clark expedition and also carried with them, also shows the connection of the rivers. A revised map drawn by King in 1808 embedding the information from that expedition shows the tentative dotted connection removed, replaced with a firm and definitive line (left, bottom).

It was not until Simon Fraser followed his eponymous river to the sea in 1808 that it was conclusively proved that the rivers were not the same. In that year, obviously before news of Fraser's explorations had reached Britain, Mackenzie showed he still thought the river he had reached to be the Columbia, for he wrote, in a proposal to Viscount Castlereagh, the British Secretary of State for War and the Colonies, "I . . . [was] the first, who crossed . . . to the Columbia, and from the Columbia to the Pacific Ocean, in the year 1793."

In 1811, fellow Nor'Wester David Thompson followed the Columbia to the sea, and the geographical conundrum posed by that river was sorted out and mapped for the first time. It was David Thompson's famous map of 1814, utilizing information from Simon Fraser in addition to his own, that was the first to show the world the correct relationship of the two rivers.

One wonders at the state of his mind at this juncture, for he wrote in another letter to Roderic: "I could not close my eyes without finding myself in company with the Dead. I had some visions of late which almost convinced me that I lost a near relation or a friend."

Mackenzie was at this time considering the ways in which the business of the North West Company, in which he was a partner, could benefit from the new geographical knowledge he now had; how, if you like, to turn what he had done to financial gain.

It was a turning point for Mackenzie, time to move on to other things; at the ripe old age of thirty-two (at most) he left the Athabasca country for good, traveling first to the annual meeting of the partners of the North West Company at Grand Portage, the great fur trade interchange for the interior of the Northwest, located at the western end of Lake Superior. The traveling improved his well-being, if nothing else, for he was able to write again to Roderic from Grand Portage, on 28 July 1794, that he was "a good deal recovered from [his] indisposition."

It was presumably at Grand Portage that Mackenzie related the story of his expedition to the Pacific for the first time, referred to in contemporary correspondence as "the first fruits of the creation of the North West Company."

From Grand Portage Mackenzie traveled to Upper Canada (now Ontario) and in early September visited John Graves Simcoe, the Lieutenant-Governor, at Niagara. To "prove" that he had reached the Pacific Ocean, Mackenzie presented Simcoe with a sea otter pelt. At Simcoe's request he penned a brief account of his expedition, which is the first official notice he wrote of his expedition to the Pacific.

I followed up the Waters of this River [the *Unjigah* or *Peace*] *to their Source, carried over the Height of Land which is only 700 yards; from hence I continued my route down a small River which I found discharged itself into the branch of a larger one that the Natives call Tacoutch Tesse or Tacouche River* [the Fraser, which Mackenzie thought was a tributary of the River of the West, the Columbia; see pages 234–35] . . . *from the best information I could procure judged it did not discharge itself to the Northward of the River of the West; a Branch if not the whole of which I take it to be.*

Mackenzie had more on his mind than a simple account of what he had achieved, however; he discussed at length with Simcoe the plans he had formulated over the previous winter for a radical expansion of British trade, which he felt should follow from his discoveries.

Mackenzie did not particularly propose that his new route to the Pacific should be used for trade, for he realized from a practical point of view that the route was not likely to work. He did use it to interest others in the concept, however, as he undoubtedly thought that variations on his initial route could be found, and he was right; Simon Fraser a few years later was to find the much easier shortcut from the Parsnip to the Pack River and across the Continental Divide at Summit Lake.

He did, however, propose some ideas to Simcoe that he would spend most of the rest of his life advocating, ideas that made a lot of sense commercially, which was Mackenzie's interest, but which also made sense from a British imperial expansion point of view. Unfortunately for him, the British were not at that time much interested in what is now Canada's Pacific coast. Had his ideas been implemented, the history of the west coast would likely have evolved differently.

Mackenzie's idea was that the monopolies of the British East India Company over trade in the Pacific and those of the Hudson's Bay Company over the route through Hudson Bay be somehow reconciled so that supplies of trade goods for the fur trade going into the continent, and shipments of fur pelts out, could be through both Hudson Bay and the Pacific coast. In particular, the furs produced from west of the Rockies were to be shipped through Pacific ports to China in order to open up a vast new area for the fur trade and reduce the distance the fur pelts had to be carried to a shipping point. Furs sold in China would be used to pay for tea, which would then be shipped to Britain.

Mackenzie firmly felt that it was the fur-trading system established by the Montreal traders, and of course this included him, that was the best system to extend to carry out this scheme; so, by implication, the North West Company would be merged or at least have its routes made coincident with those of the Bay Company, and would ship furs not through Montreal but through Hudson Bay. Nor'Westers would also be in charge of trading with the native population at the Pacific ports, which he felt they would do much better than the crews of the sailing ships who were trading on the Northwest Coast at the time. He was probably right. To "secure the whole traffic," as Simcoe later reported to his government, "a Post at Cookes River & another at the Southerly limit of the British Claims" should be established.

Two months later, Mackenzie was in Montreal, where he wrote to Lord Dorchester, the Governor-in-Chief of British North America, to inform him also of the details of his expedition. Mackenzie may also have met with him, but there is no record of such a meeting.

As a major partner in the North West Company, with by now a significant financial interest, Mackenzie's aim was to facilitate expansion into new territory, a process at which the company had excelled in the previous two decades, building itself into an entity that truly rivaled the Hudson's Bay Company for dominance of the entire fur trade of Canada. But now they had this geographical problem, the Rocky Mountains, and it was to the solution of this problem that Mackenzie was addressing his energies now. The streams of the western side of the mountains run west, so why fight them?

Sometime in the second half of 1794 Mackenzie accepted an appointment as one of the agents who would represent the firm of McTavish, Frobisher at the annual meeting at Grand Portage. The meeting was that of the wintering partners from the interior and the managing partners from Montreal – McTavish, Frobisher and Company.

After spending the winter in England, Mackenzie went to Grand Portage in his new role in the summer of 1795, and in November he was formally admitted to partnership in McTavish, Frobisher. The partners of the latter already held nearly a majority of the North West Company shares; the addition of Mackenzie increased that dominance. Ironically, at the 1795 meeting complaints were raised by wintering partners and their clerks that McTavish, Frobisher was too dominant in the North West Company partnership. Mackenzie took the side of the wintering partners and clerks to ensure that positions were found for up-and-coming clerks and that the number of available shares was increased. Mackenzie here reveals his good judgment in the running of a large concern such as the North West Company had become, for he recognized that it would lose its star players, probably to competing firms, if a proper place were not found for them. Accommodating them would ensure the longer-term success of McTavish, Frobisher's investment in the partnership.

The gradual implementation of the treaty of 1783, which had ended the war with the American Revolutionaries and recognized a boundary with a new United States of America, was leading to the loss of key North West Company posts. The signing of an ancillary treaty in 1794, called Jay's Treaty, made it certain that the posts of Michilimackinac and Detroit would soon be lost to the Americans, and even Grand Portage, that key interchange link in the company's transportation system, would go. Another site about 50 km or 30 miles north of Grand Portage, at the mouth of the Kaministikwia River, was selected in 1798 to replace

Montreal in 1830. A birchbark canoe is in the foreground.

it; this became Fort William and is today part of Thunder Bay, Ontario. The result of all this was that Canadian trade was being forced north of the new boundary line, with only one major direction to go – northwest. Under these circumstances, one would have expected Mackenzie's ideas to have received a more enthusiastic reception than they did. But he was ahead of his time. Many of his ideas would be implemented, but not for another twenty-five years.

Mackenzie's closest friend in the partnership was William McGillivray, Simon McTavish's nephew, who was the same age as him. (McGillivray was born in 1764.) They shared accommodation in Montreal,

William McGillivray.

and their social events, parties, and drinking became a feature of the social life of the city for a while. This in striking contrast to the life both of them had experienced at lonely outposts hundreds of difficult miles from anyone of like mind.

George Landmann, who was in Canada between 1797 and 1802, visited and traveled with both of them. He wrote about a gathering held in December 1797 which seems to have been typical of Mackenzie's life at this time (see opposite). The next year he was accompanying Mackenzie and McGillivray to St. Joseph and told of an incident that occurred while crossing Saganaw Bay, in Lake Huron (see page 242).

Despite the good relationship Mackenzie and McGillivray obviously had, a rift was slowly opening between Simon McTavish and Mackenzie. It had probably begun with the latter's support of the wintering partners and clerks against the McTavish concern in 1795. At its root was Mackenzie's advocacy of his scheme to merge the interests of the North West Company with those of the Hudson's Bay Company and the British East India Company, for this would inevitably result in a loss of business for Montreal-based traders such as McTavish, Frobisher as furs were routed through other ports.

Mackenzie spent the first part of 1798 in New York, dealing with company business. The North West Company had already found that it could get around the monopoly of the British East India Company over the China trade by using American ships, and Mackenzie journeyed to Philadelphia, where he purchased a ship, *Northern Liberties*, which was to be used to carry furs under American registry from New York to Canton, and thence to Europe. This was to some extent part of

Under the Table

A Beaver Club medal. Membership in this social club was restricted to wintering partners of the North West Company, and all had these medals. This one belonged to James McGill. 1785 is the date the club was founded, 1766 the date the member (in this case McGill) first voyaged to the Northwest.

An indication of the type of life Mackenzie was leading in the period after his Pacific voyage is given in these extracts from the diary of George Landmann, a young army engineer who was at the time stationed in Canada. This is from 1797:

In those days we dined at four o'clock, and after taking a satisfactory quantity of wine, perhaps a bottle each, the married men, viz. Sir John Johnson, McTavish, Frobisher, O'Brien, Judge Ogden, Tom Walker, and some others retired, leaving about a dozen to drink to their health. We now began in right earnest and true highland style, and by four o'clock in the morning, the whole of us had arrived at such a degree of perfection, that we could all give the war-whoop as well as Mackenzie and McGillivray, we could all sing admirably, we could all drink like fishes, and we all thought we could dance on the table without disturbing a single decanter, glass or plate by which it was profusely covered; but on making the experiment we discovered that it was a complete delusion, and ultimately, we broke all the plates, glasses, bottles, &c., and the table also, and worse than all the heads and hands of the party received many severe contusions, cuts and scratches.

Another amusing account was given by Landmann for 12 May 1798.

At La Chine we found the two canoes destined to proceed with us, by the shore opposite to a house belonging to the North-West Company; and wherein an abundant luncheon was waiting our arrival. Several officers in the army, amongst them Colonel Gordon and Lieutenant McArthur, of the 60th regiment, and some of the North-West Company, not about to form part of our expedition, had accompanied us, all of them, I believe, natives of the Highlands of Scotland, so that I was the only "foreigner" amongst them. We sat down, and without loss of time expedited the lunch intended to supersede a dinner, during which time the bottle had freely circulated, raising the old Highland drinking propensity, so that there was no stopping it; Highland speeches and sayings, Highland reminiscences, and Highland farewells, with the dioch and dorich, over and over again, was kept up with extraordinary energy, so that by six or seven o'clock, I had, in common with many of the others fallen from my seat. To save my legs from being trampled on, I contrived to draw myself into the fire-place, and sat up in one of the corners there being no stove or grate. I there remained very passive, contemplating the proceedings of those who still remained at table, when at length Sir Alexander Mackenzie, as president, and McGillivray, as vice-president, were the last retaining their seats. Mackenzie now proposed to drink to our memory, and then give the war-whoop over us, fallen foes or friends, all nevertheless on the floor, and in attempting to push the bottle to McGillivray, at the opposite end of the table, he slid off his chair and could not recover his seat whilst McGillivray, in extending himself over the table, in the hope of seizing the bottle which Mackenzie had attempted to push to him, also in like manner began to slide on one side, and fell helpless on the floor.

Canoeing in the Dark

Our friend and erstwhile chronicler George Land-mann gives us another of his colorful accounts in his diary of life with Mackenzie, this time of an exploit while voyaging – traveling in canoes. One cannot but be reminded of Mackenzie's accounts of canoeing on Great Slave Lake on his way to the Arctic in 1789; here the problem was waves and weather, but both accounts bring home the perils of this type of travel.

Early in the month of May 1799 I received an order to proceed again to the island of St Joseph [at the eastern entrance to St. Marys River, which connects Lakes Huron and Superior]; and having mentioned that circumstance to Sir Alexander Mackenzie and to Mr W. McGillivray, they very kindly offered me a passage in a canoe in which they were about to proceed by the St Lawrence to Kingston, Niagara, Detroit and Michilimakinac . . .

During the night we suffered severely from cold, the cause of which was readily explained, as soon as the daylight opened to our view the waters of Lake Erie (on the borders of which we were encamped), covered as far as we could see with packed ice. Notwithstanding this obstruction we put the canoe into the water, loaded it, and pushed off, when to my surprise, with some care, and by placing a paddle upright on each side of the bows to fend-off the ice, we very gently advanced, with setting poles forcing to the right and left as much of the floating ice as we could, so as to avoid injuring the canoe. In this manner we reached the clear surface through a distance of about four miles, and shortly afterwards arrived in a very comfortable warm atmosphere.

Then they attempted to cross Saganaw Bay, in Lake Huron.

After careful consideration, it was thought better to attempt crossing the bay at its mouth to the tedious navigation round its coast. The weather was exceedingly tranquil, the wind light from the eastward, and we still could depend on six or seven hours of daylight, which it was believed would be sufficient either to complete the traverse, or at least to gain a view of the land at the opposite point of the bay before nightfall. These circumstances had induced us to adopt the direct line across the mouth of the bay. Our men, fully aware of the importance of not waiting a moment, urged an immediate departure; and away we went in high spirits, every pipe filled and lighted, and the best singer in the canoe singing the very best canoe song, which the high cliff-like land at Point-aux-Barques re-echoed with fading voice as we advanced.

Six and even seven hours had expired, yet no land could be seen ahead, and we had for some hours past lost sight of the Point-aux-Barques. The sun had descended below the horizon, and the young moon was making haste to follow his example, yet no land was visible in any direction. Our anxiety increased, and various were the speculations as to the failure of our calculations. Some thought we had overrated our speed, others that we had stood out too far to our right, and had actually passed the northern cape of the bay out of sight of land; there might be a current carrying us out of our course; and many other conjectures were set forth without profit. The light left us, and we had not seen any land, whilst the wind, right in our teeth, was rapidly increasing. In the midst of these conjectures, two hours after the sun had left us, the man in the bow with a terrific voice screamed out, "Breakers in every direction; stop the canoe!"

"Stop her!" was the cry from every mouth at once; but our canoe was not a steamer, and the directions were more easily said than done. By the utmost efforts of the men, however, we did stop, just in time to escape total wreck, for one touch on the angular rocks surrounding, would have done it. With setting poles pushed out in all directions, we contrived to retreat, and got out into water free from breakers, whither we thought it necessary to remain until daylight should come to our rescue. The long and anxiously-desired rising of the sun at length came, and we soon discovered that we had in the darkness of the night hit exactly on the only part of the coast where rocks could be found. Had we gone to the right or to the left but a few hundred yards, we should have effected a landing on a beautifully steep shore of hard sand, whereas we had arrived on the extremity of a long reef of detached blocks of stone . . .

Notwithstanding the surf ran high, we found a tolerably sheltered spot and soon had a kettle on the fire.

Mackenzie's plan, by subterfuge, but with the furs still passing through Montreal. In addition, Britain since 1793 had been at war with the French, following the French Revolution, and American ships were safer than British ones for shipping goods to Europe. Ironically, Mackenzie didn't like these machinations, largely because of their cost.

While in Philadelphia Mackenzie met a Polish traveler named Julian Niemcewicz, who recorded their conversation in a diary. Niemcewicz noted that he had had "the pleasure of meeting the celebrated traveler Mackenzie" and that "he has made a journey which is the most astonishing that has ever been undertaken, having crossed the whole breadth of the immense continent of North America." These comments suggest that Mackenzie was becoming famous even before the publication of his book.

While in Philadelphia Mackenzie met John Jacob Astor in the street. Astor was the owner of companies competing with the North West Company, and when the latter lost posts because they were now in American territory, one of his companies had taken them over. Mackenzie recorded the encounter in a letter to McTavish.

A letter from Mackenzie to his company, McTavish, Frobisher, sent in February 1798 from New York to Montreal.

Astor overtook me in the Street this morning and gave me a hearty shake of the Hand, as If nothing had happened and a pressing invitation to go to His House, and Expressed a wish that I should call upon Him soon as If he had something to say to me; while he's polite to me I shall be so to Him.

It would be within Mackenzie's lifetime that Astor's Pacific Fur Company would establish the first post on the Pacific coast, acting on Mackenzie's scheme before the North West Company did. This occurred in 1811, when Astoria was established at the mouth of the Columbia, which was the "southern limit of British influence" where Mackenzie had advocated setting up a post seventeen years before. The post was purchased the next year by the North West Company when the Americans thought that it was about to be seized by a British naval vessel anyway – a sort of forced sale brought about by the beginning of the War of 1812. This act, technically of sale rather than seizure, greatly assisted American territorial claims to the region and was one of the reasons Britain did not hold onto the coast as far south as the Columbia in 1846, when the 49th parallel boundary was agreed upon. Mackenzie and Astor were competitors who would have made a great team!

Mackenzie returned to Montreal in the spring of 1798, but did not stay long; he set off for the annual meeting at Grand Portage. There he tended, as he had always done, to support the wintering partners against the Montreal management. He was back at the rendezvous again the following year, and there exist a large number of letters written by Mackenzie at this time that show he was still intensely looking after the business, as was his style.

But it was not to continue. In 1799 his contract with McTavish, Frobisher expired, and Mackenzie did not mean to renew it. At Grand Portage Mackenzie announced to all the partners present his intention to retire, and by all accounts (the minutes of the meeting have not survived, so we must rely on later letters by some of those present) a show of support for him followed, led especially by the younger wintering partners, who supported his ideas. The latter group saw him as an indispensable champion and tried to get him to change his mind, but he had come to a decision; he carried through with his resignation and left Canada in October 1799, sailing for England.

This was probably not a sudden decision, but an action he had resolved to take as long before as the winter of 1793–94 when, freshly returned from his Pacific expedition, he spent the winter without much in the way of intellectual stimulation. His closest associates had known it was coming for a long time. William McGillivray, his friend and business and drinking partner, wrote in September 1799 to another partner in the concern:

You will probably be surpris'd to learn that our A McKenzie is determined to leave our Concern & the Country for ever. This has long been his determination, tho' known only to a few – as he could not put it in execution till his Engagements with our House & the NWCo. were at an end. He has realized a handsome Sum of Money and quits a very troublesome Business – but at the present Juncture we could wish he still retained his Situation as we cannot be too strong.

There is some evidence that Mackenzie actually plotted a coup to oust Simon McTavish, whom he had come to dislike. Then, with the failure of the coup, he left in a huff. He may simply have had cold feet about leaving at the last moment, and then McTavish, having made other arrangements (and perhaps glad to be rid of his troublesome partner), would not let him change his mind. A different account again was given by Alexander Henry (the younger) in a surviving letter to a friend.

The Old N West Company is all in the Hands of McTavish, Frobisher, and McKensey is out, the latter went off in a pet, the cause as far as I can learn was who should be first, McTavish or McK. and as there could not be two Caesars in Rome one must remove.

There are letters that suggest that the only reason for Mackenzie's departure was that McTavish refused to add Mackenzie's name to the partnership name, or that perhaps Mackenzie wanted precedence over McGillivray, but this seems unlikely, at least as a sole cause. But there was certainly some sort of conflict between Mackenzie and McTavish resulting in a challenge to McTavish's authority by one anxious to run the show himself.

Aaron Arrowsmith's Map

Aaron Arrowsmith was arguably the finest mapmaker of his time. He produced his first commercial map for his own company in 1790, and his sons and nephew carried on his business, updating maps with the latest information, until the 1860s. Arrowsmith is particularly noted for his pioneering maps of North America, which he was able to draw because of his connections with the Hudson's Bay Company, which had information passed on to the head office in London by its own employees – information they gathered and also information they acquired from others, especially from the North West Company.

The map shown here is in three sections; part of two are shown here. Its date, 1796, is likely wrong, because the entire west coast is taken from George Vancouver's survey that was published in 1798, although Vancouver was back in England, and it is possible that Arrowsmith was privy to this information before it was published. Information from Mackenzie's 1793 expedition is not engraved on the map, even though it was coincident in time with that of Vancouver.

This was Arrowsmith's own working copy of the map, now in the British Library, and has notations added by him in red ink, including the first information about Mackenzie's Pacific voyage. "Observation Given me by Mr Colen" is written at the bottom, and there is a connection shown with a red line from Peace River Fort southwest to a point marked 56° 9′ N and 117° 45′ W, and continuing across the mountains to another point marked 53° 0′ N and 122° 42′ W, with the words "Stoney Mounts according to Mr Kinzie." The line then continues almost west to a point on the coast marked 52° 22′ N, 129° 15′ W. The latter position was close to that which Mackenzie recorded, too far west, when he was at the cove near Cape McKay.

Joseph Colen, to whom the notation at the bottom of the map refers, was in charge of the Hudson's Bay Company's York Fort, on Hudson Bay, at this time, but whether the information on Mackenzie came from him, or how else the information was obtained, is not known. We do know that Colen was very interested in the evolving knowledge of the geography of the Northwest, and had a library of some 1,400 books at York Fort.

This map by Aaron Arrowsmith is significant in that it represents the earliest surviving mapping of Mackenzie's Pacific expedition.

A Map Exhibiting all the New Discoveries in the Interior Parts of North America Inscribed by Permission To the Honorable Governor and Company of Adventurers of England Trading into Hudsons Bay In testimony of the their liberal Communications To their most Obedient and very Humble Servant, A. Arrowsmith
Charles Street, Soho January 1st 1795 ~ Additions to 1796 [1798 or 1799] With written additions.

247

Regardless, however, of the immediate circumstances, it does seem clear that Mackenzie was only carrying out a long-held plan; the only question is whether he really wanted to do so at that point in time, perhaps his only likely window of opportunity with the expiry of his contract. It also seems clear that a power struggle of sorts had developed between McTavish and Mackenzie, and that there was now no love lost between the two, for when Mackenzie reached London he had discussions with McTavish's partner there, John Fraser, who reported back to McTavish:

You know him [Mackenzie] *to be vindictive, he has got an entire ascendant over your young Men* [that is, the wintering partners supported him], *& if driven to desperation he may take steps ruinous to you. He has told myself Your Nt. West business will be completely ruin'd; to others he has thrown out the most violent threats of revenge, & I have had some hints too extravagant to mention.*

Mackenzie's former business partner William McGillivray wrote a letter in May 1800 that supports the idea that Mackenzie wanted to change his mind about leaving, but was not allowed to.

Mr. A. McKenzie after a great deal of havering & irresolution at last determined on going to England without coming to any settlement with our House – his pretensions were unreasonable and inadmissible, & I believe finding at last he had carried matters too far – he would have preferr'd things were otherwise, – tho' we parted not on the best of terms, nothing has past to prevent an amicable setttlement, which we all wish for, & I sincerely hope when he has convers'd with men of more Experience & cooler Heads than his own, he will find it equaly desirable to terminate the matter amicably. – & I have reason to believe to think this is the Case – hard indeed! would it be on us all, on me primarily if after our long intimacy, we could only look on each other as Enemies in future – the consequences are not to be thought of.

The person who replaced Mackenzie as agent and partner at McTavish, Frobisher was none other than his cousin Roderic, pleased naturally enough to move up the corporate ladder. Alexander, however, was not amused. He sent a series of letters to Roderic (all of which have disappeared); the last, Roderic recorded, began "abruptly under an impression of heavy displeasure." It would be five years before the pair, who had been regularly in communication for many years, would write to each other again.

Whatever the circumstances of Mackenzie's exile from the North West Company partnership, by the summer of 1800 he had resolved what to do about it. He was then back in Montreal. In 1798 an opposition group to the North West Company had come into being, generally referred to as the New North West Company, or XY Company, from the marks it put on its goods and bales of furs. (XY was used as a convenient marking following on from the W of NW with which the goods of the North West Company were marked.)

Just as the North West Company was organized and managed by McTavish, Frobisher, so the New North West Company was managed by Forsyth, Richardson and Company, which for years had been the chief rival to Simon McTavish. This company was the largest importer of general merchandise and exporter of staples to both Britain and the United States and was thus more diversified in its business than companies engaged solely in the fur trade. In the fall of 1800, Mackenzie joined this latter concern as a partner. Presumably from a considerable financial investment in the company, reinvesting the monies he was paid by McTavish, Frobisher, he now owned 21 percent of this business, enough for substantial control. The wider economic horizons of Forsyth, Richardson may have contributed to the views Mackenzie developed of a more globally based trading network, views that would find their way into his book published the following year.

Unable to unseat McTavish, and like many an entrepreneur wanting to run his own show, he had created an equivalent position in a rival concern. Undoubtedly his new partners would have considered getting him to join them as a major coup, for they were the underdogs in the fur trade, and would have considered it likely that Mackenzie's influence would facilitate growth at the expense of their rivals. Indeed it would be so; within a year the company was being called Alexander Mackenzie and Company.

A MAP OF AMERICA

between Latitudes 40 & 70 North and Longitudes 45 & 180 West

EXHIBITING MACKENZIE'S TRACK

From Montreal to Fort Chipewyan & from thence to the North Sea in 1789, & to the North Pacific Ocean in 1795.

The SEA
Whale Id

Deserted Encampment

Quarrellers

Isthmus

A Manitoe

Hare Indians

Small R.

The SEA seen by M. Hearne 1771

Copper Mine Hills

Copper Indians

Buffaloe L.

Stoney Mountains

Congreathewhapa

This R. by Indian report joins the Sea

Cegead Lake

very high hills

Nathana Indians

Great Bear Lake

Mountain Indians

Theye-Check L.

Indians

Paint L.

Cheaterfield Inlet

Napashish

Yath Kyed Lake

Inland Indians

Martin Lake

very hilly

Blethne Lake Stoney

Doobaunt Lake

Strong Bow Indians

Beaver Indians

Anawd L.

Cassarawth Lake Clowey

Titmeg Lake

Horn Mount River

Slave Lake

Clewey

Thie wey any Tith

Titcrey Lake

Northkined L.

Admiralty B
Cape Phipps

M. St Elias

Port Mulgrave
Cape Fairweather

Bearing R.
Cc Monticlue
Cape Fairweather

Iyan Canal

Slave R.

Wholdyai Thick Lake

High Rocks

High Rocks

Stone R.

New

Cape Spencer
Cross Sound
Cross Cape

Bay of Islands
Cape Edgecumbe
Norfolk Sound
Cape Ommany

Port Swelttisham
Holkham Bay
Pt Houghton

Lake of the Hills

Salt springs

Fort Chipewyan

Elk River

Rains Deer Lake

Cape Addington
Pt Bucareli

Observatory Inlet

Old Establishment
New Establishment

Unjigah or Peace R.

Red Willow

Pelican R.

Methy L.

Loche la loche

Primo Lake
Black Sear L.

Forresters Id

Dixons Entrance

North I. Dundas I

Hippa I

Renell's Sound

Queen Charlotte Island

Stephens Id

Finlays Bay

M.Leods R.

The Fork

Forks Fort

Lesser Slave Lake

Elk R.

Camp Ford
Buffaloe L.

Red Deer L.

Beaver Lake

Beaver R.

Rapids

Beaver I.

Cedar

Winnipic LAKE

Cape d'Lewis

Kingsell

Milbank's Sound
Cape d'Ennis

Carrying Place

Nansetud Denees or Ind Rapid

Nagailer Ind

Atnah Nation

Blood Indians

Black-foot Indians

Manchester H.

Huldimon

South Branch House

Red R.

Somerset House

Culverts I.
Fitzhugh Sound

Quadra & Vancouver Isl.

Nootka

Breakers

Wakash Nation

Tacouutche Tesse or Columbia R.

Kihimex L.

Buffaloe Lake

Eagle hill Creek

Red R.

Carlton Hou.

Ritinat

Supposed Strait of Juan de Fuca
Pinnacle Cape

Fall Indians

Great quantity of Coal in this Creek

Athew or Rad R.

Edge Coal Cc

South Branch

Grants Hou.

Thorburne Hou.

Queen Hythe

Whidbey's Har
Saddle hill
Cape Nizaria
Quicksand Bay

Cattanhowes

C. Foulweather

B.O

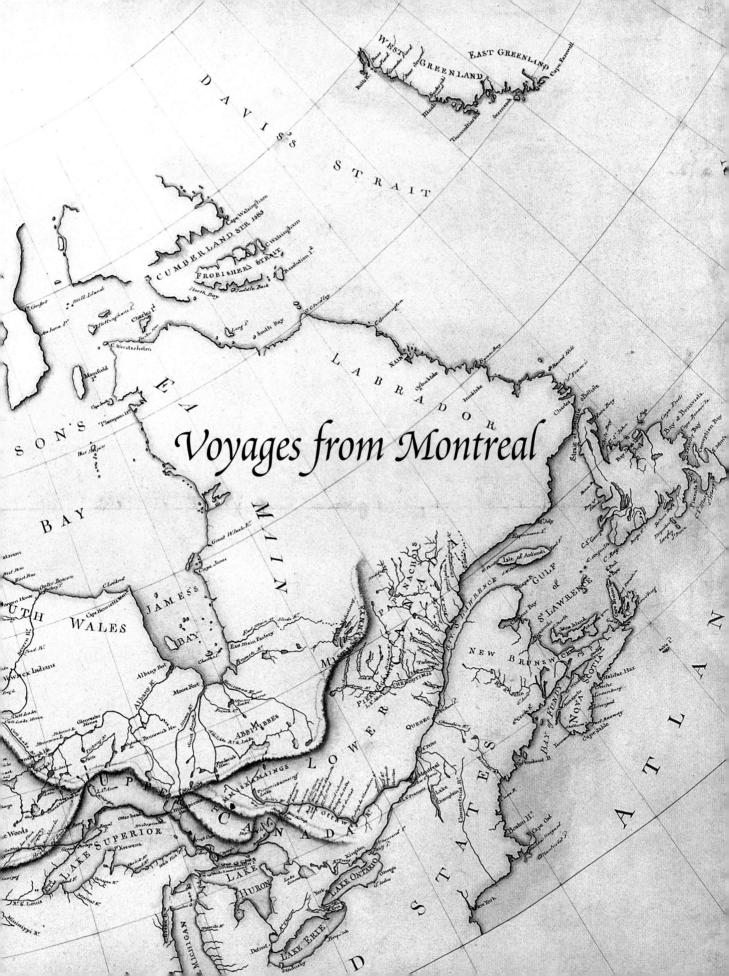

Voyages from Montreal

Though this large volume will convey but little important information to the Geographer, the naturalist, or the statesman, it will probably be perused with very general interest and satisfaction.

– *Edinburgh Review*, 1802

Previous page: The hand-drawn prototype map for the one in Mackenzie's book. It was possibly the map given to the engraver to copy. The red line is the route to the Arctic Ocean, and the yellow/orange line is that to the Pacific. Note the red "Inspector General of Fortifications" stamp. The map's title is *A Map of America between Latitudes 40° & 70° North and Longitudes 45° & 180° West Exhibiting Mackenzie's Track From Montreal to Fort Chipewyan & from thence to the North Sea in 1789, & to the North Pacific Ocean in 1793.*

We can only assume that Mackenzie worked on the preparation of his journals for publication on and off for seven or eight years. We know he found it hard going, and it may well have been frustration with the long process that finally led him to seek help. He found it in the form of William Coombe, a freelance editor and ghostwriter with a long track record of preparing books for publication. Whatever his credentials and talents for helping Mackenzie, he certainly needed the money; he finished his work on the book in the King's Bench Prison for debt, where he remained from 1799 till the end of his life, in 1823. It must have been quite a debt, for clearly assisting Mackenzie didn't help enough financially to be able to get him out of prison. One writer has pointed out the irony in that the account of Mackenzie's far-flung travels was written up by one whose own travels were considerably circumscribed.

It was not uncommon for explorers and navigators to acquire help in polishing their accounts for public consumption. Most well known was the appointment by the British Admiralty of John Hawkesworth to edit the account of James Cook's first voyage. Much to the latter's chagrin, Hawkesworth virtually rewrote Cook's work.

And Coombe was an adept hand at it; by the time he came to Mackenzie's book, he had already prepared for publication a number of exploration-type titles, including Thomas Falkner's *Description of Patagonia* (1774); John Meares' *Voyages Made in the Years 1788 and 1789 from China to the North West Coast of America* (1790), which coincidentally meant that Mackenzie had carried Coombe's work with him at least to the Athabasca country when he returned from England in 1792, if not to the Pacific in 1793; Aeneas Anderson's *Narrative of the British Embassy to China* (1795); James Colnett's *Voyage to the South Atlantic and round Cape Horn* (1798); translations of several French explorers; and a host of similar titles from exploration and travel all over the world. Blessed with the ability to vary his style depending on the character of his author, Coombe was able to do a creditable job with many projects. There are so many, in fact, that one can only assume he must have been a gambler, for he must have made substantial amounts of money from all this good work, yet never again got out of prison.

Mackenzie's own writing, judging from the surviving copy of his first journal and many letters, was quite acceptable by modern standards, given a bit of repunctuating. But at the beginning of the nineteenth century a somewhat more flowery language was in vogue, and it was this language into which Coombe translated Mackenzie's work. He also "cleaned it up," for as we have seen (page 99), some words offended Georgian sensibilities.

Mackenzie's book was finally published on 15 December 1801 by the publishing firm of Cadell and Davies, perhaps the foremost publisher of the day (and which had in 1795 published Samuel Hearne's book). It had the daunting title of

Voyages from Montreal, on the River St. Laurence, through the Continent of North America, to the Frozen and Pacific Oceans; In the Years 1789 and 1793. With a Preliminary Account of the Rise, Progress, and Present State of the Fur Trade of that Country.

Probably 750 copies were printed, that number being normal for this type of book.

But it was not enough! The book was an instant success and a new edition was soon required. There was the pirated French edition, with its interesting background (see page 262). There was a new British edition, then two American editions, then two German editions – all within a single year of the original. In 1803 a third American edition was published. One of the American editions was purchased by Thomas Jefferson, President of the United States, who was then at the

Right: Title page of the first edition of Mackenzie's book, published late in 1801. More properly an account of two voyages from Fort Chipewyan on Lake Athabasca, of course everyone concerned had first to voyage from Montreal, the headquarters of the fur trade for the North West Company.

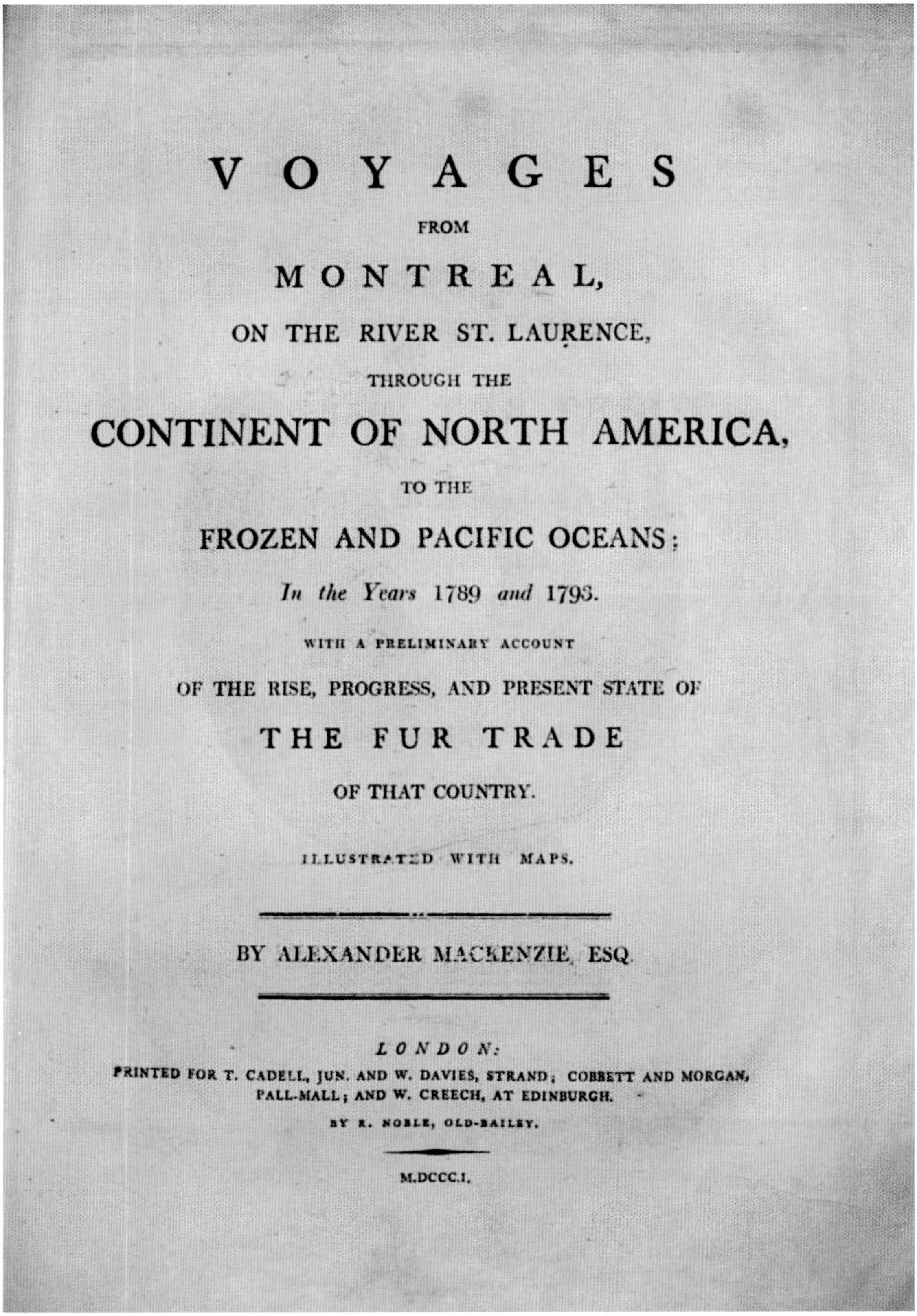

VOYAGES

FROM

MONTREAL,

ON THE RIVER ST. LAURENCE,

THROUGH THE

CONTINENT OF NORTH AMERICA,

TO THE

FROZEN AND PACIFIC OCEANS;

In the Years 1789 *and* 1793.

WITH A PRELIMINARY ACCOUNT

OF THE RISE, PROGRESS, AND PRESENT STATE OF

THE FUR TRADE

OF THAT COUNTRY.

ILLUSTRATED WITH MAPS.

BY ALEXANDER MACKENZIE, ESQ.

LONDON:

PRINTED FOR T. CADELL, JUN. AND W. DAVIES, STRAND; COBBETT AND MORGAN,
PALL-MALL; AND W. CREECH, AT EDINBURGH.

BY R. NOBLE, OLD-BAILEY.

M.DCCC.I.

advanced planning stages of organizing the Lewis and Clark expedition, to give to Meriwether Lewis. This volume would be carried by Lewis to Pacific tidewater two years later. Jefferson had already acquired from England a copy of the first edition; he was keen to obtain an American edition for Lewis because it was a smaller book, octavo instead of quarto, and thus easier to carry. In a letter to his New York agent, Jefferson wrote, "There is to be had in New York an 8vo edition of McKenzie's travels with the same maps which are in the 4to edition: I will thank you to procure it for me." Jefferson was probably more in agreement with Mackenzie's trade strategies than anyone in the *British* government at that time, unfortunately for Mackenzie.

The book even spawned imitators, in the form of a knockoff copy produced in London in February 1802 and attributed to a "Mr. Maclauries," a thinly disguised parody of Mackenzie himself (see pages 260–61). Copyright as we know it today did not exist.

That same month, Mackenzie received one of the highest accolades the British could deliver. Less than two months after his book's publication he was knighted by King George III. Now Sir Alexander, he would henceforth bring more prestige to his business dealings and would make full use of his new moniker. It must have seemed like a fitting reward for his efforts to bridge the mountains, his isolation in the wilds of Canada, and not least his struggle over so many years to bring his book to fruition.

Mackenzie's Preface

In his preface, Mackenzie felt it necessary to deny that the delay in publishing his book was due to "a misunderstanding between a person high in office" and himself. It was due, he maintained, solely to the "very active and busy mode of life in which [he] was engaged."

The latter idea arose from the publication of a book of American travels by Isaac Weld, published in 1799, in which Weld wrote the following:

At the Grand Portage, and along that immense chain of lakes and rivers, which extend beyond Lake Superior, the [North West] company has regular posts, where the agents reside; and with such astonishing enterprize and industry have the affairs of this company been carried on, that trading posts are now established within five hundred miles of the Pacific Ocean. One gentleman [Mackenzie], indeed, a partner in the house at Montreal [McTavish, Frobisher], which now holds the greatest part of the shares of the [North West] company, has even penetrated to the Pacific Ocean itself. The journal kept by this gentleman upon the expedition is, it is said, replete with information of the most interesting nature. That it has not been laid before the public long ago, together with an accurate map of his track, is to be imputed solely to an unfortunate misunderstanding which took place between him and a noble lord high in the confidence of government.

Here are two extracts from Mackenzie's preface:

I do not possess the science of the naturalist; and even if the qualifications of that character had been attained by me, its curious spirit would not have been gratified. I could not stop to dig into the earth, over whose surface I was compelled to pass with rapid steps; nor could I turn aside to collect the plants which nature might have scattered on the way, when my thoughts were anxiously employed in making provision for the day that was passing over me. I had to encounter perils by land and perils by water; to watch the savage who was our guide, or to guard against those of his tribe who might meditate our destruction. I had, also, the passions and fears of others to control and subdue. To day I had to assuage the rising discontents, and on the morrow to cheer the fainting spirits, of the people who accompanied me. The toil of our navigation was incessant, and oftentimes extreme; and in our progress over land we had no protection from the severity of the elements, and possessed no accommodations or conveniences but such as could be contained in the burden on our shoulders, which aggravated the toils of our march, and added to the wearisomeness of our way . . .

Before I conclude, I must beg leave to inform my readers, that they are not to expect the charms of embellished narrative, or animated description; the approbation due to simplicity and to truth is all I presume to claim; and I am not without the hope that this claim will be allowed me. I have described whatever I saw with the impressions of the moment which presented it to me. The successive circumstances of my progress are related without exaggeration or display. I have seldom allowed myself to wander into conjecture; and whenever conjecture has been indulged, it will be found, I trust, to be accompanied with the temper of a man who is not disposed to think too highly of himself: and if at any time I have delivered myself with confidence, it will appear, I hope, to be on those subjects which, from the habits and experience of my life, will justify an unreserved communication of my opinions. I am not a candidate for literary fame: at the same time, I cannot but indulge the hope that this volume, with all its imperfections, will not be thought unworthy the attention of the scientific geographer; and that, by unfolding countries hitherto unexplored, and which, I presume, may now be considered as part of the British dominions, it will be received as a faithful tribute to the prosperity of my country.

What the Critics Thought – A Book Review

Mackenzie's book was generally received politely by the British press, without much excitement. Expeditions up the Nile or to other more exotic places where there were evidences of advanced civilizations were more in fashion. Canada simply wasn't exciting enough. Nevertheless, by the standards of the day the book was a best-seller.

Here are some extracts from one review, which appeared in the *Edinburgh Review* in October 1802. Some of the reviewer's observations on Canada and its inhabitants are quite amusing.

Though this large volume will convey but little important information to the Geographer, the naturalist, or the statesman, it will probably be perused with very general interest and satisfaction. There is something in the idea of traversing a vast and unknown continent, that gives an agreeable expansion to our conceptions; and the imagination is insensibly engaged and inflamed by the sprit of adventure, and the perils and the novelties that are implied in a voyage of discovery.

A small band of adventurers, exposed, for months together, in a boat of bark, upon those inhospitable waters, "which (to use our author's own language) had never before borne any other vessel than the canoe of the savage, and traversing those deserts where an European had never before presented himself to the eye of the swarthy natives;" exhibit a spectacle that is well calculated to excite our curiosity and attention. They remind us of the romantic expedition of Orellana, and carry back the imagination to those days of enterprise and discovery, when the Genius of Europe broke into all the continents of the world, and performed and discovered wonders, that made the marvellous familiar, and obtained credit even for impossibilities. Though that great harvest, both of invention and discovery, be now over, the gleanings that remain for this later age, are neither few nor inconsiderable: and Mr. Mackenzie, who has travelled for them over a large and rugged field, certainly has neither lost his labour nor misemployed it.

He has brought back, indeed, no report of prodigies either of nature or of art, and has not found in his way the materials of those descriptions which animate the narratives of more fortunate travellers. He has discovered, in the wilderness, no traces of ancient civilization, and no indications of surpassing wisdom and virtue among the savages: he has found no pyramids, nor labyrinths, nor deserted cities, nor splendid ruins, and neither reasoned with the superb philosophers of El Dorado, nor exercised himself, in gallantry and arms, with the nymphs of an Amazonian community. His adventures, however, have all the interest that sober probability will admit of, or that his situation was capable of exciting. He followed a painful course, through difficulties and dangers, to an unknown termination; and went steadily forward, without knowing where he was to issue, amidst the roaring of cataracts, and the solitude of mountains; exposed to the daily hazard of shipwreck, and famine, and mutiny; and to the danger of treachery or assault from the melancholy savages that roamed across his course, or reluctantly consented to direct it. His narrative, if sometimes minute and fatiguing, is uniformly distinct and consistent; his observations, though not numerous, are sagacious and unassuming; and the whole work bears an impression of correctness and veracity, that leaves no unpleasant feeling of doubt or suspicion in the mind of the reader . . .

Of the importance of his geographical discoveries, we do not indeed think very highly. The nonexistence of any practicable communication by sea, from the eastern to the western shores of North America [the Northwest Passage], we conceive to have been satisfactorily established, before either the expedition of Mr. Mackenzie, or the voyage of Vancouver: and the passage which the former has discovered by land, is such as few people could have doubted to exist . . .

Mr. Mackenzie himself, indeed, appears to be of the opinion, that the route by which he came would be altogether unfit for the purposes of trade, and rather points at a communication between the Tacoutche or Columbia River [the Fraser], and the head waters of the Saskatchewine. It is needless to observe, however, that the existence of such a communication must be established by another voyage of discovery; and the lower course of the Columbia may present obstacles, of a nature even more formidable than those of which Mr. Mackenzie's experience and information have already given us warning. [Of course, the lower reaches of the Fraser, which Mackenzie thought was at least a tributary of the Columbia, did present obstacles, as Simon Fraser was to find out in 1808, six years hence.]

The countries which Mr. Mackenzie has brought to our knowledge by these expeditions, are certainly the least interesting of any with which modern enterprise has made us acquainted – the barrenness of the soil, the severity of the climate, the remoteness of their position, and the small number and intractable character of their inhabitants, place them very low indeed in the scale of political importance, and reduce their influence upon the rest of the world to a very humble denomination. The believers in perfectability expect, of course, to see the whole universe covered with the miracles of polity and art; but these regions will probably be the last to put off their original barbarity; and philosophy will have native apostles among the Manchew Tartars and New Hollanders [Australians], before any progress has been made in the conversion of the Knisteneaux [Cree] and the Chepewyans.

Mr. Mackenzie makes no pretensions to literary attainments; and the merit of his work is not to be estimated by the elegance of its composition. His style is, in general, sufficiently perspicuous; and we willingly pass over its deficiencies in harmony or correctness.

Literary Pirates!

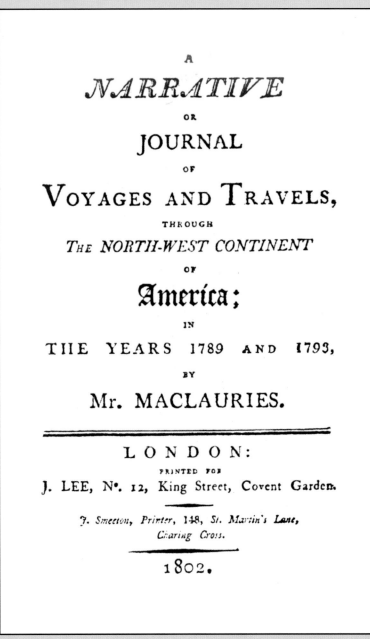

A

NARRATIVE

OR

JOURNAL

OF

VOYAGES AND TRAVELS,

THROUGH

THE NORTH-WEST CONTINENT

OF

America;

IN

THE YEARS 1789 AND 1793,

BY

Mr. MACLAURIES.

LONDON:

PRINTED FOR

J. LEE, N°. 12, King Street, Covent Garden.

*J. Smeeton, Printer, 148, St. Martin's Lane,
Charing Cross.*

1802.

Title page of the pirated book.

The publication of Mackenzie's book in the fall of 1801 was very well received, and it would lead to his knighthood. In an attempt to grab some of this glory and translate it into hard cash, someone published a pirated version of the book in 1802. In these days before copyright, writers copied each other's ideas, particularly if they were best-selling ideas, but this attempt was a particularly bare-faced theft. The writer extracted Mackenzie's book, dumbing it down and thinning it out to the point that much of it no longer makes any coherent sense. Substituting for Mackenzie is a character called Mr. Maclauries.

The deed was perpetrated by someone with no feel for what had been achieved and absolutely no idea of the reality of the Canadian West. The frontispiece, illustrated here, shows a scene that looks distinctly African rather than Canadian; clearly the illustrator had no idea what the natives of Canada might look like, drawing African-looking natives with togas! The landscape contains trees that look more like palm trees than conifers.

Many of the names mentioned in Mackenzie's book are changed, often to meaningless ones. On the first voyage, the island in the Arctic Ocean Mackenzie named Whale Island becomes "Whole Island," thus completely missing the point. Instead of the details regarding the rise of the water that Mackenzie finds in his book to be the tide, Maclauries simply states that "the tide here appeared to rise sixteen or eighteen inches," missing the revelation.

On his second voyage, to the Pacific, the Maclauries version totally omits the culmination of the westward thrust at Mackenzie Rock and the writing of his epithet on that rock; in fact, there is no clue to the fact that the party has even begun to retrace its steps. Thus the whole point of the second voyage, the reaching of salt and tidal water that is indeed the ocean, is missed.

To a reader familiar with the real Mackenzie, Maclauries offers only a little pathetic fun. The book was never reprinted, and perhaps it is just as well that few copies of this book still exist. Ironically, the Maclauries book is now rarer than the first edition of Mackenzie's book, being held by only half a dozen North American libraries today.

The meeting of the Guide & his relations.

Pub.ᵈ Feb. 27. 1802.

Africa in Canada! The frontispiece of the Maclauries volume.

The Napoleon Connection

Above: Napoleon Bonaparte.

Right: Napoleon's personal copy of Mackenzie's *Voyages from Montreal.*

Far right: Jean-Baptiste Bernadotte, Napoleon's marshal, and later, King of Sweden.

Mackenzie's book was quickly translated into French and published in France in 1802, the first other edition and first translation to be done. Yet France and Britain were at war at this time; the great naval Battle of Trafalgar, which would finally destroy French ambitions for an invasion of England, was three years away. So how did this publication of a French edition of *Voyages* occur?

The answer was discovered in 1824, when a boyhood namesake friend of Alexander Mackenzie, one William Mackenzie, visited the King of Sweden, Karl Johan Bernadotte, who as Jean-Baptiste Bernadotte had been one of Napoleon's marshals. Bernadotte told him, and the information was later passed to Alexander Mackenzie's son George in a letter, that Napoleon had hit upon the idea of diverting British attention from his real schemes in Europe by planning a diversionary attack on Canada.

This attack was to be a surprise, in that it was to come up the Mississippi Valley from New Orleans. This was, remember, before France unloaded Louisiana onto the Spanish and then to the Americans, which would come the next year, 1803, with the Louisiana Purchase.

The task of planning the invasion of Canada was given to Bernadotte, who in 1802 was a French councillor of state and in that year became commander of the French Army of the West.

As Bernadotte told William Mackenzie,

The organization and command of this gigantic enterprise was given to me by the Emperor with instructions to make myself master of any work which could bear upon it, and the facilities the nature of the country afforded. Foremost amongst these the work of your namesake was recommended.

Mackenzie's *Voyages* was clearly one of the most up-to-date references available on conditions in Canada .

The difficulty was to get a copy of the book to France, when all communication was cut off. "However," as William Mackenzie recorded Bernadotte's words,

as every one knows, my then master, L'Empereur, was not the man to be overcome by such small difficulties. The book, a huge quarto, was procured through smugglers, and in an inconceivably short space of time most admirably translated into French for my especial use.

Needless to say, the plan to conquer Canada never got off the drawing board; Bernadotte procrastinated, and Napoleon soon had more pressing concerns on his front doorstep and could not plan campaigns and allocate men and resources half a world away. Some thought Bernadotte was in the United States, for a secret dispatch sent from New York to the Governor of Lower Canada in 1804 stated that "Jerome Bonaparte" had been in that country for some time and that it would be "desirable to keep watch on his movements." Jérôme Bonaparte was Napoleon's youngest brother.

Napoleon's personal copy of *Voyages*, stamped with the French eagle, was found in his library in St. Helena, his final exile. Somehow this book, in three volumes, came into the possession of Alexander Mackenzie's granddaughter, and on her death in 1931 it was presented to the National Archives of Canada. When it was transferred to the National Library of Canada in the 1980s it came with a plaintive note written by an archivist: "Can we really give this up?"

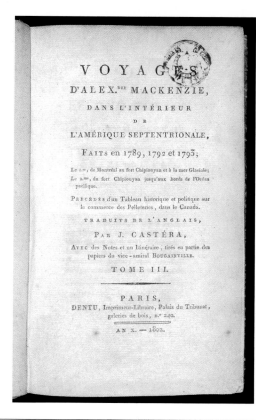

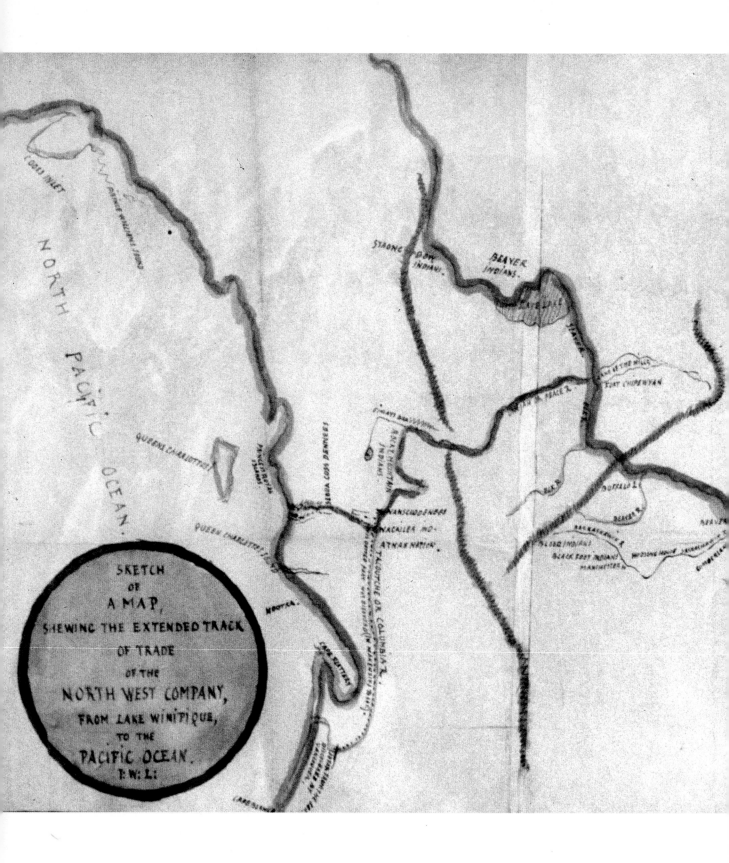

SKETCH
OF
A MAP,
SHEWING THE EXTENDED TRACK
OF TRADE
OF THE
NORTH WEST COMPANY,
FROM LAKE WINIPIQUE,
TO THE
PACIFIC OCEAN.
T: W: L:

NORTH PACIFIC OCEAN.

QUEEN CHARLOTTE'S

QUEEN CHARLOTTE'S S.

NOOTKA.

STRONG BOW INDIANS.

BEAVER INDIANS.

FORT CHIPEWYAN

BLACK FOOT INDIANS

Opening This Intercourse between the Atlantic and Pacific Oceans

The non=existence of a practicable passage by sea, and the existence of one through the continent, are clearly proved; and it requires only the countenance and support of the British Government, to increase in a very ample proportion this national advantage, and secure the trade of that country to its subjects.

– Alexander Mackenzie

Previous page: Sketch of a Map, Shewing the Extended Track of Trade of the North West Company, from Lake Winipique, to the Pacific Ocean. J:W:L: A map drawn by James Winter Lake in 1805. He was the Governor of the Hudson's Bay Company. His family had virtually run the company for the last hundred years; both his father and grandfather had been governors. Fort Edmonton was named after the Lake family estate, north of London. This map is a copy by one company of the other's work, illustrating the rivalry between the two. This map also has an attached map of the entrance to the Columbia River from George Vancouver's survey (not shown here). Clearly the Hudson's Bay Company was concerned about the progress their competitor was making and probably used this map in their discussions of strategy.

$\mathcal{P}$ublication of Mackenzie's book was just one part of an overall strategy he had for the promotion of his ideas for the expansion of British trade to the Pacific coast and China. The book contained a major section entitled "General History of the Fur Trade," which may not have been written by Mackenzie himself. It is often attributed to Roderic, but it seems unlikely that the latter would have wanted his work published as his cousin's work, since they were not on speaking terms at that time.

On the other hand, the inclusion of Roderic's piece may have been planned for some time and, communications being what they were, it was not possible to prevent it. Nevertheless, its inclusion in Mackenzie's book gave it a prominence it would not otherwise have attained. The purpose of its inclusion was to provide background information as to circumstances in the Canadian fur trade so that Mackenzie's later entreaties would be better understood.

The initial salvo was fired by way of his book's conclusion, wrapping up the accounts of the two expeditions. It was essentially the same idea he had originally presented to John Graves Simcoe in 1794, the combining of the efforts of the two fur-trading monopolies, the Hudson's Bay Company and the North West Company, to which he would of course now add his New North West Company, so that furs could be shipped to Europe from Hudson Bay. At the same time the East India Company was to be forced to allow the shipping of furs to China from some newly established west coast ports.

The final part of Mackenzie's book included a wide-ranging description of Canadian geography, probably the first essentially comprehensive description of the territory which now forms Canada, and certainly the first written by someone who had actually visited the three ocean shores of that country.

One of the more interesting points Mackenzie discussed was the establishment of the boundary between British and American territory, now the boundary between Canada and the United States. The treaty of 1783 had laid down that the boundary west of Lake Superior was to be along the line of the Pidgeon River to Lake of the Woods (which is why the North West Company lost its great interchange post of Grand Portage), then due west to meet the headwaters of the Mississippi. But a line due west from Lake of the Woods does not in fact touch the Mississippi at all. Mackenzie advocated a boundary line lower than 47° 38′ N, where he placed the farthest headwaters of the Mississippi, a line probably at 45° N, and then continuing west, "till it terminates in the Pacific Ocean, to the South of the Columbia."

This was the first proposal for a boundary that would have made all of today's British Columbia and Washington State British – and later Canadian – territory. The 49th parallel would be established as this east-west boundary in 1818, as far west as the Rocky Mountains; beyond them a region of "joint occupancy" was agreed upon, which lasted until 1846, when the United States managed to establish the boundary as 49° N except for Vancouver Island.

Mackenzie also included a description of the Rocky Mountains,

the immense ridge, or succession of ridges of stony mountains, whose Northern extremity dips in the North Sea, in latititude 70 North, and longitude 135 West, running nearly South-East, and begins to be parallel with the coast of the Pacific Ocean, from Cook's entry [Cook Inlet] and so onwards to the Columbia.

This section of the book, we can be sure, would have been read very carefully by Thomas Jefferson, for one of the imponderables of the Lewis and Clark expedition was the width, height, and number of ridges of the barrier of the Rocky Mountains.

Then Mackenzie introduced what would become his main theme, the merging of the interests of the trading monopolies, through a discussion of the Northwest Passage. He began:

The discovery of a passage by sea, North-East of North-West from Atlantic to the Pacific Ocean, has for many years excited the attention of governments, and encouraged the enterprising spirit of individuals . . . The non-existence, however, of any such practical passage being at length determined, the practicability of a passage through the continents of Asia and America becomes an object of consideration. The Russians, who first discovered that, along the coasts of Asia no useful or regular navigation existed [that is, there was not a usable Northeast Passage], *opened an interior communication by rivers . . . Our situation . . . is in some degree similar to theirs; the non-existence of a practicable passage by sea, and the existence of one through the continent, are clearly proved; and it requires only the countenance and support of the British Government, to increase in a very ample proportion this national advantage, and secure the trade of that country to its subjects.*

Engraved portrait of Alexander Mackenzie as published in his book. It is based on Thomas Lawrence's painting (see page 9).

Then he presented his case:

Experience . . . has proved, that this trade, from its very nature cannot be carried on by individuals. A very large capital, or credit, or indeed both, is necessary, and consequently an association of men of wealth to direct, with men of enterprise to act, in one common interest, must be formed on such principles, as that in due time the latter may succeeed the former, in continual and progressive succession. Such was the equitable and successful mode adopted by the merchants of Canada.

Here Mackenzie was describing the organization of the North West Company, and it is clear from his thoughts why he supported the wintering partners, "the men of enterprise," against the managing partners – support that helped lose him his job. He concluded:

The junction of such a commercial association with the Hudson's Bay Company, is the important measure which I would propose . . . as the trade might then be carried on with a very superior degree of advantage . . . under their charter.

And the North West Company should not be left out of this, he pointed out, because their trading system was inherited from the French system, which was taken over by the British in 1763 and the geographical area expanded,

having themselves been the discoverers of a a vast extent of country since added to his Majesty's territories, even to the Hyberborean and the Pacific Oceans.

The latter, of course, was a plug for Mackenzie's own contribution.

Mackenzie planned to use the Columbia River for one of his coastal transshipment points, but he thought it was the same river that he had been on when he had in fact been on the Fraser, which he called the Tacoutche-Tesse.

By "opening this intercourse between the Atlantic and Pacific Oceans," he wrote,

and forming regular establishments through the interior, and at both extremes, as well as along the coasts and islands, the entire command of the fur trade of North America might be obtained, from latitude 48 North to the pole, except that portion of it which the Russians have in the Pacific. To this may be added the fishing in both seas, and the markets of the four quarters of the globe.

It was truly a wide-ranging scheme, which made a lot of sense in its broad outline if not in every detail.

The British government, naturally enough, was interested in the scheme, but never got around to ensuring that it happened, being distracted principally by events nearer to home – the threat of Napoleon. It was unfortunate for Mackenzie that government involvement was essential, in order to force the cooperation of the trade monopolies. Unfortunately for the British, the Americans had no such problem with trade monopolies, and it would be an American company, John Jacob Astor's Pacific Fur Company, which in 1811 would be the first to establish a post at the mouth of the Columbia to trade on similar lines to those envisaged by Mackenzie.

Even as his book was being published, the far-ranging Mackenzie had submitted a memorandum to Lord Hobart, the British Colonial Secretary, proposing the construction of a canal from Montreal to Lake Ontario, in order to "render fruitless," as he put it, a canal the Americans were proposing to build from Albany to that lake. The latter was eventually built, in 1817–25, and became known as the Erie Canal. Mackenzie's proposal had to wait a bit longer; it was not until 1957 that the St. Lawrence Seaway opened, although I guess it would only be fair to say that that project was likely on a somewhat bigger scale than foreseen by Mackenzie.

Now his ideas were in full flow. Mackenzie submitted a detailed plan to Lord Hobart the next month, entitled *Preliminaries to the establishment of a permanent British Fishery and Trade in Furs &c on the Continent and West Coast of North America.* He wanted to "form a Supreme civil and Military Establishment" on the "centrally situated and Navally defencible Island of Nootka," pointing out that under the Nootka Convention of 1790 with Spain, the principle of sovereignty had been agreed, at Britain's behest, to follow from actual occupation, not just "discovery."

He proposed the removal of the exclusive rights of "Fishery Trade and Navigation" from the East India Company and the South Sea Company, or force both to issue licenses allowing free trade in the Pacific, and that the Hudson's Bay Company be forced to grant "Licenses of Transit" to allow the use of Hudson Bay by all.

Mackenzie also proposed to set up in England a new company called "The Fishery and Fur Company," which, with these licenses, would set up trading posts at Nootka; at "Sea Otter Harbour" (a name given to a bay at about 55° N by William Duncan in 1788, but the identity of which is confused); and at the mouth of the Columbia. Whaling ships were to bring trade goods from Britain to these posts and bring back some of the furs; the rest were to go to Canton.

Overall, the plan was a reasonably feasible one that foresaw what would actually happen later on. Had it been implemented when it was proposed, it likely would have led to a Canadian coastline at least as far south as the Columbia.

Lord Hobart felt that the first step for this plan was to unite the fur-trading companies based in Montreal, and to this end Mackenzie returned to Canada in 1802. He quickly found that there was no chance that the North West Company partners and those of his New North West Company, or XY Company, would bury their differences; his personal antagonism to Simon McTavish saw to that.

Mackenzie went to Grand Portage in the summer of 1802. One of his XY partners, John Richardson, requested of the British government that it extend the legal system of Lower Canada into the Northwest in order to prevent lawlessness between the men of the old and new companies; this was done by act of the British Parliament in 1803. Richardson, who has been called the chief architect of the Canadian commercial state, was later one of the founders of Canada's first bank, the Bank of Montreal, in 1817.

Another of Mackenzie's partners, Edward Ellice, acting for the XY Company, made an offer to purchase the Hudson's Bay Company outright for £103,000; this would certainly have solved the monopoly problem, but the offer was not accepted.

The partnerships of the XY Company were expanded in 1803 to include the London firm of Phyn, Inglis and Company, whose financial strength probably increased that of the XY Company to the level of the larger North West Company.

The North West Company mounted a direct challenge to the Hudson's Bay Company monopoly in the same year, sailing into Hudson Bay and establishing a post on Charlton Island. The next year they started negotiations with the Hudson's Bay Company to try to find an accommodation that would allow them to use the bay, but after eighteen months these talks reached a stalemate; the monopoly was just too valuable to be given up lightly.

Mackenzie achieved part of what he wanted in 1804, for in July of that year Simon McTavish died unexpectedly, and with his death the antagonisms were able to be overcome enough to allow him to negotiate a merger of the old and new North West Companies. However,

Mackenzie was not able to negotiate any say in the running of the combined concern, and was specifically excluded from any interference. Mackenzie's old XY Company was to own a quarter of the combined concern, but the business was to be conducted by the old North West Company. Four years of cutthroat competition had driven wedges even between old friends. Isaac Todd, a longtime Nor'Wester, wrote that despite the commercial reconciliation, "with [Mackenzie] and McGillivray there will I fear, never be intimacy."

Mackenzie personally now had 4 percent of the combined company. Negotiating the details of this merger was to prove essentially the last fur trade negotiation he would carry out, and from this point on he retracted from day-to-day dealings.

He had been persuaded to enter politics. He was elected to the Legislature of Lower Canada in 1804 and sat officially until 1808, although his attendance was sporadic; he soon found out that politics were not for him. In fact he went to Britain in 1805, and from then on he paid only several short visits to Canada.

Advice to a Son – Follow in Mackenzie's Footsteps

In 1803 Harry Munro was the surgeon-in-residence at Fort Kaministiqua, the North West Company's new fort at the western end of Lake Superior built to replace Grand Portage, farther south, which by Jay's Treaty of 1794 had in 1796 fallen into American hands. His father wrote to him from Montreal:

[Mackenzie] *was presented to the king with his book & made a Knight of in consequence. So you must grease your boots & travel up to find the N. West Passage . . . & . . . come out with the title Lord Munro of the S. Sea.*

Needless to say, the advice went unheeded!

VIEW of the GRAND PORTAGE on LAKE SUPERIOR.

Fort Kaministiqua in 1815.

Thomas Douglas, Earl of Selkirk, was a Scottish philanthropist who in 1803 had settled some 800 dispossessed Scottish Highlanders on land he had purchased on Prince Edward Island. By 1808, he had decided that another good place for a settlement would be on the Red River, in what is now Manitoba. Since this area was within the lands draining into Hudson Bay, the region called Rupert's Land, he hit on the idea of buying up enough shares in the Hudson's Bay Company to be able to persuade its committee to grant him land for a settlement.

His initial partner in this venture was none other than Alexander Mackenzie. It is virtually inconceivable that Mackenzie realized Selkirk's motives, for the last thing he would have wanted was a settlement that would potentially hinder the collection of furs. But he assisted Selkirk in a series of transactions that bought up the Bay Company's shares in 1808.

It seems that Mackenzie's money was tied up in his business ventures in Canada and he could not quickly get at his capital. The attraction of Selkirk was that he had available money to use on such a project.

At this very time Mackenzie was still barraging the British government with his schemes; in March 1808 he submitted another proposal to Viscount Castlereagh, the British Secretary of State for War and the Colonies, in which he advanced a

Thomas Douglas, Earl of Selkirk.

> *system of exclusive privilege . . . in preference to urging the necessity of making such Military and Naval Establishments, with Expensive appointments, as would be absolutely necessary to protect an open and general Trade.*

He seems to have come to the conclusion (correctly) that the government was not going to spend a lot of money nor expend much in the way of resources, still having Napoleon to beat. So now he was proposing that the North West Company, which of course was, in his view,

> *the best calculated to execute the Plan here proposed[,] be granted the exclusive right of Trade in the Columbia and its tributary Waters, and along a certain extent of Coast for a given period.*

In addition, a "Licence of transit" would need to be granted for import and export through all ports on both coasts.

Mackenzie had heard of the Lewis and Clark expedition, despite the fact that it had only returned to St. Louis eighteen months before. He was concerned that the Americans would use their expedition as a reason to claim the Columbia for themselves,

it being evident from the exertions of the American Government, that it is their intention to claim under the right of the Discoveries of Captains Lewis and Clark . . . exclusive Privileges to the intermediate Country, as well as to the Coast Northward from the Spanish Boundary to the Latitude of 50.

He noted that these claims could be resisted because the whole of the Northwest Coast had been previously visited by the British – he was referring to Cook and Vancouver – and also "because I myself, [am] known to have been the first, who crossed thro' it [the intermediate territory] to the Columbia, and from the Columbia to the Pacific Ocean, in the year 1793." Mackenzie, of course, still thought that the Fraser was the Columbia.

Poor Mackenzie. It would be another two years before the British government got around to considering his somewhat modified plan, and even then no action would be taken.

By 1810 Mackenzie had realized that Selkirk was proposing a larger settlement than he could condone and turned to opposing him. On 30 May 1811 Selkirk's application for a land grant for his Red River Colony was submitted to the Hudson's Bay Company for approval. Mackenzie, assisted by other North West Company partners, tried hard to prevent the approval, but their efforts were in vain; Selkirk got his grant. The first settlers left Scotland in July and arrived at the new colony in August 1812. Mackenzie and his partners then tried to convince the Hudson's Bay Company directors to agree to a partition of the fur country between them, as advantageous to both companies, but again the proposal was rejected.

Mackenzie seems to have given up at this point, and no further trade proposals were made either to the Hudson's Bay Company or to the government. But seeds had been sown; in 1821, the year after

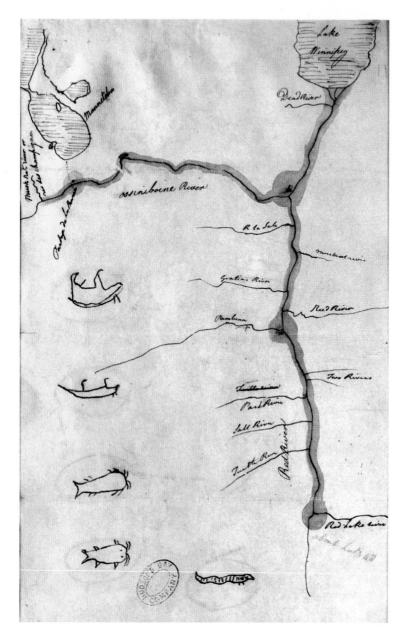

What Mackenzie strove to avoid: the map from the deed conveying land in the valleys of the Red and Assiniboine Rivers from native chiefs to Lord Selkirk, 18 July 1817. The animal figures are the chiefs' signatures.

Mackenzie's death, the North West Company and the Hudson's Bay Company did merge, under the name of the latter.

In 1812 Mackenzie married a young Geddes Mackenzie, from the same clan, but not related; he was forty-eight or fifty, she certainly only a teenager. At the same time Mackenzie purchased the estate of Avoch, on Moray Firth on the east coast of Scotland, which had belonged to Geddes' grandfather and which now belonged jointly to Geddes and her sister through an inheritance, her father having died three years previously. The pair settled down to a domestic life unlike anything Mackenzie had been used to. Thus Mackenzie retired and married at the same time.

Like many financially secure landowners at this time, the Mackenzies spent quite a lot of their time in London, where they had a townhouse. The couple had three children: a daughter, Margaret Geddes, born in 1816, and two sons, Alexander and George, born in 1818 and 1819.

But Mackenzie's happy domestic life was not to last, for his health was failing. In his last letter to his cousin Roderic, in January 1819, he wrote that he had "been overtaken with the consequences of my sufferings in the North West." Under doctor's orders he had become "a water drinker and milk sop," quite a change from his days in Montreal.

His symptoms were such that

the exercise of walking, particularly if uphill, brings on a headache, stupor, or dead pain which at once pervades the whole frame, attended with a listlessness and apathy.

What a depressing situation for one once so driven. Mackenzie's first biographer, Mark Wade, noted, "When he wrote that letter to his cousin, the grim reaper was even then lurking near at hand ready to cut him down while still a comparatively young man."

Early in 1820 he was strong enough to travel to Edinburgh to see his doctors, but on the return journey he was suddenly taken ill, and died before he could return to Avoch. It was 12 March 1820; Mackenzie was at most fifty-eight.

Mackenzie's company did not last long afterwards; not because of his death, for he was no longer actively involved in the running of the company, but from the merger, or rather take-over, of the North West Company, with its quarter share belonging to Sir Alexander Mackenzie and Company, by its longtime rival, the Hudson's Bay Company, in November 1821. Now the country first explored for commercial purposes by Mackenzie, the Mackenzie Valley and New Caledonia, would fall exclusively within the domain of the Hudson's Bay Company.

Here I had intended to place a photograph of Mackenzie's grave in Avoch, Scotland. But this image, of Mackenzie's portrait painted by Sir Thomas Lawrence and shown hanging in the National Gallery of Canada, is a much better monument to a man who influenced the shape of the country of Canada as it exists today. The National Gallery of Canada gave special permission for it to be used in this book.

Alexander Mackenzie was a hard-driving man, who expected others to work as hard as he did, if not harder, in pursuit of *his* objectives. In a letter to Roderic on the day of his departure from Fort Fork on his Pacific expedition he noted, "Alexr. Mackay [his second-in-command] desires his Compliments to you. I kept him so at work that he has no time to write you."

His single-mindedness in pursuit of a goal is illustrated nowhere better than during his two expeditions, and the Pacific one in particular, when he daily drove his men forward, often against their better judgment. And he clearly had strong leadership skills and a good ability to persuade others to the path he wished to take; he probably would have made an excellent modern chief executive officer.

He may not have been a very "nice" person; CEOs often aren't. The brouhaha surrounding his rift with Simon McTavish when he left Canada at the end of 1799 is an example. It seems Mackenzie left vowing revenge on McTavish for having crossed him, threatening to ruin his business and even uttering "some hints too extravagant to

This ninteenth-century Ordnance Survey map shows the area where Mackenzie lived after 1812. Avoch House is named; it is just northwest of the village of Avoch on the north shore of Moray Firth.

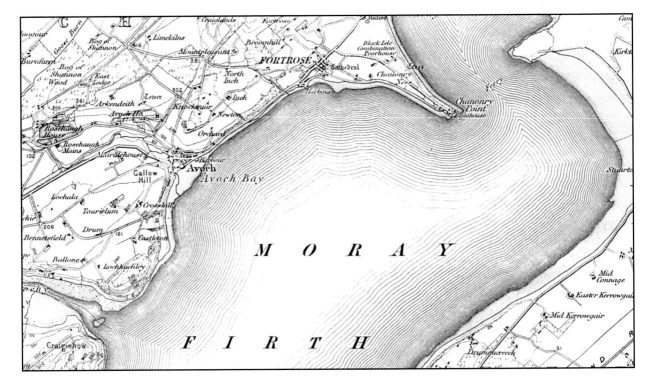

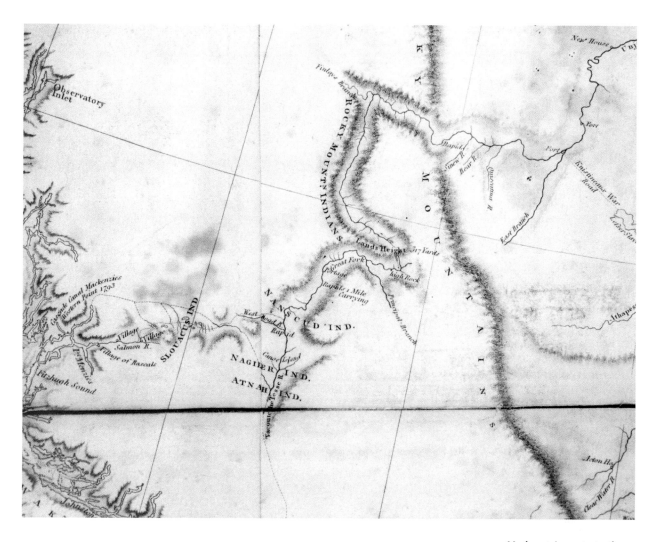

Mackenzie's route to the Pacific Ocean, as shown on Aaron Arrowsmith's map of North America, 1802.

imagine," whatever they were. Clearly McTavish was getting in the way of his vision of the way the company's business should be conducted, and he didn't like it.

Mackenzie was a man of enormous energy and resourcefulness. Never swerving from the path he wished to tread, he had a dominating personality, yet still was given to private moments of introspection and doubt, which he would confide to none but his closest associates and certainly never to the men he commanded.

But through his resolve and vision, he joined the Pacific coast to the rest of the country that would one day be called Canada.

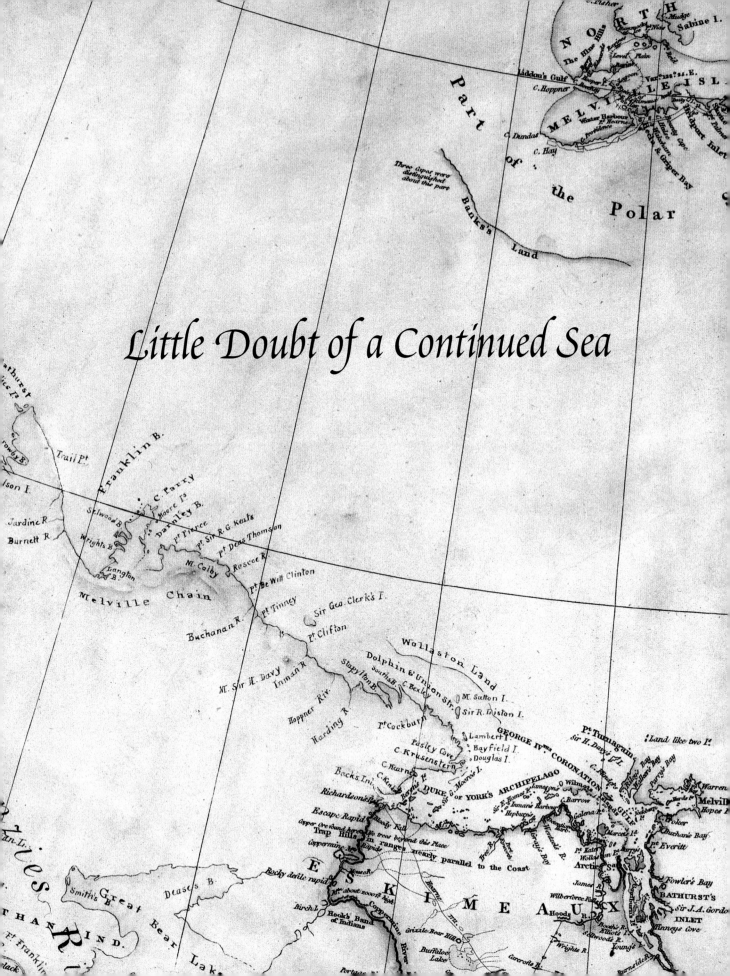

To amend the very defective geography
of the northern part of North America

Sir John Franklin.

Previous page: Part of Aaron Arrowsmith's map of North America, 1824 edition. This particular map belonged to the Hudson's Bay Company and is from its archives. As such, the printed map has been updated in pen and ink, and paper patches have been applied to change information. The Arctic coast in both directions from the mouth of the Mackenzie has been drawn in to reflect the new knowledge gained from John Franklin's expeditions.

*A*fter Alexander Mackenzie, the first European explorer to reach the shores of the Arctic Ocean was John Franklin, later to gain worldwide fame for being the subject of perhaps the most massive and long-lasting search for a missing explorer in the nineteenth century, if not ever. Franklin conducted two land expeditions before the ship-based search for the Northwest Passage that he is better known for, and which would lead to his demise in 1847.

His first land expedition was in 1819–22, instigated by the British government in an effort to map the unknown coast of the Arctic Ocean, to determine "the latitudes and longitudes of the Northern Coast of North America . . . to amend the very defective geography of the northern part of North America."

Franklin met with Mackenzie before he left on his first land expedition. In his book Franklin noted:

A short time before I left London I had the pleasure and advantage of an interview with the late Sir Alexander Mackenzie, who was one of the two persons [Hearne being the other] who had visited the coast we were to explore. He afforded me, in the most open and kind manner, much valuable information and advice.

Franklin and four others – surgeon John Richardson, midshipmen George Back and Robert Hood, and seaman John Hepburn – sailed into Hudson Bay on a company supply ship and landed at York Fort at the end of August 1819. From there they traveled to Cumberland House,

Mackenzie's Advice to John Franklin

In May 1819, before Franklin set off on the first of his two land expeditions to the Arctic, he met with Mackenzie to obtain his advice, the latter being then the only living person in Britain who had actually travelled overland to the Arctic. The following are extracts from the letter Mackenzie wrote to Franklin after the meeting. It is dated 21 May 1819.

Independent of your own Baggage & stores with the Quantity of Provision necessary for your Voyage you should have to embark in these Canoes pieces of Goods for Trade and Barter, Fishing tackling &c for fear you should by the Season or Accident be prevented arriving at the regular Establishments of either Company on your Route to Athabasca and should contain 5 Indian Guns, 1 Keg Powder, 1 Keg Balls, 2 Bag of Shot, 1 case with Iron work assorted i Roll of Twist Tobacco, two or three Bales of Dry Goods suitable to the Trade, and if you could provide yourself with shirts & some other Articles that are given to Men as Equipments it would be necessary as they are Articles which used to be scarce and not to be had in the Interior of the Country at the Season you may require them to give to the People that have to accompany you from Athabasca. I should have added to the above Articles a quantity of spirits . . .

In selecting your guide I wish you could fall in with my old Friend if alive Nestabeck commonly called the English Cheif, he would be invaluable as he was as I told you often in that Country. Presuming you have surmounted all your difficulties and reached the Sea at the discharge of the Copper Mine River –it will I think be absolutely necessary to find some of the Natives, say the Esquimaux, make your Peace with them & persuade some of them to accompany you along the Coast until they give you over to some of their Friends to the East. One of their Large Canoes, or their Womens Canoes, will carry your whole Party, and if they consent to allow some of their Wives and Children to embark it will secure the Men to you who of course will accompany you in their own small Canoe which fair all weather. Should you get to the Sea and could Establish this understanding with the Esquimaux I have no doubt of its being possible to succeed in that object of your ambition, as I am persuaded that the Nation are the same People, and have communication together along the Sea Coast from Hudson's Bay to Behrings Straits which may be and I suppose is interrupted by Ice at different Periods of the year.

If you can glean any thing from this that can assist you in the prosecution of your arduous undertaking it will be gratifying my anxious wish, as I feel earnestly interested in the results of your exertion under such perilous circumstances and believe me

Yours Most Sincerely
Alex Mackenzie

then to Fort Chipewyan. Franklin then found he was unable to acquire all the provisions he needed, because the rivalry between the Hudson's Bay Company and the North West Company had descended to open warfare and both were thus hard-pressed to feed themselves, let alone spare supplies for Franklin. He also was forced to pay a premium for his voyageurs, who were to prove very troublesome.

In July 1820 Franklin headed north to Great Slave Lake, where he persuaded a group of natives to accompany him as hunters and guides. Now, instead of descending the Mackenzie River, he tried to retrace Samuel Hearne's route (in reverse) to the Coppermine River. He found the Yellowknife River, which leads north from today's city of Yellowknife.

Midshipman George Back was quite an artist, and Franklin used his drawings and paintings to illustrate his own book. This one showed a Cree family.

By 19 August, the natives had had enough, feeling that it was too late in the season to continue north, and so Franklin stopped on the shores of a lake they called Winter Lake and built a winter camp, which was dubbed Fort Enterprise. It was not until 14 June the following year that they started north again. They descended the Coppermine River, the native group deserting Franklin as soon as Inuit country was reached, still fearing revenge for the attack that Samuel Hearne witnessed in 1771 (see page 30).

On 17 July 1821 Franklin reached the point where Hearne had first seen the Arctic Ocean exactly fifty years before, to the day. Here he named

Manner of Making a Resting Place on a Winter's Night, March 15th, 1820. This engraving from Franklin's book is after another drawing by George Back. All the details are here in this superb illustration.

the most conspicuous cape we then saw "Cape Hearne" as a just tribute to the memory of that persevering traveller. I distinguished another cape by the name of Mackenzie, in honour of Sir Alexander Mackenzie, the only other European who had before reached the Northern Ocean.

Franklin set out eastward to map the Arctic coastline, following his instructions; he mapped about 900 km or 550 miles of

coast before deciding to turn back. On 18 August, at his farthest east, he named Point Turnagain, writing that his

researches . . . favour the opinion of those who contend for a North-West Passage . . . The general line of the coast probably runs east and west . . . and I think there is little doubt of a continued sea.

He nearly didn't make it back. Ascending another river, named for Hood, he split his party, leaving a sick Robert Hood with surgeon John Richardson and John Hepburn and sending George Back ahead. Franklin made it to Fort Enterprise on 11 October, but the food had gone. Back had gone south to pursue the native group that had left them or, if that failed, to go to Fort Providence, a North West Company post 240 km or 150 miles south, in search of food. Then Richardson and Hepburn arrived with terrible news: one of the voyageurs had gone insane and shot Hood, perhaps to get rid of him because he was slowing the others down, or perhaps, as Richardson believed, to eat him. Richardson, in fear for his life and those of the others, had in turn shot the voyageur at the first opportunity.

In one of those episodes seemingly typical of nineteenth-century heroic British naval Arctic exploration, Franklin's party managed to survive at Fort Enterprise, boiling hides and scraping lichens, although three more voyageurs died, until 7 November, when Back arrived with food, having caught up with the natives he was pursuing south. With native help, the men were nursed back to health.

They eventually arrived back at York Fort in July 1822. Franklin had achieved his objective of mapping the Arctic coast, though at great cost, losing nine men. The book Franklin produced on his return to England was a big success, with his Gothic tale of hardship, death, and possible cannibalism being devoured by the public. Franklin and his publisher, needless to say, made a lot of money from the story, and Franklin was off to a good start in his career as a tragic hero.

In 1824 the British Admiralty, determined to settle the question of a northern Northwest Passage, had come up with a scheme to resolve the doubt, involving several simultaneous expeditions. Edward Parry, already the veteran of two maritime attempts to find the Northwest Passage, was to attempt to sail through Lancaster Sound; George

Lyon, Parry's sometime second-in-command, was to go to Repulse Bay, and then strike out overland for Franklin's easternmost point, Point Turnagain. Franklin was to again go overland, but this time he was to descend the Mackenzie River to the Arctic Ocean, then go westward to meet with a fourth expedition, that of Frederick William Beechey, another officer who had sailed with Parry. Beechey was to go north through Bering Strait, then eastward to meet Franklin.

Determined to prevent a recurrence of the disaster that beset Franklin on his first expedition, the Admiralty this time provided large quantities of food; the route was carefully planned using maps derived from Mackenzie's expedition, and food caches were made along the route. Four specially made boats were constructed, waterproof clothing was supplied, and the party was to include British marines and sailors to avoid disciplinary problems with voyageurs, such as the extreme example on Franklin's first expedition.

As a result, the preparations took a year. An advance party built a wintering post on the shores of Great Bear Lake even before Franklin left England. This was Fort Franklin, which was the name of the modern community until 1993, when it was changed to Déline.

Franklin left Fort Chipewyan on 25 July and took four day to get to Great Slave Lake. Like Mackenzie, Franklin had weather problems on the lake. He wrote:

We were detained . . . by a strong south-west gale; and even when we embarked, the wind and waves were still high, but time was too precious to allow of our waiting.

They started up the Mackenzie River on 3 August, traveling fast – so fast that one night they didn't even stop to sleep in order to take advantage of a following wind. By 14 August they were, wrote Franklin,

gratified by the delightful prospect of the shore suddenly diverging, and a wide space of open water to the northward, which we doubted not would prove to be the sea.

That day the water, Franklin noted, was entirely fresh, but he had read Mackenzie; the next day a tide pole was put up when they

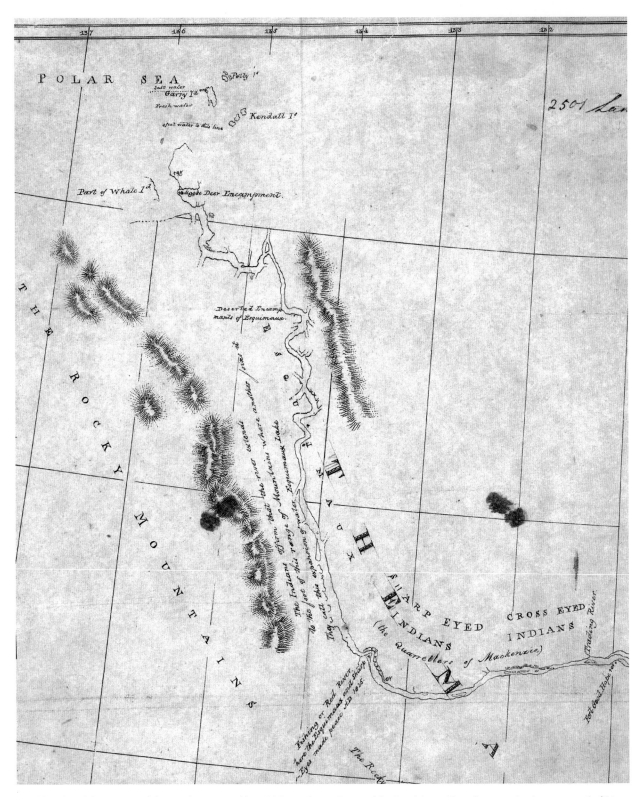

Franklin's hand-drawn map of the northern part of his 1825 expedition, *Route of the Land Arctic Expedition under the command of Lieut. J. Franklin R.N. from Great Bear Lake River to the Polar Sea. Surveyed and Drawn by Mr. E. A. Kendall R.N. Assistant Surveyor,* 1825.

landed for the night and they "perceived the water to rise about three inches." The next morning they

pulled across a line of strong ripple which marked the termination of the fresh water; that on the seawrd side being brackish; and in the further progress of three miles to the [Garry] island, we had the indescribable pleasure of finding the water decidedly salt.

It was 16 August 1825. They had reached the Mackenzie Delta fully a month later than Mackenzie, but Franklin did not have to retrace his steps that season.

By coincidence Franklin had landed on Mackenzie's Whale Island, which he named after his "much-esteemed friend Mr. Garry, the Deputy Governor of the [Hudson's Bay] Company." He also named Pelly Island, which was within sight, after the Governor of the Company "for his earnest endeavours to promote the progress and welfare of the Expedition."

It had taken Franklin only fourteen days to descend the Mackenzie River from Great Slave Lake to Garry Island, exactly the same time it had taken Mackenzie.

Franklin's complete party of fifty-one people spent the winter at Fort Franklin. The next season two parties set out: one under Franklin would push westward to attempt to rendezvous with Beechey; while the other, under John Richardson, would go eastward to connect with their previous survey at the mouth of the Coppermine River.

Franklin made it to a place he called Return Reef, near today's Prudhoe Bay, which was within 250 km or 160 miles of where Captain Beechey and the *Blossom* waited for him at Point Barrow. The latter place was named after John Barrow, the Second Secretary of the Admiralty, who was for forty years the guiding light and chief promoter of the British naval effort to navigate the Northwest Passage. It was 16 August 1826; Beechey waited until 26 August and then retreated.

The survey of the Mackenzie made on this Expedition differs very little in its outline from that of its discoverer, whose general correctness we had often occasion to admire. We had, indeed, to alter the latitude and longitude of some of its points, which he most probably laid down from magnetic bearings only; and it is proper to remark, that in comparing our magnetic bearing with his, throughout the whole course of the river, they were found to be about fifteen degrees more easterly; which may, therefore, be considered as the amount of increase in variation since 1789.

– John Franklin, August 1825, from Narrative of a Second Expedition to the Shores of the Polar Sea, in the Years 1825, 1826, and 1827 (1828)

The gap in geographic knowledge for the coast between Return Reef and Point Barrow would be filled in 1837 by two Hudson's Bay Company traders, Peter Dease (who had been with Franklin on his second expedition) and Thomas Simpson.

Richardson meanwhile went eastward to the mouth of the Coppermine and successfully made his way back to Fort Franklin. Between them, Franklin and Richardson had mapped 2 400 km or 1,500 miles of coast. After overwintering again at Fort Franklin, they finally reached England again in September 1827. Unlike Mackenzie, Franklin had worked on his account of his travels while overwintering at Fort Franklin, and his book was published the next year.

The exploration of the last major river flowing into the Arctic Ocean was achieved in 1833 and 1834 by George Back, Franklin's lieutenant, in an expedition originally conceived to search for John Ross, whose ship was presumed lost while searching westward for the Northwest Passage and had been gone since 1829.

The river was the Back, named after the explorer; at the time it was called the Great Fish River, or Thlew-ee-choh. It was accessible through a maze of lakes and rivers from the eastern end of Great Slave Lake, and was supposed to, as Pierre Berton so eloquently put it, "wriggle through the Precambrian schists of the naked tundra" to Chantry Inlet, itself only about 250 km or 150 miles, from the northwesternmost extension of Hudson Bay, Wager Bay. The latter had been explored by sea from the east by Christopher Middleton in 1742.

Back and nineteen others descended the Great Fish River in 1834. It was not an easy river; Back counted no less than eighty-three falls or rapids in its course. Back recorded that it had a "violent and tortuous course . . . running through an iron-ribbed country without a single tree on the whole line of its banks." The expedition did not continue beyond Chantry Inlet, for by this time Back knew Ross had been found, and he was himself running short of supplies; Back returned to England the following year. Like Mackenzie and Franklin, Back produced a book about his exploits, feeding an increasingly ravenous British public appetite for things Arctic.

In 1837 Hudson's Bay Company men Peter Warren Dease and Thomas Simpson connected the map from the westernmost point reached by Franklin to Point Barrow, completing an initial mapping of the coastline from the Mackenzie west to the Pacific, a route to that ocean Mackenzie himself had at one point considered. Simpson wrote that he had the honor of "uniting the Arctic to the great Western Ocean." In 1838 and 1839 Simpson and Dease explored the coast east of the easternmost point Franklin had reached in 1826, his Point Turnagain. They saw and named Victoria Island after the new queen and in 1839 found the mouth of Back's Great Fish River, even finding one of his food caches. They went a little farther and were now on the western side of the Boothia Peninsula; had the latter been an island instead of a peninsula, they would probably have made it through to previously explored territory and thus have had the distinction of filling in the final gap in the true Northwest Passage.

As it was, they had completed the map of the major part of Canada's Arctic coastline. Simpson wanted to try again, to close the final gap in the Northwest Passage, but when traveling to England to press his case with the committee of the Hudson's Bay Company in the summer of 1840, he was killed somewhere in the Dakotas under circumstances that are still mysterious to this day.

The final link in the Northwest Passage was made by Robert McClure, on foot, after his ship had become trapped in the ice at Mercy Bay, on the north coast of Banks Island. He had sailed through Bering Strait, around Alaska, in 1850 and spent another three years trapped in the ice before being rescued by Lieutenant Bedford Pim from the *Resolute,* one of several British ships anchored at the western end of Lancaster Sound that had approached the passage from the east. McClure was able to abandon his ship and make his way by sledge to the other ships, thus becoming the first to conquer the Northwest Passage.

PARSONS DEL.

To Seize All We Possessed

To the waters which flow
on the other Side of the Mountain

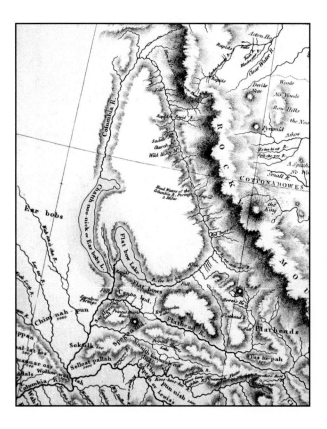

Above: Part of an Aaron Arrowsmith map dated 1811. The puzzle of the river systems on the west flank of the Rocky Mountains has nearly been solved.

Previous page: Fort Astoria, the post at the mouth of the Columbia established in 1811 by John Jacob Astor's Pacific Fur Company and taken over by the North West Company in 1813.

When Alexander Mackenzie, fresh from his Pacific expedition, was at Grand Portage in August 1794, Duncan McGillivray, William's younger brother, was also there, in his capacity as a clerk. Although there is no record of any conversation between the two, it surely took place, and this may have been from where the younger McGillivray would date his own interest in penetration to the Pacific. At any rate, seven years later he would make the attempt to cross the Rockies.

After 1800 Simon McTavish developed several strategies for combating the new organized competition from Mackenzie's New North West or XY Company in Montreal, as well at that from the Hudson's Bay Company. One was to establish a post on Charlton Island in Hudson Bay, a short-lived challenge to the English company's monopoly; Fort St. Andrews was built there in September 1803.

Another strategy was to try to find a practical trade route overland to the Pacific. Duncan McGillivray was put in charge of the project, and with David Thompson as his clerk, he wintered at the newly built Rocky Mountain House on the Saskatchewan River. The pair arrived in October 1800 complete with a copy of George Vancouver's recently published *Voyage of Discovery to the North Pacific Ocean,* which certainly depicted the Pacific coast more or less correctly, and in its correct location longitudinally.

Some initial reconnaisance was carried out immediately; the early hope was that the North Saskatchewan River would provide a route through to the Columbia River, which was shown on Vancouver's map as far as William Broughton, Vancouver's second-in-command, had

The Columbia River, from a nineteenth-century print.

surveyed it, which was to Point Vancouver, later the site of Fort Vancouver, across the river from Portland.

But McGillivray became ill with rheumatism and was unable to cross the mountains; he appointed James Hughes, in charge of Rocky Mountain House, to go instead. Thompson and Hughes set out on 6 June 1801 with horses, voyageurs, and native guides. But they did not manage to make it over the Divide that year. Thompson's guide, not wanting trade developed with other tribes on the west side of the mountains – trade his tribe was currently involved in – was uncooperative, and the voyageurs, facing difficulties, were unable to be persuaded to go on. Thompson figured out that they needed to start earlier, when there was less water cascading from the Rockies, and intended to try again the next year. "Whoever wishes to cross the Mountains for the Purposes of Commerce," he wrote in a letter to William and Duncan McGillivray,

ought to employ a Canoe, & start early in the Spring . . . the Water . . . being low & the Current not half so violent as in the Summer; then there are Beaches all the way, either on one Side or the other of the River even in the Mountains, by which people may track on the Shore where the Pole cannot well be used. In this Season, they would cross a great Part of the Mountains without any extraordinary Difficulty, and meet the Flushes of high Water where they would have need of it, that is, near the Head of the River – from whence there is said to be a short Road to the waters which flow on the other Side of the Mountain.

Alexander Mackenzie referred to these 1800–1801 westward attempts in a letter to John Sullivan, the British Under-Secretary of State for War and the Colonies, written on 25 October 1802.

An attempt had been made by one of the Partners of the old Fur Company to penetrate in a more Southern direction than I did to the river Columbia in which he failed through ill health; a second attempt has been made by another Partner of the same concern [James Hughes, sent by Duncan McGillivray] *with no better success, owing to a Mutiny of the men employed, arrising as I Judge from the Want of the appropriate Talent for such an undertaking in the leader.*

Supporting his own long-held view was David Thompson: "The Astronomer who went upon both expeditions declares Positively that the object [a trade route through the mountains] is not impracticable."

The next year, 1802, saw the North West Company cutting costs, as they were finding the competition with Mackenzie's company difficult, so Rocky Mountain House was shut down and Thompson reassigned to the Peace River. In 1804 Thompson was made a partner in the North West Company and the same year the two Montreal concerns merged, following the death of Simon McTavish. Now there was renewed interest in opening up new fur regions west of the Rockies. Simon Fraser was to concentrate on the northern region, on what is now central British Columbia, and Thompson was to set up a fur trade network to the south. Searching for a practicable route to the Pacific, both would reach the ocean, but both would be beaten by an American expedition led by Meriwether Lewis and William Clark.

From the United States by Land –
Meriwether Lewis and William Clark, 1804–1806

American president Thomas Jefferson's Corps of Discovery – the Lewis and Clark expedition – has almost become part of the American national psyche. It was the second expedition to make it to the Pacific north of Mexico, and not, as has often been stated, the first, which was of course Mackenzie's.

It was different from the Canadian efforts in that its motives were first and foremost political: to establish a claim to territory beyond the Louisiana Purchase and perhaps to a Pacific outlet. But while claiming to the world that it was a scientific expedition, Jefferson secretly emphasized the potential commercial benefits to Congress, the first of which was for an American fur trade.

Quite unlike the efforts of the North West Company, the Lewis and Clark expedition was an immense logistical exercise, and technically a

Above: Meriwether Lewis.

Left: William Clark.

military one at that, involving years of planning, forty-five men, and 1 600 kg or 3,500 pounds of supplies, initially in four boats. The expedition left Camp Dubois, upstream of St. Louis, on 14 May 1804, wintering at Fort Mandan in what is now North Dakota. They carried with them a copy of Mackenzie's book, including its maps, which had been specially acquired for them by Jefferson.

Lewis and Clark spent four months finding a tortuous route through the Rocky Mountains.

In an interesting parallel with the experience of Mackenzie on the Fraser River, Lewis and Clark at one point in August 1805 found themselves at the Salmon River, which Clark named Lewis's River, which was impassable according to native report. This turbulent river is today sometimes referred to as the "River of No Return"; thrill-seeking rafters speed downriver, but never up. As a result, Lewis and Clark were forced to travel overland, though in their case on horses borrowed from the Shoshone. Waterborne again, they followed the Columbia downstream from its confluence with the Snake, finally reaching the mouth of the Columbia on 3 December 1805.

Arrowsmith's map of 1802 shows the information Lewis and Clark had about their route to the Pacific. Mackenzie's route was shown (north of this section), and the coast was that of George Vancouver's survey, published in 1798. The Columbia is surveyed to Point Vancouver (near Portland); everything else is tentative.

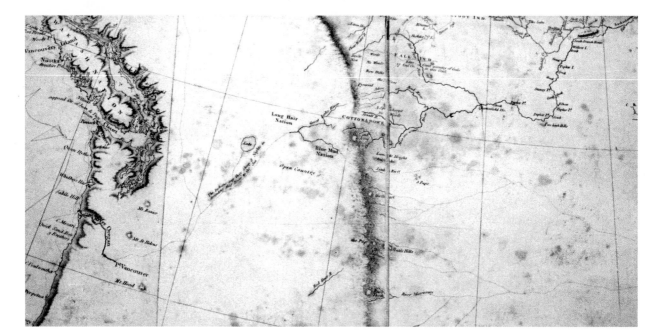

In an unmistakable emulation of Mackenzie, Clark carved into a pine tree on the banks of the Columbia the words "Capt William Clark December 3rd 1805. By Land. U. States in 1804–1805."

A temporary post was built, Fort Clatsop, on the banks of a small river flowing into the south side of the Columbia estuary near Astoria, where they remained until March 1806. That Lewis and Clark reached the mouth of the Columbia before British or Canadian explorers was to have immense ramifications for American sovereignty in the region. One wonders what Mackenzie, from Canada by land, would have thought of this, from the United States by land. There is, alas, no record.

This River, Therefore, Is Not the Columbia
– Simon Fraser, 1806–1808

At the same time that the Lewis and Clark expedition reached the mouth of the Columbia, Simon Fraser, who had been instructed to do the same thing, was camped near the wrong river, unable to proceed from lack of supplies.

Simon Fraser had become a partner in the North West Company in 1801 and had extensive experience in the Athabasca country; he had been chosen to head the operations of the North West Company west of the Rockies on McTavish's death in 1804. His plan, following his instructions, was to go up the Peace River in the footsteps of Mackenzie, establish trading posts west of the mountains, and trace the Columbia River, which the upper Fraser was still thought to be, to its mouth.

In the fall of 1805 Fraser went up the Peace River and established a post at Rocky Mountain Portage, at the bottom of the Peace River Canyon, near today's Hudson's Hope, B.C. Fraser, who had a copy of Mackenzie's map with him, then continued up the Peace and, branching southward, followed Mackenzie's route up the Parsnip. However, while pushing up the Parsnip, Fraser found a river Mackenzie had missed, which the next time he reached this point, on 5 June 1806, he would attribute to Mackenzie

Simon Fraser.

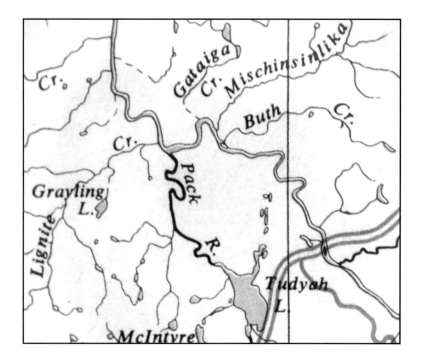

This 1959 map shows the Pack River connecting the Parsnip with Tudyah Lake, which in turn connects to McLeod Lake (Fraser's Trout Lake) and Summit Lake and a much easier route across the Continental Divide; it is close to the route followed today by Highway 97. The confluence of the Pack and the Parsnip is today under Lake Williston, behind the W.A.C. Bennett Dam.

taking a nap. This was the Pack River, a small river that joined the Parsnip about 12 km or 7½ miles north of the present-day bridge that carries Highway 97 over the Parsnip River. The Pack led to Tudyah Lake and then to McLeod Lake, and would soon be found to provide a much easier route across the Divide, continuing south along the Crooked River to Summit Lake, and to the Fraser River first via the Salmon River and later via the Giscome Portage.

It seems that Fraser may only have had his attention called to the Pack River by a chance encounter with a group of natives who knew about it. In a letter to his partners written at Stuart Lake in August 1806, he noted:

Before our arrival at the height of land, we found a small band of Indians that had never seen white people before, they seemed quite peaceable and industrious. They informed us of another Road that lead[s] into the Columbia [which river he thought the Fraser to be], which is much shorter and more safe than the one we came by. It falls in a little below the Knights [Mackenzie's] first encampment on the Columbia [Fraser]. It is a fine navigable River, with no great current[,] and report says that there is only a carrying place of about a couple of miles at most . . . It will be the means of avoiding the Bad River [James Creek].

At the end of 1805 Fraser built a post on the shores of McLeod Lake that he called Trout Lake Post; it was the first permanent European settlement west of the Rockies in what is now British Columbia. Fraser left three men to winter there and returned to Rocky Mountain Portage. The men deserted the post during the winter and also returned to Rocky Mountain Portage. One of Fraser's men, sent to investigate, carried out a notable reconnaissance early in 1806; James McDougall penetrated to Stuart Lake, where Fraser later that year established another post, Fort St. James. McDougall had determined from the natives that the Nechako River, which connects with the river flowing out of Stuart Lake, joined the "Columbia" – the Fraser – but Fraser, not yet knowing this, in 1806 followed Mackenzie's route across the Divide via Arctic, Portage, Pacific, and the unnamed lake, and down his "Bad River" (James Creek) to get to the river he had been instructed to descend. In so doing, Fraser spent a week getting down James Creek, a descent equally as difficult as Mackenzie's had been thirteen years before.

From Fort St. James, Fraser intended to begin his descent of the Fraser River, but a shortage of food and other supplies changed his mind. He wrote that "it would have been little short of madness to attempt going down the Columbia in a starving state, without an ounce of any kind of provisions."

An aerial photograph from 1929 showing the confluence of the Pack River (flowing from the south, at the bottom of this photograph) and the Parsnip (flowing right to left). Unless the pattern of mudbanks and islands was radically different in 1793, Mackenzie would have looked straight up the Pack from his position on the Parsnip. But the main stream is clearly the continuation of the Parsnip itself, and if Mackenzie was taking a nap (as Fraser maintained), his men would as normal have kept to the main stream lacking any other instruction. Simon Fraser, on the other hand, knew from native information to look for the Pack.

It was not until much later, the fall of 1807, that fresh men and supplies would arrive from east of the mountains. Fraser then established another trading post, Fort George (later Prince George), at the confluence of the Nechako and the Fraser, and by the spring of 1808 he was ready to begin his expedition down the Fraser River.

His party was twenty-four in number: nineteen voyageurs; two clerks, John Stuart and Jules Quesnel; two natives; and Fraser himself. They embarked in four canoes from Fort George on 28 May 1808. Later the same day they passed the West Road River on their right, the place from which Mackenzie had left the river to go overland, and three days later they passed the point at which Mackenzie had turned back upriver.

Fraser found no reason to criticize Mackenzie's decision not to proceed farther south than Alexandria; his epic voyage was a continuous set of rapids, impassable water, and portages around them that were often just as difficult. On 9 June, at French Bar Canyon, Fraser wrote in his journal:

Here channel contracts to about forty yards, and is inclosed by two precipices of great heighth, which bending towards each other make it narrower above than below. The water which rolls down this extraordinary passage in tumultuous waves and with great velocity had a tremendous appearance. It being absolutely impossible to carry the canoes by land, yet sooner than to abandon them, all hands without hesitation embarked, as it were a corp perdu [à corps perdu, recklessly] *upon the mercy of this Stygian tide. Once engaged, the die was cast, and the great difficulty consisted of keeping the canoes in the* [current]. . . *clear of the precipice on one side, and of the gulphs formed by the waves on the other. However, thus skimming along like lightening, the crews cool and determined, followed each other in awful silence. And* [when] *we arrived at the end we stood gazing on our narrow escape from perdition.*

On 15 June, just below Lillooet, Fraser had his first hint that the river he was on might not be the Columbia when natives drew a map for him. They "drew at my request," Fraser wrote,

a chart of the Country below this to the sea. By this sketch the navigation seems still very bad, and dificult. At some distance to the East appears another large river which runs parallel to this to the sea.

This was the real Columbia.

Fraser passed the Thompson River on 20 June, naming it after his fellow partner David Thompson, whom he supposed had built a post, Kootenae House, farther upstream. In fact the post was on the Columbia. In a nice historical tit-for-tat, it would be Thompson who would later name the Fraser River, the river that Fraser had shown not to be the Columbia.

The going got worse. Now the Fraser Canyon had to be traversed. Impossible for the canoes, the country was almost impossible by foot, for "hanging rocks, and projecting cliffs at the edge of the bank made the passage so small as to render it difficult even for one person to pass sideways at times." Sections had native-made steps like ladders and were strung with tree boughs as railings. On 26 June Fraser penned his often-quoted lines that nevertheless bear repetition:

I have been for a long period among the Rocky Mountains, but have never seen anything equal to this country, for I cannot find words to describe our situation at times. We had to pass where no human being should venture.

Eventually they made it out of the canyon, and on 30 June they emerged into the lower Fraser Valley. Two days later Fraser took the north arm of the river and "at last . . . came in sight of a gulph or bay of the sea . . . On our right we noticed a village called by the Natives Misquiame [Musqueam]," where they landed. It was 2 July; it had taken Fraser thirty-six days to travel from Fort George.

The reception Fraser received from the natives was recorded by him as unfriendly and threatening. That night they camped "within 6 miles of the Chief's village." If Fraser had any doubts that they had reached the sea, these were soon dispelled, for "they were not long in bed before the tide rushed upon the beds and roused them up." An interesting contrast to Mackenzie's arrival on the Arctic coast!

Fraser wanted to sight the "main ocean," which he thought was very close, but had to make do with the Strait of Georgia, as he judged that it would be unwise to proceed any farther due to concerns about the natives. He recorded that "here I must . . . acknowledge my great

Hell's Gate in the Fraser Canyon, much as Fraser would have encountered it. This photograph was taken in 1913, before a slide caused by the construction of the Canadian Northern Railway. Unfortunately, the relatively long exposures required of early photography mean that the churning waters of the river appear placid when they are anything but.

A native canoe lies beached
on a riverbank in the upper
part of the lower Fraser Valley
in this late-nineteenth-century
photograph.

disappointment in not seeing the main ocean, having gone so near it as
to be almost within view." Like Mackenzie before him, he had discovered
that the coastline of the Northwest is highly indented; Mackenzie also
did not see the "main ocean."

But then in his journal he records his main and most significant
finding:

*The latitude is 49° nearly, while that of the entrance to the Columbia is
46° 20´. This River, therefore, is not the Columbia.*

Though a negative conclusion that must have been bitterly dis-
appointing to Fraser after all his trials and tribulations, it was an important finding. Not only was this river not the Columbia, it was clearly

impracticable as an alternative route to the sea. Fraser's clerk Jules Quesnel summed it up: "This journey did not meet the needs of the Company and will never be of any advantage to them, this river not being navigable." From now on the North West Company knew that it must find the Columbia and a practical route for trade elsewhere.

The Great Geographer – David Thompson, 1806–1811

At the North West Company's summer rendezvous at Fort William in 1806, it was decided that David Thompson would lead an expedition to cross the Rockies and set up a fur trade network initially with the Kootenais, who lived just west of the Divide. This was to the south of the network Simon Fraser was to establish.

In the summer of 1807 Thompson crossed the Rockies through Howse Pass (named after his Hudson's Bay Company counterpart, Joseph Howse) to the headwaters of the Columbia, which he called the Kootenae River. Over the next four years, he found the routes and sites for posts that would add a Columbia department to the regions of the North West Company.

He explored and mapped three routes: from Rocky Mountain House to Kootenae House through Howse Pass, from the Columbia headwaters to Kullyspel House and Saleesh House on Clark Fork River, and overland from Pend Oreille Lake to Spokane House. These "houses" were fur-trading posts set up by Thompson to receive furs from the new region. It seems that by 1809, any urgency to follow the Columbia to the sea had disappeared, for he later wrote:

1809. The Partners of the Coy. allow of no further Discoveries but only trading posts upon a small scale, and I have means for nothing else.

But this situation was to change suddenly the next year.

In 1810, Thompson was on his way east to a well-deserved furlough – "going down on rotation," as was the practise of North West Company wintering partners – and reached Rainy Lake on his way to Fort William and Montreal. There he heard about John Jacob Astor's efforts to reach the mouth of the Columbia first. "The critical situation

The Hudson's Bay Company Crosses the Mountains

Howse Pass, the spectacular pass through the Rockies now in Jasper National Park at the headwaters of the North Saskatchewan River, was named after Joseph Howse, one of the best-educated of the explorers, who was later to write books on native language grammar. He was exploring potential routes across the Rockies for the Hudson's Bay Company, and hot on Thompson's heels, Howse journeyed into and across the mountains in 1809 and 1810–11.

Although he too found the Columbia, in 1810 near present-day Golden, B.C., Howse made no attempt to follow the river to the sea and instead went upstream and built a trading post in opposition to one of Thompson's.

Howse has probably not been given due credit for his contribution to geographical knowledge, as he was not given any instruments for fixing his position, had not "laid down his track" on a map, and his journals and letters are all missing.

One of the company's most seasoned explorers, Howse was the only Hudson's Bay man to find his way through the Rockies prior to the merging of that Company with the North West Company in 1821; all other penetrations to the Pacific slope were by Nor'Westers.

of our affairs in the Columbia [department] obliged me to return," he wrote in a letter, the only surviving document.

It has often been assumed that Thompson was instructed to get to the mouth of the Columbia before Astor's men, but he also transported trade goods west, which surely would have been left for others to bring had this been the case. Thompson's journals for this period are missing.

To avoid natives who did not want him to take guns and other trade goods to their enemies across the mountains, Thompson this time decided to try another route farther to the north, the Athabasca Pass, crossing the Rockies at today's Jasper, Alberta. Thompson crossed in December 1810 and January 1811, in the middle of winter. He spent the rest of the winter at Boat Encampment, right at the northern bend of the Columbia, which he named because it was here that he and his men, with considerable difficulty, built a new canoe with which to continue their expedition. Thompson now knew he was on the Columbia, but since he did not know the terrain below that point, he continued along the routes he already knew: *up* the Columbia, across Canal Flats to the Kootenay River, to the Pend Oreille River, and across to Spokane House on the Spokane River.

The Spokane was unnavigable below Spokane House, so Thompson went north to the Colville River and emerged at the confluence of that river with the Columbia on 19 June 1811. Now he was on the Columbia again and only had to follow it to the sea.

Thompson now made a habit of stopping at every native encampment to introduce himself: "smoking with the Natives," as he put it. This was to ensure that when he came back up the river, slower, against the current, he would meet a friendly reception.

On 9 July he was at the Snake River, which Thompson recognized as Lewis and Clark's Lewis's River, and which he called the Shawpatin. Thompson had Lewis's calculation of the latitude of this point in his notebook, taken from Patrick Gass' published journal. Gass was one of Meriwether Lewis' men; his journal was published before that of Lewis. Following the custom, here he

erected a small Pole with half sheet of Paper well tied about it, with these words on it: Know hereby that this Country is claimed by Great Britain as part of it's Territories and that the NW Company of Merchants from Canada, finding the Factory for this People inconvenient for them, do hereby intend to erect a Factory in this Place for the Commerce of the Country around. D. Thompson. Junction of the Shawpatin River with the Columbia, July 8th, 1811.

Continuing downstream, on 10 July he noted, "Heard news of the American Ship's arrival." At this point Thompson probably realized that the Americans had beaten him to it, but he makes no comment on the fact in his journal, which suggests that he was not concerned about priority.

On 15 July 1811, after many delays, Thompson reached Astoria. But a fort was already built and the Stars and Stripes flew above it. Thompson's journal entry for that day records simply:

At 1 Pm, thank God for our safe arrival, we came to the House of Mr Astors Company – Messrs McDougall, Stuart & Stuart – who received me in the most polite Manner, & here we hope to stay a few days to refresh ourselves.

Gabriel Franchère, one of Astor's Pacific Fur Company men, recorded the event in his journal this way:

Toward midday, we saw a large canoe, carrying a flag . . . We did not know who it could be, for we did not yet expect our own men [an overland party led by Wilson Price Hunt]. *The flag she bore was the British, and her crew was composed of nine boatmen in all. A well-dressed man, who appeared to be the commander, was the first to leap ashore; and addressing us without ceremony, he said that his name was David Thompson, and that he was one of the partners of the North West Company.*

Franchère also commented that

Mr. Thompson had kept a regular journal and had traveled, it seemed to me, more like a geographer than a fur trader. He was provided with a sextant, and . . . had an opportunity to make several astronomical observations.

Cape Horn, on the Columbia, in an 1880 engraving.

Despite not arriving before the Americans, Thompson had finally found and mapped what Mackenzie had been seeking but not found: a *navigable* route through the Rocky Mountains to the Pacific Ocean. It was a route that would be followed by many, right up to the completion of the Canadian Pacific Railway in 1885.

Thus the Gentlemen of the North West Company Took Over Astoria

In 1810, John Jacob Astor had determined to establish a trading post at the mouth of the Columbia River so as to enable furs from the Pacific slope and beyond to be shipped out by sea. To achieve this objective, he organized two separate groups, one to go by ship round Cape Horn and another to strike out overland.

The first group, which included Alexander Mackay, who had been Mackenzie's trusted second-in-command in 1793, arrived on the *Tonquin* in March 1811 and established the trading post of Astoria the following month. The overland expedition was led by Wilson Price Hunt, who canoed and portaged from Montreal, leaving Lachine on 2 July 1810 and arriving at an already established Astoria on 15 February 1812, having crossed the continent in nineteen and a half months. It was the second American overland expedition to reach the Columbia, though starting from Montreal.

In April 1813 the North West Company's John George McTavish reached Astoria with nineteen voyageurs. He expected that the ship *Isaac Todd* was to arrive shortly with supplies for them. But the ship did not arrive, and McTavish's men were supplied by the Astorians, enabling them to leave again for the interior in July.

In September of the same year the men of the Pacific Fur Company at Astoria were surprised to see one of their canoes recently departed return in the company of two canoes bearing British flags. The British canoes were those of the North West Company bearing John McTavish and Angus Bethune. These were express canoes, and had gone ahead of eight others containing furs. McTavish now showed the Astorians a letter confirming that their ship the *Isaac Todd* was en route but was now in company with the frigate *Phoebe,* with orders from the British government to seize the post, "represented to the

Lords of the Admiralty," as Gabriel Franchère wrote in his journal, "as being an important colony founded by the American government."

The Astorians had learned of the war between Britain and the United States in January 1813, but now it was to affect them more directly. Although working for an American company, most of the Astorians were British subjects. What happened next is again related by Franchère:

As the season advanced and their ship did not arrive, the Northwesters found themselves in a very disagreeable situation, without food and without merchandise with which to bargain with the natives. The Indians, in turn, regarded them with distrust. They had good hunters but lacked ammunition; and finally, disgusted at having to ask us constantly for food, they proposed that they buy our establishment and its contents.

Situated as we were, expecting from day to day the arrival of an English man-of-war to seize all we possessed, we listened to their proposition. We held several consultations, and the negotiations between us extended over a long period. At length the price of the goods and furs in the establishment was agreed upon, and the bargain was signed by both parties on October 23, 1813.

Thus the gentlemen of the North West Company took over Astoria . . . [and] I lost in a moment all my hopes of fortune.

Fort Astoria.

Thus was Mackenzie's scheme of having coastal fur-trading posts finally achieved. Here at last was a North West Company post at the mouth of the Columbia River, the river Mackenzie thought he was on when he traveled the upper Fraser River in 1793, and one of the primary thrusts of the trade policies advocated by him since his return from his Pacific expedition.

In fact it was the British corvette *Racoon,* which had joined the other ships at Rio de Janeiro, which made it first to the Columbia. That ship's captain, William Black, was irritated to find that Astoria was already under British control and on 1 December 1813 insisted on cermonially seizing the fort, smashing a bottle of Madeira wine across the flagstaff flying the British flag and renaming the post Fort George.

This act, being one of seizure rather than purchase, was later to be used by the Americans to advance their case for American sovereignty over the area, achieved in 1846. Thus did the British establishment of a post at the mouth of the Columbia finally become an American one, confirming Mackenzie's concerns first voiced so long before.

Notes

Mackenzie's own journals and letters are the source for most information. Others are given below. References are to page numbers.

Abbreviations used:

BCA – British Columbia Archives, Victoria
HBCA – Hudson's Bay Company Archives, Winnipeg
NAC – National Archives of Canada, Ottawa
PRO – Public Record Office, London
UBC – University of British Columbia, Vancouver

21   The first mapping of the coast of British Columbia was by the Spaniard Juan Pérez in 1774.

22–23 Quote about Henry Kelsey is from Rich, 1958, Vol. 1, p. 296.

39   Mackenzie's year of birth: emigrant record according to Gough, 1997; grandson according to Bryce, 1906; sister's descendants according to Lamb, 1970.

41   Quote is from Bryce, 1906, p. 11.

53   Pond quote is from the journal *Connecticut Magazine*.

55   The Frobisher petition is in PRO CO 42/47 ff. 317–18.

55   Pond memorial is in PRO CO 42/72 ff. 323–24; the map (page 56) is PRO MPG 425.

61   The document attached to the British Library Crevecoeur map is BL Add. 15332E; here it has been translated from the French.

64   Ogden's letter is in PRO 42/72 ff. 245–76; the map did not accompany the letter but was sent a few months later.

66–67 The note regarding Pond's assertion is in Mackenzie's letter to Lord Dorchester, 17 November 1794.

67   DeVoto's comment, 1958/1980, p. 303.

68   Morton's comment, 1939/1973, p. 410.

68   Letter from Alexander Mackenzie to Roderic McKenzie dated Lac La Loche, 17 February 1788; Masson papers, in Lamb, 1970, p. 432.

73   Quote is from Masson, *Les Bourgeois,* 1960.

74   Kane quote is from a book on Kane: Eaton and Urbanek, 1995, p. 37.

75   Quote re Mrs. Mackenzie: 30 October 1799, Masson papers, NAC.

76   Quote re Andrew Mackenzie is a footnote in Harmon book, ed. Lamb, 1957.

76   Quote from Hosie is a letter to A.S.G. Musgrave, BC Archives; Mackenzie vertical file (microfilm) 85 2224.

76   Jean Steinbruck, *The Yellowknife Journal,* Nuage Editions, Winnipeg, 1999, has the story of this fascinating journal, with the text in both English and French.

82   Mackenzie's route from Point Separation on has been well analyzed by Bredin, 1962.

102   Bredin (1962) and Stager (1965) demonstrated that Whale Island was Garry Island.

108   Information about the "river that took them to the sea in five days" is from Franklin's second expedition, p. 182.

124   From *A few Remarks to Eludicate my Tracks from Athabasca Latitude 58.38 North and Longitude 110½ West from Greenwich to the North Sea and Western ocean as delineated on Mr. Arrowsmith's Map.* Written in the back of the manuscript copy of the journal of the first voyage, now in the British Library Manuscript Department.

128–29 Dene publication from Dene Cultural Institute, 1989.

132   Information that the Dene "never had to travel very far" is from the Dene Cultural Institute, 1989, p. 31.

132   Franklin, 1828, pp. 39–40. The name "Great River" may have been used in the fur trade in the mid-1820s, but "Mackenzie's River" was certainly used by the world before. The name was used on a printed map by Arrowsmith, on his world map of 1794.

133   Holland's "Lucrative Furr trade" quote is from Morton, 1939/1973, p. 412.

140   Holland's plan and his expenses and instruments list are in PRO CO 42/72 ff. 260–63.

141   Turnor quote is from Tyrrell, Turnor journal, p. 317.

142   "Not having been furnished with proper Instruments" quote is a footnote in a letter to Lord Dorchester, 17 November 1794.

144   Turnor quote: HBCA B9/a/3.

148   Ship Cove is now Resolution Cove; see map of Nootka, map 69 in Hayes, 1999.

148   References to Mackenzie's journal for his second voyage are from his book, as the original journal has not survived.

155   Thutade Lake is not only the source of the Finlay, but one of the main sources of the Peace, and the ultimate source of the entire

173   Mackenzie River system. Water from this lake flows 3 780 km or 2,350 miles to the Arctic Ocean.

177   Simon Fraser's words are from *Letters and Journals of Simon Fraser*, pp. 196–97; Fraser had established a post on Trout Lake in 1805, which was soon renamed McLeod Lake. It was the first North West Company post in British Columbia.

189   The quote about "this Great River being Navigable with Canoe and Boats to its mouth" is from *A few Remarks to Elucidate my Tracks* . . . found in the back of the surviving journal of the *first* voyage. See note for pages 128–29.

214   Point Menzies, nearly opposite Green Bay (Mackenzie's Porcupine Cove) had been passed by Mackenzie the day before. It had been named by Vancouver the year before, 1792, and had marked the northern limit of Vancouver's survey for that year; Vancouver had just returned to the point where he left off the year before to resume his monumental survey of the coast.

215   A description of the archeological investigation of Mackenzie Rock is given in Hobler, Philip M., n.d.

225   "Rascal's" name advanced as the epitome of all that was wrong: Ken Brealey, Geography Department, UBC; lecture 8 December 1999, Vancouver Maritime Museum.

226   Au Kvalla's words as told to B. Fillip Jacobsen: BCA, "Sir Alexander Mackenzie vertical file" (microfiche) 85-2275-6. Detail on Jacobsen is from Cliff Kopas, *Bella Coola*, 1970.

235   The letter to Viscount Castlereagh is in PRO BT 1/59 ff. 62–67.

236   The reference "referred to in contemporary correspondence" is quoted in Campbell, 1975, p. 55.

236   John Graves Simcoe was the Lieutenant-Governor of Upper Canada, the predecessor of Ontario. It had been formed in 1791 by the division of Quebec into Upper and Lower Canada. Simcoe, the first Lieutenant-Governor, had arrived in 1792.

238   Simcoe's report is in a report from the Committee of the Privy Council for Trade and Foreign Plantations to the House of Lords, and is dated 11 September 1794, the day after Simcoe met with Mackenzie. PRO CO 42/318, ff. 267–68 verso.

244   Mackenzie's comments about his meeting with Astor are in a letter to McTavish, Frobisher and Company dated at New York, 30 January 1798. HBCA F. 3/1, ff. 273–74.

245   McGillivray's letter is quoted in Mitchell, 1960.

248   John Fraser's letter is quoted in Wallace, 1954, pp. 40–42.

248   William McGillivray's letter was to Aeneas Cameron, 8 May 1800, quoted in Mitchell, 1960.

253   Pointing out Coombe's own travel was circumscribed is a footnote in Montgomery, 1937.

256   Jefferson's letter re getting a copy of *Voyages* is in a letter from Thomas Jefferson to James Cheetham, 17 June 1803, quoted in Allen, 1975 (1991), p. 131.

262   Letter from William Mackenzie to George Mackenzie, 24 May 1856, is quoted in Bryce, 1906, pp. 94–97.

262   Jean-Baptiste Bernadotte was a one-time French Revolutionary general and marshal of France who was elected crown prince of Sweden in 1810, and who was king of Sweden and Norway from 1818 to 1844. In 1810 the Swedish crown prince Christian August had died, and the Swedes searched for a successor for the childless king Charles XIII. Bernadotte became viewed as a possible contender when they turned to Napoleon for advice. On 21 August 1810 Bernadotte was elected Swedish crown prince, taking the name Karl Johan (Charles John).

263   The dispatch about Jérôme Bonaparte is from Jean Ritchie Anderson, "With Mackenzie to the Pacific," in the *Family Herald and Weekly Star*, Montreal, 23 November 1927, BCA "Sir Alexander Mackenzie vertical file" 85-2208.

272   John Richardson as "chief architect of the Canadian commercial state" is from Denison, 1966.

273   Harry Munro quote is from Campbell, 1975, p. 65.

274   Castlereagh's quote about the "system of exclusive privilege" is from PRO BT 1/59 ff. 62–67.

277   The "grim reaper" quote is from Wade, 1927, p. 253.

283   Franklin's quote about meeting Mackenzie is from the introduction to his book, 1824, p. xiv.

284   Mackenzie's Advice to John Franklin, 1819, from Scott Polar Research Institute, Cambridge, England, MS 248/276, pp. 29–31. London, 21 May 1819.

285   The "conspicuous cape" quote is from Franklin, 1824, p. 191.

290   The "wriggle" quote is from Pierre Berton, 1988, p. 127.

290   George Back's "iron-ribbed" quote is from his book, p. 202.

290   Peter Warren Dease was chief factor for the Hudson's Bay Company's Athabasca District; Thomas Simpson was the cousin of the Governor of the company, George Simpson.

296   David Thompson's "ought to employ a Canoe" quote is from his report to William and Duncan McGillivray, *Account of an attempt to cross the Rocky Mountain by Mr James Hughes, nine men & myself on the part of the NWⁿ Company in order to penetrate to the Pacific Ocean, 1801*, Belyea (ed.), 1994, p. 21.

297   Quote about "the Astronomer" is David Thompson, PRO CO 42/330 ff. 189–90v.

300   Simon Fraser's letter "Before our arrival": August 1806, the original is in the Bancroft Library, University of California. Lamb, 1960, pp. 229–34.

307   "Erected a small Pole": David Thompson's journal entry for 9 July 1811, Belyea (ed.), 1994, p. 152.

307   "At 1 Pm": Thompson, Belyea (ed.), 1994.

308   Franchère quotes are from Franchère's book, 1820, in French; translation by Hoyt Franchère, 1967.

310   "Gentlemen of the North West Company," Franchère, 1820 (1967).

Sources and Further Reading

Alexander Mackenzie's own book is *Voyages from Montreal, on the River St. Laurence, through the Continent of North America, to the Frozen and Pacific Oceans; In the Years 1789 and 1793. With a Preliminary Account of the Rise, Progress, and Present State of the Fur Trade of that Country.* London: Printed for T. Cadell, Jun. and W. Davies, Strand; Cobbett and Morgan, Pall-Mall; and W. Creech, at Edinburgh. By R. Noble, Old-Bailey. M.DCCC.I [1801, first edition]; there are several other editions as well.

By far the best way of reading Mackenzie's work is the annotated and footnoted Hakluyt Society edition of *The Journals and Letters of Sir Alexander Mackenzie*, edited by **W. Kaye Lamb** (Hakluyt Society, Cambridge University Press, 1970; there is also a Canadian edition published by Macmillan), which also contains selected letters. It is a book well worth reading and I thoroughly recommend it.

The following books and articles were used in the writing of this book, and many are excellent for further reading.

Allen, John Logan   *Lewis and Clark and the Image of the American Northwest*   Dover, Mineola, NY, 1991. (Originally published as *Passage through the Garden: Lewis and Clark and the Image of the American Northwest,* University of Illinois Press, Urbana, 1975.)

Belyea, Barbara (ed.)   *Columbia Journals: David Thompson*   McGill–Queen's University Press, Montreal, 1994

Berton, Pierre   *The Arctic Grail: The Quest for the Northwest Passage and the North Pole, 1818–1909*   McClelland and Stewart, Toronto, 1988

Birchwater, Sage   *Ulkatcho: Stories of the Grease Trail: Anahim Lake, Bella Coola, Quesnel*   Ulkatcho Indian Band, Anahim Lake, BC, 1993

Bishop, R. P.   *Sir Alexander Mackenzie's Rock: End of the First Journey across North America*   Department of the Interior, Ottawa, 1924

Bliss, Michael   "Conducted Tour"   *Beaver*, Outfit 69, 2, pp. 16–24, April–May 1989

Bredin, T. F.   "Whale Island and the Mackenzie Delta: Charted Errors and Unmapped Discoveries 1789–1850"   *Arctic*, Volume 15, No. 1, pp. 51–65, March 1962

———   "Mackenzie, Slave Lake and Whale Island"   *The Beaver*, Outfit 294, pp. 54–55, Summer 1963

Bryce, George   *Mackenzie Selkirk Simpson* Makers of Canada series   Morang, Toronto, 1906

Burpee, Lawrence J.   *The Search for the Western Sea*   Alston Rivers, London, 1908

Campbell, Marjorie Wilkins   *The North West Company*   St. Martin's Press, New York, 1957

———   *Northwest to the Sea: A Biography of William McGillivray*   Clarke, Irwin and Company, Toronto, 1975

Camsell, Charles   *The Mackenzie River Basin*   Geological Survey of Canada, Ottawa, 1921

Daniells, Roy   *Alexander Mackenzie and the North West*   Oxford University Press, 1969

———   "The Literary Relevance of Alexander Mackenzie"   *Canadian Literature*, No. 38, pp. 19–28, Autumn 1968

Davidson, Gordon C.   *The North West Company*   University of California Press, Berkeley, 1918

[Dene Cultural Institute]   *Dehcho: "Mom, We've Been Discovered!"* Dene Cultural Institute, Yellowknife, NWT, 1989

Denison, Merrill   *Canada's First Bank: A History of the Bank of Montreal*   2 vols. McClelland and Stewart, Toronto, 1966

DeVoto, Bernard   *The Course of Empire*   Houghton Mifflin, New York, 1952 and 1980

Eaton, Diane, and Urbanek, Sheila   *Paul Kane's Great Nor-West*   UBC Press, Vancouver, 1995

Franchère, Gabriel; Franchère, Hoyt C. (trans. and ed.)   *Adventure at Astoria 1810–1814*   University of Oklahoma Press, Norman, 1967

Franklin, John   *Narrative of a Journey to the Shores of the Polar Sea, in the Years 1819–20–21–22*   John Murray, London, 1824

———   *Narrative of a Second Expedition to the Shores of the Polar Sea, in the Years 1825, 1826, and 1827*   John Murray, London, 1828

Gates, Charles M. (ed.)   *Five Fur Traders of the Northwest: Being a Narrative of Peter Pond and the Diaries of John Macdonell, Archibald N. McLeod, Hugh Faries, and Thomas Connor*   Minnesota Historical Society, St. Paul, 1965

Gough, Barry *First Across the Continent: Sir Alexander Mackenzie* University of Oklahoma Press, Norman, 1997

Harmon, Daniel *Sixteen Years in the Indian Country: The Journal of Daniel Williams Harmon 1800–1816* W. Kaye Lamb, ed. Macmillan, Toronto, 1957

Hayes, Derek *Historical Atlas of British Columbia and the Pacific Northwest* Cavendish Books, Vancouver, 1999. (Also published as *Historical Atlas of the Pacific Northwest* Sasquatch Books, Seattle, 1999.)

Hobler, Philip M. *Archeological Survey of Alexander Mackenzie Provincial Park and Environs, B.C.* Environment Canada, no date. British Columbia Archives microfiche Df–23, No. 422.

Hearne, Samuel *A Journey from Prince of Wale's Fort in Hudson's Bay, to the Northern Ocean, Undertaken by Order of the Hudson's Bay Company for the Discovery of Copper Mines, A Northwest Passage, etc., in the Years 1769, 1770, 1771, and 1772* London, 1795

———— *A Journey from Prince of Wales's Fort in Hudson's Bay to the Northern Ocean 1769 · 1770 · 1771 · 1772* Richard Glover, ed. Macmillan, Pioneer Books, Toronto, 1958

Howay, F. W. "An Identification of Sir Alexander Mackenzie's Fort Fork" *Transactions of the Royal Society of Canada*, third series, 22, Section 2, pp. 165–74, 1928

———— "Maclauries' Travels through America: A Pirated Account of Sir Alexander Mackenzie's Voyages" *Washington Historical Quarterly* 23, pp. 83–87, 1932

Innis, Harold A. "Peter Pond and the Influence of Capt. James Cook on Exploration in the Interior of North America" *Transactions of the Royal Society of Canada*, Section 2, pp. 131–41, 1928

———— *The Fur Trade in Canada* University of Toronto Press, Toronto, 1999 (Originally published in 1930.)

———— *Peter Pond: Fur Trader and Adventurer* Irwin and Gordon, Toronto, 1930

Karamanski, Theodore J. *Fur Trade and Exploration: Opening the Far Northwest, 1821–1852* University of Oklahoma Press, Norman, 1988

King, Richard *Narrative of a Journey to the Shores of the Arctic Ocean in 1833, 1834 and 1835; Under the Command of Capt. Back, R.N.* Bentley, London, 1836

Lamb, W. Kaye (ed.) *The Letters and Journals of Simon Fraser 1806–1808* Macmillan, Pioneer Books, Toronto, 1960

Landmann, George *Adventures and Recollections of Colonel Landmann late of the Corps of Royal Engineers* Colburn and Co., London, 1852

McDonald, T. H. (ed.) *Exploring the Northwest Territory: Sir Alexander Mackenzie's Journal of a Voyage by Bark Canoe from Lake Athabasca to the Pacific Ocean in the Summer of 1789* University of Oklahoma Press, Norman, 1966

Mackenzie, Alexander *Voyages from Montreal on the River St. Laurence . . .* John W. Garvin (ed.); Volume 3 of *Master-works of Canadian Authors*. Introduction by Charles W. Colby. Radisson Society of Canada, Toronto, 1927

Maclaren, I. S. "Alexander Mackenzie and the Landscapes of Commerce" *Studies in Canadian Literature*, 7, pp. 141–50, 1982

Masson, L. R. *Les Bourgeois de la Compagnie de Nord-Ouest* Coté, Québec, 1889–1890. Reprint, Antiquarian Press, New York, 1960

Meares, John *Voyages Made in the Years 1788 and 1789 from China to the North West Coast of America* Logographic Press, London, 1790

Mitchell, Elaine Allan "New Evidence on the Mackenzie-McTavish Break" *Canadian Historical Review*, 41, pp. 41–47, 1960

Montgomery, Franz "Alexander Mackenzie's Literary Assistant" *Canadian Historical Review*, 18, pp. 301–4, 1937

Morse, Eric W. *Fur Trade Canoe Routes of Canada / Then and Now* University of Toronto Press, 1995

Morton, Arthur S. *A History of the Canadian West to 1870–71* Thomas Nelson, London, 1939

Niemcewicz, Julian Ursyn *Under Their Vine and Fig Tree: Travels through North America in 1797–1799* 1805. Reprint, Grassman Publishing, Elizabeth, NJ, 1965

Nisbet, Jack *Sources of the River: Tracking David Thompson across Western North America* Sasquatch Books, Seattle, 1994

Pond, Peter "Journal of 'Sir' Peter Pond – Born in Milford, Connecticut, in 1740" Introduction by Mrs. Nathan Gillett Pond. *Connecticut Magazine,* 1906, facsimile edition, no date.

Rich, Edwin E. *The History of the Hudson's Bay Company, 1670–1870* 2 volumes. Hudson's Bay Record Society, London, 1958

———— *The Fur Trade and the Northwest to 1857* McClelland and Stewart, Toronto, 1967

Ronda, James *Astoria and Empire* University of Nebraska Press, Lincoln, 1990

Sage, Walter N. "Sir Alexander Mackenzie and His Influence on the History of the North West" *Queen's Quarterly*, 29, pp. 399–416, 1922

Smith, James K. *Alexander Mackenzie, Explorer: The Hero Who Failed* McGraw-Hill Ryerson, Toronto, 1973

Stager, J. K. "Alexander Mackenzie's Exploration of the Grand River" *Geographical Bulletin*, 7, pp. 213–41, 1965

Steinbruck, Jean *The Yellowknife Journal* Introduction by Harry Duckworth. Nuage Editions, Winnipeg, 1999

Stuart-Stubbs, Basil *Maps Relating to Alexander Mackenzie: A Keepsake for the Bibliographical Society of Canada* Jasper Park, AB, June 1968

Swannell, Frank C. "On Mackenzie's Trail" *The Beaver*, Outfit 289, pp. 9–14, Summer 1958
——— "Alexander Mackenzie as Surveyor" *The Beaver*, Outfit 290, pp. 20–25, Winter 1959

Tyrrell, J. B. (ed.) *The Journals of Samuel Hearne and Philip Turnor* Champlain Society, Toronto, 1934

Wade, M. S. *Mackenzie of Canada: The Life and Adventures of Alexander Mackenzie, Discoverer* William Blackwood and Sons, London, 1927

Wagner, Henry R. *Peter Pond: Fur-trader and Explorer* Yale University Library, New Haven, 1955

Wallace, W. S. *The Pedlars from Quebec and Other Papers on the Nor'Westers* Ryerson Press, Toronto, 1954
——— **(ed.)** *Documents Relating to the North West Company* Champlain Society, Toronto, 1934

Weld, Isaac, Jr. *Travels Through the States of North America and the Provinces of Upper and Lower Canada, During the Years 1795, 1796 and 1797* London, Printed for John Stockdale, Piccadilly, 1799

Woodworth, John, and Flygare, Hälle *In the Steps of Alexander Mackenzie: Trail Guide* Kelowna, BC, 1981

Woollacott, Arthur P. *Mackenzie and His Voyageurs: By Canoe to the Arctic and the Pacific 1789–93* London and Toronto, J. M. Dent, 1927

Wrong, Hume *Sir Alexander Mackenzie: Explorer and Fur-trader* Macmillan, Toronto, 1927

Index